Beyond Our Selves

Books written and edited by Catherine Marshall

Mr. Jones, Meet the Master
A Man Called Peter
Let's Keep Christmas
The Prayers of Peter Marshall
To Live Again
The First Easter
Christy
Something More
Adventures in Prayer
The Helper
Meeting God At Every Turn
The Best of Peter Marshall
Julie

Beyond Our Selves

Catherine Marshall

 Chosen Books
A Division of Baker Book House
Grand Rapids, Michigan 49516

© 1961 by Catherine Marshall

Published by Chosen Books
a division of Baker Book House Company
P.O. Box 6287, Grand Rapids, MI 49516-6287

Second printing, February 1995

Printed in the United States of America

Library of Congress Catalog Card Number: 61-17599

ISBN 0-8007-9089-8

Cairns, D. S., from *The Faith That Rebels*. Richard R. Smith, New York, N.Y., 1930.
By permission of Harper & Brothers.

Davenport, Russell, from *The Dignity of Man*, 1955. By permission of Harper &
Brothers.

Gossip, Arthur John, from *The Interpreter's Bible*. By permission of Abingdon Press.

Jung, C. G. from *Modern Man in Search of a Soul*. By permission of Harcourt, Brace
and World, Inc., and Routledge and Kegan Paul, Ltd., London, England.

Kunkel, Fritz and Kickerson, Roy E., from *How Character Develops*. By permission of
Charles Scribner's Sons.

Lewis, C. S., from *Beyond Personality*. By permission of The Macmillan Company
and Geoffrey Bles, Ltd.

Moffatt, James, from *The Bible: A New Translation*, 1922, 1935, and 1950. By permission of Harper & Brothers.

Montague, Margaret Prescott, from "Twenty Minutes of Reality," 1916, by the
Atlantic Monthly Company, Boston, Massachusetts.

Oursler, Fulton, from *Why I Know There Is a God*, 1950. Reprinted by permission of
Doubleday & Company, Inc. and Mrs. April Armstrong.

Phillips, J. B., from *The Gospels Translated into Modern English*. By permission of The
Macmillan Company and Geoffrey Bles, Ltd.

Simpson, A. B., from *The Gospel of Healing*, 1935. By permission of Christian
Publications, Inc., Harrisburg, Pennsylvania.

To
Len

Acknowledgments

I wish to express my appreciation to Elizabeth Sherrill for her constructive criticism and wise counsel; to my husband, Leonard Earle LeSourd, who has assumed responsibility for my manuscript as though it were his own; to Dr. Dudley Zuver, who has checked the manuscript for biblical and theological accuracy; to Miss Patricia Harris, who has done a herculean job of typing and retyping manuscript; to the Fleming H. Revell Company for their generosity in loaning me Hannah Whitall Smith's out-of-print books; to the kind ladies at the Chappaqua Library; and to Mr. Robert F. Beach and his associates at the Union Theological Seminary Library; finally, my lasting gratitude to the friends who have been so gracious in allowing me to share their personal experiences with the readers of this book.

When *Beyond Our Selves* was published in 1961, it did not become an instant best seller like *A Man Called Peter* and *To Live Again,* two of Catherine Marshall's earlier books. Instead, *Beyond Our Selves* has performed over the years a steady but solid ministry to countless thousands of seekers throughout the world. By 1983 sales of all editions had topped 2,000,000. As the title implies, people are challenged to stretch their beliefs, deepen their faith, revitalize ineffective lives. These excerpts indicate how it happens:

> I tried suicide and failed, after reading *Beyond Our Selves.* I turned myself over to God, was led to seek help from AA and have been sober for two years. My life has changed so completely it's hard to believe.
>
> S.K., Iowa

> . . . The book opened a whole new world of joy for me.
>
> C.S., Michigan

> . . . it brought me freedom, growth and awareness of Jesus as Best Friend and Lord.
>
> T.M., Oregon

> . . . *Beyond Our Selves* opened the door and there was God waiting for me.
>
> D.W., Ohio

> . . . The most remarkable book I've ever read

. . . gave me answers to questions I've struggled with for so many years.

K.D., North Carolina

The continuing vitality of *Beyond Our Selves* stems from its basic practicality as a handbook on Christianity. In it is a mine of helpful material as Catherine focuses the blazing light of her own faith on subjects which concern us all: our will, commitment, forgiveness, guidance from God, ego slaying and deeper dimensions of prayer.

Contents

Foreword

Back in 1943, when illness hemmed me within the four walls of my bedroom certain questions presented themselves to me with terrible urgency:

Is it really possible for us to get in touch with the God who created our world?

Why does God allow evil, if He has the power to destroy it?

Can God heal where medicine fails?

Can prayer affect the outward circumstances of our lives?

Does God guide people today?

The search for the answers to these questions has brought adventure beyond anything I could have imagined. *Beyond Our Selves* is the story of that search.

Many others have shared in the explorations that made this book possible. Three persons especially have had a part in it, the first being a woman who died before I was born. I first met her in the pages of one of her own books.

It was in the fall of 1944 that a copy of Hannah Whitall Smith's *The Christian's Secret of a Happy Life* fell into my hands. Superficially the volume was anything but inviting. The print was small and cramped, the language quaint, the writing style outdated. All of this was understandable, as the book had been written in 1870. Since then—with almost no advertising—this little volume had sold about three million copies. I wondered why.

I soon found out. Here was a practical how-to book written in the days before there was any such thing. The chapter headings read like a table of contents still damp with printer's ink: "How to Enter In" (that is, into the Christian life); "Difficulties Concerning Guidance"; "Difficulties Concerning Doubts"; "Difficulties Concerning Faith" . . . .

The zest and decisivness of her writing revealed Hannah Smith as a woman who knew what she believed and why she believed it. In her day, hell and damnation were still major emphases across Christendom. Instead, her emphasis was that the Christian life is the happiest of all lives. Yet hers was no easy cult-of-happiness teaching, for she insisted that Christian joy could not be bought cheaply. There was no evading the total surrender of one's life and resources, no avoiding the giving up of doubt and the giving in to a costly obedience.

I read the book through, then read it again. Certain chapters I returned to, over and over. If I had a spiritual problem puzzling me, I could always find an answer in *The Christian's Secret*, provided—provided I meant business about getting straightened out. Someday, I told myself, I would like to write the same kind of helping book for my time. In it I would want to share, as Hannah Smith had, the discoveries—great and small—which had been of value to me in my Christian walk.

The second person whose mark is indelibly on *Beyond Our Selves* is Peter Marshall. When I was a college girl in Atlanta, Peter first caught my attention by the recurring note in his preaching of conviction based on personal experience. In a hundred different ways he said, "I know this is so, because I have experienced it."

He talked often of God's guidance, since he was an example of one whom the Lord had guided. He spoke ringing words about God's ability to provide material needs; God had provided his needs.

He had much to say about Christianity being a joyous life. Those who bowled with him or accompanied him on fishing trips or to baseball games saw the joy firsthand. He insisted that a man need not be a sissy to love the Lord. Other men listened to him, because he was walking proof.

To us college girls, the surety of his conviction and firsthand faith was more fresh and more impressive than any preaching we had ever heard.

Then after he became my husband, he continued to mold me. Here was the love of God pouring through as warm and vivid a personality as I have ever known. Through Peter I saw that our love for God should involve the emotions. Why not? For emotion need not be maudlin. It can also have a virile strength.

He taught me, and many another, the difference between going through the mechanical motions of a church service and the art of corporate worship. Through him I learned what worship is.

Peter imparted to me his knowledge of immortality. His sureness about it was a trumpet call of faith. He was certain of the continuation of a life beyond this one, certain in a way that few persons ever are.

He took my tendency toward snap judgments of people and situations and taught me that "there, but for the grace of God, go I."

And I can never forget his insistence that women should be women, that in our femininity is our glory.

All of this Peter did for me. Not often is there such a combination of husband and teacher. So far as Christianity is concerned, I sat at his feet as did thousands of others. I find now that his ideas, his convictions, even his word-pictures, have become a part of me, tissue and sinew. That is why any book I write is Peter's book too.

I also owe to Peter, in a strange sort of way, my present happiness. For he engrafted into me the truth that in God's scheme of things there is no place for rivalry or jealousy. Each beloved person's place is secure, his own for this life and for eternity. No one can take it from him, nor does it impinge on anyone else's place. That is why Peter is and always will be a part of my life. It is also why Leonard LeSourd, whom I married in

1959, can share him with me and is as grateful as I for Peter's influence on our life together.

I find that having an editor in the family has many compensations, along with a few drawbacks. As the executive editor of *Guideposts* and a writer himself, Len understands the hours that every writer must keep, the needed isolation. He is patient with me when I fall into a black mood because ideas are not flowing, sentences are wooden, and what I am turning out is just plain terrible. Always he gives me unstintingly of his fine editorial judgment.

There are times, however, when I want to slam the office door on my manuscript and not think or speak of it until the next day.

But ideas do not keep hours for Len. "Now, Catherine, if you shifted this section from the middle of Chapter Six to the end—" Or, "I hate to mention it, but the material slows down here." Once he even telephoned me from a tollbooth along the New Jersey Turnpike: "I've been thinking about that chapter on forgiveness all the way down here. The opening paragraph still isn't quite right—" Then of course, like all editors, he is ruthless with the blue pencil.

But somehow he always knows when I need to shut the door on my writing for longer periods of time. "I want you to write FUN on your calendar for x number of days," he will say every so often. "See what you think of this plan for a trip."

Someday perhaps I shall write about the adventure of rearing a second family. Just at the point when I thought child-rearing was over, Len's three children have joined Peter John in calling me *Mother*.

There is Jeffrey, mischievous and lovable. Standing beside Peter John's six feet, four-and-a-half inches, Jeff appears even tinier than he is. Chester, quiet and sensitive, has enormous deep brown eyes and a well-developed passion for baseball. Peter John has earned his adoration by coaching him for Little League. Then there is Linda, who has always wanted a big brother, and looks on the one she acquired as a dispensation straight from heaven. Linda is also ecstatic over having a writer "for a mommy." She will be even more ecstatic, I hope, when she finds something about herself in this book.

Many experiences have tested me in my lifetime, but none more than this one. And none has made me happier. But writing about it must come later. A man swimming a horse across a turbulent stream does not stop to take a picture of the experience. I'll get my colts across the stream, see them thoroughly dried off, well fed, and on their way—then perhaps, the picture.

Thus, with these three people—Peter, Len, and Hannah— always at my shoulder, *Beyond Our Selves* has been written. Though so different, each of them has one characteristic in common: enthusiastic delight in what Peter Marshall liked to call "spiritual research unlimited." All too often this enthusiasm is the missing ingredient in Christian circles. So if I have succeeded in transferring to the pages that follow one one-hundredth part of the excitement that I feel about Christianity, I shall have achieved my purpose.

C.M.

Beyond Our Selves

1

Something More

If you are satisfied with your life and feel no need for any help outside yourself, this book is not for you. The search for God begins at the point of need.

Most of us feel this need either because of some problem for which we have no answer or because of a nagging consciousness that we should be getting more out of life or putting more into it. There is the realization that we are going through but the motions of living. Surely our half-somnolent existence is not living as it was meant to be! We yearn for something more.

I first felt this need for something more during my college days. Recently I came across these comments, written in a journal that I began about the middle of my freshman year:

> People bustle and strive and hurry. Their eyes are mostly on material considerations. They die, and apparently it's all over. What are we here for anyway? There must be some purpose in living, but I haven't found it yet.
>
> All of my life I've thought that I was possessed with a wanderlust. Now I know that the trouble lies within myself, and I cannot escape myself. I'm restless and unhappy.

Some of the restlessness may have been typical of late adolescence. But not all, for this search for something that I had not yet experienced lasted for ten years or more—into my late twenties.

I think of many of all ages who are on the same search. For example, a man named Alex. He is tall and lean, with the high forehead of the intellectual, the eyes of a thoughtful man. Alex is the product of one of the best of the Ivy League colleges and is now a successful free-lance writer.

Where religion was concerned, until a few years ago Alex was an agnostic—and proud of it. With a mind trained in materialism and rationalism, he suspected in all religion a form of elaborate self-deception.

"The truth is that my god has been reason," Alex told me recently. "And reason seemed a god worth worshiping until—"

Until Alex came squarely up against problems in his family life that no amount of reasoning could solve.

"It was hard for me to admit that there are areas in life for which reason has no answers—like man's emotional life and the knotty problem of human relationships. Realizing that shook me," he said. For the first time, he was encountering the indisputable truth that there must be something more.

And I think of Sheila Goshen, a housewife in Birmingham, Alabama, who asked for my help in her search:

> . . . After ignoring God for fifty years, I recently got a new look at myself and believe me, I did not like what I saw. So now I've been trying to change myself into what I want to be, but I find that I can't make myself over.
>
> For the first time I know that I need God and faith. So now the question is, how does an ordinary person like me go about gaining an "intimacy" with God?

This is an easy question to ask, a hard one to answer. I puzzled for weeks, then months over it. In a way, this book is my answer.

There is abundant proof that vocational and material success fail utterly to satisfy the inner hunger. The famous Hollywood actress, Mary Astor, has known the fairy-tale magic of movie stardom. An Academy Award, glamorous marriages, two children, several Beverly Hills mansions, furs, jewels, publicity—what more could any woman want?

Yet Mary Astor admitted in print that "for years—even in the midst of fame and glamor—I yearned for contentment, happiness. It took me almost twenty years to go from idle curiosity about religion . . . to meeting God as a Person and a Father, and knowing that walking in faith meant growing up."

I have seen this search in college students, especially during their senior year. One such incident happened during one of my weekend visits to Yale University to see my son, Peter John. Three of Peter's friends and I had been chatting over lunch in the cafeteria. The tall, dark-haired boy directly across from me rose. "Sorry to have to rush like this, but I have a one o'clock class. This has been an interesting conversation—"

An odd look, one that I could not interpret, crossed his face, and he hesitated before he spoke again. "Now that I'm a senior, I'm spending quite a lot of time these days trying to figure out what life is all about. Isn't it queer that we get so little help with this in college? I mean why we're here and how to handle life and all that. Well—g'bye, all."

Often the inner hunger catches up with those most immersed in materialism. One day I was talking with a man in the investment business. "During the last year," he told me, "I've experienced a kind of restlessness that baffles me. I've tried working late at the office, even plunged in the stock market so that I won't have time to think about myself. I've gone out on the town more, trying to have some fun. Even tried drinking more than usual. Nothing is ever as gratifying to the taste, sight and touch as I hope it will be. I've tried to find some satisfaction in new sports equipment, two expensive cars. Nothing helps.

"What I'm about to ask may sound strange—especially from a Wall Street broker who spends his time thinking about Dow-Jones averages rather than religion. But I wonder—could this gnawing inside be . . . well, my inner spirit crying out for its Maker and refusing to be satisfied with anything less? If this is a possible explanation, what can I do about it? How does one go about finding God?"

In every community, in every land, at every social and economic level, are individuals just as eager as the investment broker to find their way to God, though many are too shy to voice it as he did. They have questions to ask, problems to solve. They wonder if Christianity really does have answers for them.

To know where answers cannot be found is at least a step in the right direction. Until the first World War, many people were certain that the *something more* was right here on earth. Of course, we thought it wise to give lip-service to a Higher Power. *In God We Trust* was stamped on our coins. A sentence or two mentioning a Supreme Being appeared in most political speeches, rather like a sprig of parsley for garnish. But through all this there was the tacit understanding that we could work out our destinies, both personal and national, by ourselves. We did not really need God.

In fact, as the twentieth century dawned Americans were probably the most optimistic people on earth. Industry, stimulated by mass production and distribution, made the end of poverty seem in sight. Eventually all the inhabitants of earth could be provided with at least minimum requirements of food, clothing, and shelter. Given time, medicine would virtually stamp out disease. More inventions and gadgets would give us leisure time for fun and culture, perhaps even a little self-examination.

Best of all, education would finally convince men that war

was folly. During the late 1920s, in high schools across the United States, boys and girls were studying about the League of Nations. I know, because I spent many a winter evening curled up in an easy chair near a gas heater, preparing for a stiff examination on the subject. The prize (which I did not win) was a trip to Geneva, Switzerland, to see the League in action. My generation was confident that intelligent arbitration guided by the League and the World Court would soon replace the senseless outrage of war. It was all a part of the doctrine of inevitable progress.

Without realizing what was happening, most of us gradually came to take for granted the premises underlying this philosophy of optimism. We proceeded to live these propositions, though we would not have stated them as blandly as I set them forth here:

> Man is inherently good.
>
> Individual man can carve out his own salvation with the help of education and society through progressively better government.
>
> Reality and the values worth searching for lie in the material world that science is steadily teaching us to analyze, catalogue, and measure. While we would not deny the existence of inner values, we relegate them to second place.
>
> The purpose of life is happiness. And happiness we define in terms of enjoyable activity, friends, and the accumulation of material objects.
>
> The pain and evil of life—such as ignorance, poverty, selfishness, hatred, greed, lust for power— are caused by factors in the external world. Therefore the cure lies in the reforming of human institutions and the bettering of environmental conditions.
>
> As science and technology remove poverty and lift from us the burden of physical existence, we shall

automatically become finer persons, seeing for ourselves the value of living by the Golden Rule.

In time, the rest of the world will appreciate our demonstration that the American way of life is best. They will then seek for themselves the good life of freedom and prosperity. This will be the greatest impetus toward an end of global conflict.

The way to get along with people is to beware of religious dictums and dogma. The ideal is to be a nice person and to live by the Creed of Tolerance. Thus we offend few people. We live and let live. This is the American way.

So we believed. So we acted.

Then came the first World War and its hideous aftermath. In Europe and the British Isles, the disillusionment was deep and real. Europeans were no longer convinced of the inherent goodness of man.

But in the Western Hemisphere we had had no cities shelled, no countryside devastated. The ink was scarcely dry on the Versailles Treaty before our philosophy of optimism reasserted itself. The trouble that caused the 1914-1918 war, we assured ourselves, was not unredeemed human nature but the munitions-makers and kindred institutions inherited from an unenlightened nineteenth century. On college campuses, lecture platforms, and in church groups our indignation was loud and vociferous. I remember taking part in intercollegiate debates—some of them with international teams from Oxford, Cambridge, and the University of London—in which we aired our loathing for the armament-makers and the peddlers of war propaganda.

The fault was never in ourselves. No, this had nothing to do with man and his God. It was just a matter of ironing the kinks out of our society. Meanwhile technological developments rose to ever greater heights. The Golden Twenties gave certitude to the doctrine of inevitable progress. And while the Depression that struck in late October 1929 was, for a time, a shattering experience, once again most people felt that the trouble was not in man but in his institutions—in this case, monopolies, the stock market, buying on margin, greedy big business. Franklin Delano Roosevelt's New Deal with its relief, recovery, and reform would take care of all that.

Suspicions that mankind might not be working out salvation for our world came with Adolf Hitler. Czechoslovakia, Poland, Denmark, Norway, the Netherlands, Belgium, France—one by one they fell before the tide of Nazism. But it was not so much the war itself as the Nazi atrocities that finally shattered our philosophical optimism about man. These shocked us to our depths, destroying once and for all the pretty picture of man as inherently good. Certain pictures can never be erased. . . .

The year was 1941. The scene a Polish village called Minsk. Adolph Eichmann, Hitler's specialist for Jewish Affairs for the Third Reich, had been sent to witness the extermination of five thousand Jews.

The morning was cold. The condemned men, women and children undressed down to their underwear or their shirts. They walked the last hundred yards and jumped into a pit that had been prepared for them. Eichmann was impressed by the fact that they offered no resistance, apparently by this time reconciled to death.

Then the rifles and machine pistols opened fire. Children in the pit were crying, clinging to their parents. Eichmann saw one woman hold her baby high above her head, pleading, "Shoot me, but please let my baby live. Take my baby. Please take my baby—"

Eichmann had children of his own. For a moment he felt a twinge of compassion. He almost opened his mouth to order, "Don't shoot. Hand over the child." Then the baby was hit.

"I scarcely spoke a word to the chauffeur on the trip back," he reported later. "I was thinking. I was reflecting about the meaning of life in general. . . ."

What conclusions did Eichmann reach? Years later he summarized how he felt about the mass-execution program that destroyed some six million Jews. "I was a little cog in the machinery of the Reich. I merely carried out orders. Where would we have been if everyone had thought things out in those days?

"After all, the people who were loaded on trains and buses [for extermination] meant nothing to me. It was really none of my business." [1]

What had happened to the German people? Americans who had traveled in Germany between the two world wars remembered the charm of the tidy countryside, the friendliness of the people on the city streets and in the shops, the love of music, the gaiety. We had acquired a healthy respect for the typical German businessman; his approach seemed so akin to ours. And as more and more Americans had roamed the globe, one conclusion had seemed paramount: surely men everywhere are much the same.

So it was not only the enormity of the Nazi cruelties that appalled us but the ugly suspicion that imperfect man might commit other brutalities—anywhere, at any time. Was it really true that man was innately good, that education, science, technology, and a better environment would ultimately perfect him? The German people had had all those advantages.

But there was still one corner in which we as Americans might hide from the truth about human nature, so we fled to it. It was undeniable that evil things had happened in the rest of the world. But Americans, we reasoned, were different. We were people of good will. We hated war. We coveted no empire. Our intentions were of the best. We were a generous people.

And then, just at the close of the second World War, a bomb was dropped on Hiroshima. It made dubious our carefully drawn distinction between us and the evil of the rest of the world. It had not been merely German evil that had been responsible for unspeakable brutalities: it was human evil. And we, too, were a part of that humanity.

Some occurrences during the Korean conflict threw further light on man's potential for weakness, evil, even depravity. There were events involving Americans. Take, for example, an incident that took place in February 1951, just ten years after the mass murders of the Minsk pit. It happened in the mountains of North Korea, near Pyoktong. Forty-three American prisoners were huddled in a hut trying to keep warm. Two of the men had severe cases of diarrhea, not pleasant in the close quarters.

In the course of the evening, an American corporal suddenly got to his feet, picked up one of his sick comrades and dumped him outside. Then he came back and threw the other sick soldier out. Not a man stirred, not a voice was raised in protest. It was thirty degrees below zero outside; the exposed men were dead within minutes.

The merciless corporal who was thus responsible for the death of two fellow countrymen was tried after the war, convicted of manslaughter, and sentenced to life imprisonment.

But what of the forty witnesses? All of these were questioned about the incident by Army psychiatrists. The typical interview, as reported by the psychiatrists, went something like this:

"Soldier, did you see that man throw the two sick soldiers out of the hut?"

"Oh, yes sir."

"What were you doing at the time?"

"Oh, I was just huddling together with the rest of the guys, trying to keep warm. That's the only way you could stay alive."

"Then you knew that it would destroy these men to be exposed?"

"Well—sure."

"But what were you doing about it?"

"I wasn't doing anything—except trying to keep warm."

"Why *didn't* you do something about it, soldier?"

"Because," the reply came, "it wasn't any of my business."

The words echo strangely: "It was really none of my business."

To be sure, there were many examples of American self-sacrifice and heroism in the Korean war, as in every war in which Americans have been involved. Yet something about the attitudes and conduct of a percentage of men in the Korean conflict has seriously disturbed our leaders. These were American boys from all across the nation—a nation presumed to be "under God." They had come up through our public school system, a percentage of them also through our Sunday schools. Since childhood they had heard about the worth of the individual, about liberty and human rights, and "loving thy neighbor." How was it that these values had not become a part of them?

Obviously something had happened back home, something that had allowed them to grow up insecure children of an age of anxiety, with a sense of isolation and a desperate need to make contact with other human beings. As prisoners in the cold wasteland of North Korea, they found that the Something More was not where they had thought it. Materialism had provided them pleasure, but it had given them no answers about the meaning of life.

These boys were no better, no worse than the rest of us Americans. For the raw drama of the Korean hut has been repeated often in the years since then . . . Bystanders along the shore watched while an elderly man drowned a hundred feet from shore; no one tried to save him. A man attacked a woman during daylight in an apartment courtyard. Though her screams were heard by dozens of people, no one rushed to her aid. A twenty-six-year-old father, his hair burned from his head, stood naked in front of his burning home screaming for help from passing motorists for his wife and six children trapped inside. The cars sped by him; his wife and children— seven to six months old—were burned to death. And the words echo back, "It's really none of my business."

Though the lack of personal involvement was still with us, as the sixties progressed, a creeping national frustration was added to it. The "course of human events" was not going well. In spite of our much-vaunted military might, the war in Vietnam dragged on and on. Terror in the once-peaceful streets of American cities, riots in the ghettos, the assassination of leaders, ever-rising inflation—all fed this frustration. There was the terrifying feeling that the control of our national destiny was slipping from our grasp and that perhaps no leader could be found to help us rediscover the American Dream.

Yet still we cling to our philosophy of materialism, though we have had abundant evidence that this ideology which ignores the spirit has failed time and again. "Happiness is . . . the accumulation of things" our television commercials keep reassuring us. Then the Great Society, we assume, must be a bigger and better handout to more citizens, so minority groups march and camp and riot for their rightful share.

But man—where is man in all this? Jammed into our cities of concrete and steel and glass, crowded and threatened by our fellows, the air polluted, the soil and water poisoned, so much of the countryside and farmland desecrated, our lives dictated increasingly by centralized government—where are we, the people, now?

What we write and say about ourselves reveals that we believe ourselves not so much citizens of a republic, but a body of consumers. The difference is significant. As citizens of a republic we would still be concerned with the national destiny, with our individual creativity, with what we could contribute to our time. As consumers we have become a nation of takers, frantically scrambling to get ours while there is anything left to take. Instinctively we know that this is a diminishing proposition: "out there" somewhere is point zero, extermination—unless—

Unless we can find a way for man once again to control his own science and technology. But that brings us back full circle to man. Why is man on earth? What are his goals? How can we handle the evil intertwined in human nature so that the golden age can come? Force does not achieve it. Wars solve nothing. Atomic weapons in the hands of unredeemed human nature bequeath us the ultimate in fear.

And so our only hope lies in a change inside man. Are we finally to the place where we know that only with the help of a power greater than ourselves can any man, can any nation be redeemed?

Is this too slow a way, now that civilization has arrived at the eleventh hour? No, for we have tried all other ways. And the influence that can be wielded by a single great man in the grip of a spiritual passion can never be measured. Even as a handful of leaders in the grip of evil have wrecked the lives of millions, so other leaders who are willing to put themselves into the mainstream of God's power may yet be able to grant us a reprieve.

The stakes are higher than they have ever been. For the first time mankind faces the possibility of self-extermination. But in these stakes there is challenge and high adventure, along with the danger.

A few years ago, there were those who said that the atom could not be split. The atom has been split. Why should we not go forward in the same spirit to explore the spiritual world where lies the answer to a greater riddle—the riddle of the nature of man and his relation to the universe?

This spiritual world is a real world. Of that some of us have abundant evidence. There is terrain still to be discovered; peaks yet to be scaled; new truth to be mined; in short, the spiritual atom to be split.

We can learn much from the spiritual explorers who have sought and found some of that truth. They can lead us at least a part of the way, to the foothills beyond which rise the mountains that challenge our time. Some of them, like Hannah Whitall Smith, lived in other centuries, and we have the privilege of sharing their discoveries through the written word.

Many are contemporaries. A number are friends whom I have found eager to share anything that they have learned, so that others can go on to further discoveries. Some of their stories are in the pages that follow.

This book, then, is the story of a pilgrimage. The end has not yet been written. In a sense, you and I will be doing that in the days and years ahead. What I have written here is for anyone who longs for Something More and who wants to be a part of the quest.

2

The Unselfishness of God

I know a young scientist who admits he does not believe in God. He is warm-hearted and likable, is good to his family, but has a restless uncertainty about the meaning of life.

From talking to him I know that at intervals he goes through a certain cycle. Some experience or reasoning process will bring him to the conclusion that there has to be "something more" in life than birth, struggle, death, nothingness. He will thirst for things of the spirit, hunger to believe in God. Then just at the point where there could be a spiritual breakthrough, he encounters tragedy somewhere—possibly the death of a child, the disfigurement of a beautiful girl, cancer in someone well known and well loved.

"How can a good and loving God permit this, if He made and runs the world?" he asks then. Rather than seek an explanation, he shrugs off religion as something too baffling to comprehend.

If there is a Creator, what could His nature be? That is what the scientist wants to know. It is a question over which many would-be believers stumble. It is the question with which all of us who want the adventure of exploring the spiritual world must begin. Its answer is pertinent to our happiness.

Unless each of us can find answers that satisfy, we cannot trust that Creator with our dearest hopes, and so we shall have no basis for faith in God.

All of us have had contradictory experiences of the nature of God. I know I have. They run like threads through my childhood. In the very beginning, the love of my father and mother taught me of the fatherliness of God lying at the heart of the universe. Looking back at that childhood, feelings of glorious freedom and of rushing joy rise even now to meet me. Safe and loved we were, in God's world.

My brother, Bob, and sister, Emmy, and I used to roam the woods and mountains that surrounded our small West Virginia town. We waded mountain streams to pick mint and watercress and violets on far banks. We skipped smooth stones across the water, dared one another to run across swinging bridges. There is the memory of struggling up a mountainside, gulping deep drafts of the cool air, all of the aching effort worth that moment when we would stand on the summit to survey the world we knew so well lying at our feet, with more mountains beyond pushing back the horizon.

There was the exhilaration of lying on our stomachs, coasting down long, snow-packed hills in the winter; skimming down the same hills on our bicycles in the summer, the wind in our faces. There was the way we would stand and "pump" in our swing: Begin slowly. Bend the knees in rhythm with the swinging. Make it go higher ... higher ... up and down. Now again, swishing through the air, until finally the jerk of the chains told us that the swing had gone as high as it could. Then "let the cat die ..."

There were the twilight hours of long summer evenings when all the children of the neighborhood gathered to play "Kick the Can ..." The breathless dash out of hiding to give the can a swift kick and listen to the music of its careening, crashing, clinking progress down the street.

This was the freedom of the child who is loved and knows that he is loved. It was not that we children were free to disobey or to do as we pleased. But neither did we have to strain to earn love by being good. For we had constant evidence that Mother and Father would keep on loving us even when they disapproved our actions.

How well I recall one spring day when an irate neighbor called upon Father to inform him that a portion of the wall in his back yard had collapsed. The neighbor was sure that this was no act of God; the Wood children were mixed up in it somewhere.

Father's investigation proved that the man was right. We had been using a coal house behind the neighbor's property as a clubhouse. All our spare time for several weeks had been used in digging a secret tunnel. Soon, our toy wagon had hauled out quite a mound of dirt. As a result the tunnel which had begun underneath the coal house had veered too close to the neighbor's stone wall.

At such times the parental temper could flare. Em and I, being girls, knew better than Bob how to placate this one weakness of Father's. What usually developed was a highly dramatic scene with Bob and Father in the leading roles, Em and I standing by trying to give Bob support.

"You know perfectly well," Father would begin in that strong booming voice he had developed in seminary, "that you had no business doing all that digging in someone else's yard. The mere fact that you kept it a secret proves that——"

Already Bob was in tears, his cowlick jerking. "But—we *had* to keep it secret. All three of us had signed a pledge in blood——"

"In *what?* Never mind—I don't care *what* you signed the pledge in. I have warned you over and over——"

By now, Em was behind Mother's back, signaling to Bob. All of us were a captive audience for Father's eloquent oration. Like his well-organized sermons, the oration had several clear points: first, reminder of previous warnings; second, our total lack of respect for parental authority; third, the uncertain destiny of the younger generation; fourth, the futility of trying to raise good, obedient children; fifth, this time was the last straw.

By the time the rising crescendo of the fifth point had been reached, Mother was saying, "Pl–lease–e, John, *lower* your voice. Must we tell all the neighbors?"

Father's mien was that of a wounded lion. "Leonora, it *so* happens that in this case, the neighbors already know *only* too well." Then, with giant stride, the great man would storm out of the back door, decisively snap a small switch off the privet hedge, re-slam the back door, and stalk back in.

This was the cue for Bob to increase the anguish of his wails: "I'm sorry, Dad, I'll never do it again—never—never—" And for me to try to make myself heard: "Father, Bob wasn't the only one. Em and I——" And for Em to burst into tears: "Don't switch Bob, Dad. I dug the tunnel too——"

But after the tempest had subsided and peace was restored, it was Father who patiently helped us rebuild the stone wall. Through his lecture and even the punishment that followed, his love (which was God's love to us then) shone through. Thus even in our wrongdoing we discovered that our father and mother would always be beside us in the midst of trouble, still loving us.

As a younger child, I can remember the warmth and strength of Father's arms as I nestled there, content to sit silently while he carried on leisurely conversations with grown-ups. Just as clearly I can remember Mother's firm hand on my forehead when I was sick, the deliciousness of ice-cold apple scraped with a silver spoon for a fevered tongue, the stories she read aloud during bouts with the measles or chicken pox. I learned early that stories were experiences, entrancing lands to which the gates were always invitingly open.

In the same awareness of God's love at its simplest and most profound, I remember the fragrance of the first hyacinths in the spring and of the reddish-brown blossoms of the sweet scrub.... The feel of bare feet on moss under our giant oak trees.... The luxuriance of the purple wisteria that made beautiful even the old coal house.... The way we children would bite off the tip of a honeysuckle blossom and suck out the honey.... And, toward the turn of the year, the smell of balsam Christmas trees, of candle wax and wood smoke.

One day my mother and I stood at a window watching the fury of a thunderstorm of near-hurricane strength. It seemed drama on a cosmic scale—the clash of cymbals in the sky, the rolling of drums, fireworks of lightning. Rather than being afraid, I felt like shouting and applauding as the ferocious wind shook the great trees backward and forward as though they had been twigs clenched in the jaws of a dog. All the while, my mother's arm lay protectively around my shoulders.

Only in retrospect would I one day see the connection between these childhood experiences and my understanding of the nature of God. Then I would know that it made no sense at all that God would create my parents with a greater capacity for loving than He has Himself.

At the same time, there was another strand of experience in my childhood. As I grew up, I could not but become aware of the evil and suffering in the world. In any clergyman's home, as in any physician's, the raw drama of life passes steadily before the eyes.

I vividly recall my first encounter with suffering—the winter's night Father was called to the local hospital to minister to a woman who was dying of first-degree burns over most of her body. A stove had exploded when she had tried to start a fire with kerosene. When, after a vigil of many hours, Father wearily returned home, we children found ourselves backing away from him. The odor of burned flesh clung to his clothes. For days Father was so haunted by what he had seen that he had difficulty eating.

Then there was the night the mayor of our town banged

on our door at three A.M. to tell Father that the body of our friend and neighbor, Mr. Fisher, had been discovered on the Baltimore and Ohio railroad tracks near Harpers Ferry. Apparently he had lost his balance and had fallen off the rear platform of the Capitol Limited.

"I just can't bear to be the one to break this awful news to Mrs. Fisher," the mayor said. "You're a minister. You'll know what to say."

But Father was also a human being. His family knew that he found it just as hard as anyone to be the bearer of such tidings.

In a sense, Mother was as much a minister as Father. She had been appointed by the mayor to serve on the Board for County Relief because she had a reputation for always being on the side of the down-and-outers. Every Christmas she supervised the assembling of a hundred-odd baskets of food, clothes, and toys for the poor. And a spot like Radical Hill—the chief slum district of our town, where most of the baskets were taken—lay heavily on her conscience. There many families lived in shacks with no plumbing and little heat.

Then came the afternoon when Mother's deep conviction that something must be done spilled over into action. She spent the day tramping over Radical Hill surveying the situation. When she returned home, we children were awed to see her weep at the remembrance of what she had seen. Then she gingerly stripped herself of every garment, dumped her clothes in the washing machine, took a bath, even washed her hair.

Later, during my undergraduate days at Agnes Scott College, I was to have an experience reminiscent of Mother's. A group of college men and women were asked to give an afternoon to the Syrian Mission in Atlanta, Georgia. I was among the volunteers.

The mission was in the heart of Atlanta's worst slum district, close to the state capitol building, as is often the case. The afternoon was to include a short service at the mission and visiting afterward—two by two—in some of the homes. It was the visiting that brought the revelation. I had dimly realized that such squalid, dirty places did exist, but I had never been personally exposed to them.

Pictures still come back: Men around a fireplace, slinking away as we went in.... Broken window panes stuffed with rags and paper.... A sick child doubled up on a dirty bed in a corner.... Air so stale that we felt polluted to breathe it.... An absurdly young mother wearing ankle socks, nursing her baby before us.... In another room an old woman who had been ill, she told us, for six months, her yellow skin stretched tight over gaunt cheekbones.... A lamp on an old-fashioned dresser made grotesque shadows on flyspecked walls.

I wanted to flee. But even as we headed back toward college, I wondered—was this, too, God's world?

It was sometime during my teens that I received my first clear shaft of light on the riddle of evil. There was growing larger and larger in my mind the contrast between my loving, compassionate parents and a God who allowed such terrible things. One day I took this puzzling question to a woman who had become a very special friend.

Mrs. MacDonald was one of those remarkable people who love all young people. Because she never talked down to teen-agers, many of us gave her our complete confidence. She was married to a Scotsman, a successful lawyer. On occasions when he had to be away from home on law cases, I would spend the night with her. Those evenings were talkfests.

The flavor of Mrs. Mac's life was reflected in her home. Windows were filled with African violets. On the stair landing stood a grandfather clock whose musical chimes marked the quarter-hours. There were current books of history and travel lying about. Just before bedtime Mrs. Mac and I would always have heaping bowls of ice cream,—more ice cream than I could eat. Then she would tuck me under an eiderdown in a mahogany bed with tall pineapple posts.

On one of these evenings I found myself spilling out my

inner rebellion against a God Who permitted suffering and evil when He had the power to stop it.

"Catherine," she said thoughtfully, "you know how often I speak of Kenneth?"

I nodded. Quickly my mind reviewed what I knew about Kenneth. He had been the MacDonalds' only son, had died of diabetes as a teen-ager. It had compounded their sorrow that insulin had been discovered just a few months too late to save their boy. Here then, close at home, was an example of the kind of tragedy that made me question the love of God.

"Well," my friend went on, "if I had reasoned as you suggest, I could have railed bitterly against God for allowing Kenneth's death. God has power. He could have prevented it, so why didn't He?

"Even now, I can't give you a complete answer to that. But I can't be bitter either, because during Kenneth's long illness, I had so many examples of God's tender father-love. Like that time soon after Kenneth himself suspected that he was going to die and asked me, 'Mother, what is it like to die? Mother, does it hurt?' "

Even as Mrs. Mac repeated the questions, tears sprang to my eyes. "How—did you answer him?"

The white-haired woman seemed to be seeing into the past. "I remember that I fled to the kitchen, supposedly to attend to something on the stove. I leaned against the kitchen cabinet. Queer, I'll never forget certain tiny details, like the feel of my knuckles pressed hard against the smooth, cold surface. And I asked God how to answer my boy.

"God did tell me. Only He could have given me the answer to the hardest question that a mother can ever be asked. I knew—just knew how to explain death to him. 'Kenneth,' I remember saying, 'you know how when you were a tiny boy, you used to play so hard all day that when night came, you would be too tired to undress—so you would tumble into Mother's bed and fall asleep?

" 'That was not your bed. It was not where you belonged. And you would only stay there a little while. In the morning —to your surprise—you would wake up and find yourself in your own bed in your own room. You were there because someone had loved you and had taken care of you. Your father had come—with his great strong arms—and carried you away.'

"So I told Kenneth that death is like that. We just wake up some morning to find ourselves in another room—our own room, where we belong. We shall be there, because God loves us even more than our human fathers and takes care of us just as tenderly."

We were both silent for a moment. Then Mrs. Mac said softly, "Kenneth never had any fear of dying after that. If— for some reason that I still don't understand—he could not be healed, then this taking away of all fear was the next greatest gift God could give us. And in the end, Kenneth went on into the next life exactly as God had told me he would— gently, sweetly." There was the look of profound peace on my friend's face as she spoke.

After Mrs. Mac tucked me in that night, I lay in the mahogany bed under the eiderdown, pondering her words. What she had really been telling me was that those on the inside of tragedy are often initiated into something that outsiders may not experience at all: the love of God—instant, continuous, real—in the midst of their trouble. With the presence of the Giver, they have something more precious than any gift He might bestow.

Not until years later, after my marriage to Peter Marshall, did I experience this for myself. During our first happy year in Atlanta, we had a close friend who had known much trouble—the death of children, financial reverses, the misunderstanding of friends. She used to look quizzically at us— young, so in love, fresh in our faith in the goodness of God.

"Neither of you has really had any trouble," she would say.

"You're bound to have some sooner or later. Everyone does. When trouble comes to you, I wonder if you will feel as you do now?"

The friend's prediction was right. We did have trouble—much illness, and finally Peter Marshall's death at forty-six. So now I am in a better position to answer the friend's question. The answer is yes, I still believe in God's love, believe more firmly than ever, because my faith has stood trial.

A few hours before Peter's death I found out what the Hebrew poet meant when he wrote about "the everlasting arms." [1] I experienced the comfort of those arms. It happened in the early morning hours after Peter had been taken by ambulance to the hospital. I was forced to stay behind, so that our young son Peter John would not be in the house alone.

There was no doubt that Peter's life hung in the balance. I sank to the floor by the bed, put my head in my arms, pondering how should I pray. Suddenly there was the feeling of being surrounded by the love of God the Father—enveloped in it, cradled with infinite gentleness.

Awe swept through me, followed by the conviction that it was not necessary to *ask* for anything. All I had to do was to commit Peter and me and our future to this great love. At the time I thought this meant that Peter's heart would be healed.

Much later—when I had trodden the long way through the Valley of the Shadow—I realized that God had given me this experience in the hours preceding Peter's death so that I might have absolute assurance that He was beside Peter and me every minute, loving us, sharing Peter's glory and my grief.

That is how I came to know personally that the Apostle Paul's glowing assertion is literally true that nothing—neither death, nor life, nor tribulation, nor peril of any sort shall be able to separate us from the love of God. . . . [2]

Then, in the years that followed Peter Marshall's death, I thought I glimpsed another shaft of light illuminating the dark night of human sorrow. Not only is God always beside us in trouble, identified with our suffering, but He can also make everything—even our troubles and sorrows—"work together for good." [3]

How many times I have received letters from readers whom I have never met, who marveled at how God accomplished this in our case... "How I wish that I might have heard Dr. Marshall preach! But so far away here in New Zealand, I would never have known about him at all, had it not been for *A Man Called Peter*. And now, to think that he is preaching to more people than ever today."

This is not to say that God willed Peter's death in order that He might bring about a widened ministry. Rather that given his death, God could turn even that to good.

I remember a poignant letter I received from a reader posing a difficult question—why small children must be taken:

Our little boy was hit last spring in the street in front of our home by a truck. He died a week later. Billy was our only child. He had seemed like a gift from God, because we had hoped and prayed for a baby for two years....

Then was it God's will that this little boy die such an unnecessary death? In trying to bring themselves to say with honesty, "Thy will be done," these parents found themselves confused. For along with the best physicians and surgeons they could find, they tried everything medical science knew to save their child. Then had they been working during those days against the will of God?

I understood the questions of this mother, because I had faced them all when death had invaded my life. Surely there is a difference (and it is not just a quibble) between God's ideal will and His permissive will. Thus, in my case, I cannot believe that it was God's ideal will that Peter Marshall die at forty-six. But given a certain set of circumstances—among them Peter's inherited physique, so fine that he was inclined to overtax it—

God had an alternate plan by which He could bring unimagined good even out of early death.

In the same way I could not believe that it was God's ideal will that three-year-old Billy die in such a cruel way. But given a motorized society, given our congested cities, given human free will that resulted in a driver's and a child's carelessness, God would still not suspend the operation of His universe to violate the free will that conspired to bring about this tragedy.

And so illumination came to me. By giving humans freedom of will, the Creator has chosen to limit His own power. He risked the daring experiment of giving us the freedom to make good or bad decisions, to live decent or evil lives, because God does not want the forced obedience of slaves. Instead, he covets the voluntary love and obedience of sons who love Him for Himself.

This, then, is a large portion of the answer to my early question: Why does not a compassionate God hasten to remedy every wrong? I remember the way Peter Marshall answered this in a memorable sermon, "God Still Reigns,' preached in Washington during the second world war:

> There is no use trying to evade the issue.
> There are times when God does not intervene—
> The fact that He does nothing is one of the most
>   baffling mysteries in the Christian life.

> It was H. G. Wells who voiced the dilemma
> that many troubled hearts have faced in war-time:

>> "Either God has the power to stop all this
>> carnage and killing and He doesn't care,
>> or else He does care, and He doesn't have the
>> power to stop it."

> But that is not the answer . . .
> As long as there is sin in the world.
> As long as there is greed

selfishness
hate in the hearts of men
there will be war. . . .

It is only because God is God that He is reckless
enough to allow human beings such free will as has led
the world into this present catastrophe.

God could have prevented the war!
Do you doubt for a moment that God has not the
power?
But suppose He had used it?
Men would then have lost their free agency . . .
They would no longer be souls endowed with the
ability to choose . . .

They would then become puppets
robots
machines
toy soldiers instead.

No, God is playing a much bigger game.
He is still awaiting an awakened sense of the
responsibility of brotherhood in the hearts of
men and women everywhere.
He will not do for us the things that we can do
for ourselves. . . .

A few years ago I was asked to conduct a Sunday-evening
seminar at an exclusive girls' boarding school in the Virginia
countryside outside Washington, D.C. When I arrived I found
the high school sophomores grouped informally around a large
living room, some sitting on the Oriental rugs before a blazing
fire.

The students had been told that they might ask any questions they wished. After the first few minutes it became obvious that while these were intelligent girls, their questions
uncovered the most basic misunderstanding of God. One girl
voiced the query that is always asked at every church young-

people's conference: "What about people in remote parts of Africa or certain jungles of South America who have never heard of Jesus Christ? Will they be condemned to eternal torment? What would be fair about that?"

Another girl, who had obviously been studying sociology, chimed in, "Let's bring the question closer home. What about individuals who become criminals because they were born into slums or other terrible surroundings where they had no chance from the beginning? How could God be just and blame them?"

A beautiful fifteen-year-old posed the one that really tugged at my heart: "There's something that really bothers me...." I saw that she had tears in her eyes as she tried not to make obvious what she most wanted to ask: "My mother and father seldom go near any church. Will God condemn them to eternal damnation for that?"

I was shocked at the terrifying illusion of God that those questions revealed. The mother and father of the fifteen-year-old were dear to her. Did God love them less than she? And how would she ever be able to trust her Creator with her own happiness so long as her only emotion toward Him was terror?

The family love that was so implicit in this girl's questioning reminded me of what my own joyous childhood had taught me: God would scarcely give fathers and mothers a greater capacity for loving their children than God Himself has for loving all His children. I suggested to the girls that God would not have bothered to create father-love and mother-love in the first place, if He Himself did not have it in great abundance.

Then as I told them of my own gropings toward this answer, I thought of how grieved God must be that any of His children should cower before Him in fright. And I realized how often we attribute emotions and deeds to God that we would ascribe only to the most depraved of human minds. Probably no personality in the universe is so maligned as that of the Creator.

Soon after the evening at the girls' school, I came across this same thought in one of Hannah Whitall Smith's books:

... The amazing thing is that all sort of travesties on the character of God and libels on His goodness can find a welcome entrance into Christian hearts.... Nothing else matters as much as this, for all our salvation depends wholly and entirely upon what God is; and unless He can be proved to be absolutely good, and absolutely unselfish, our case is hopeless....[4]

Then Hannah Smith relates how she discovered for herself the unselfishness of God. Between the ages of sixteen and twenty-six, she had passed through a period of skepticism. During this period God had seemed far-off, an unapproachable Being, a stern and selfish Taskmaster, an Autocrat. She asked exactly the same questions that the sophomores in the girls' school asked me that Sunday evening: What about those born into circumstances for which they are not responsible and from which they cannot escape? Would vast numbers of fellow human beings therefore be doomed to eternal punishment for what they cannot help? Most of the church groups of her day taught that they would be. But, Mrs. Smith wondered, would that be justice from a Creator whose tender mercies were said to be "over *all* His works?"[5]

Hannah Smith began to see in every face the anguish which resulted from sin's entrance into the world. She came to be grateful that the fashion of her day dictated veils for women in public; at least the faces before her would be blurred.

One day she was riding in a tram-car along Market Street in Philadelphia. Two men came in and sat down opposite her on the straw seat. When the conductor came for the fare, she was forced to raise her veil to count out change.

She looked up and saw clearly the faces of the two men opposite her. They were lost, debauched-looking. Not only that, but one of them was blind. A new flood of emotion rose to engulf her. In her thoughts she railed against God: "How can You bear it? You might have prevented all this misery, but You did not. Even now You might change it, but You do not. How can You go on living and endure it?"

Suddenly, there in the tram car, God seemed to answer her. The word *lost* blazed with a tremendous illumination: nothing can be lost that is not first owned. Just as a parent is compelled by civil law to be responsible for his family and property, so the Creator—by His own divine law—is compelled to take care of the children He has created. And that means not only caring for the good children, but for the bad ones and the lost ones as well.

So the word *lost* came to be for Mrs. Smith a term of greatest comfort. If a person is a "lost sinner," it only means that he is temporarily separated from the Good Shepherd who owns him. The Shepherd is bound by all duties of ownership to go after all those who are lost until they are found. For Hannah Smith the question about the plight of individuals who have had little chance in life was forever answered. "Who can imagine a mother ever dropping a search so long as there is the least chance of finding a lost child?" Mrs. Smith wrote. "Then would God be more indifferent than a mother? Since I had this sight of the mother-heart of God, I have never been able to feel the slightest anxiety for any of His children. We can trust Him ... trust Him.

In my dealings with people I have been surprised to find that so many honestly do not believe that God wants our happiness and fulfillment. We have heard all of our lives that God is Love, but we insist on "spiritualizing" this. Many Christians have been taught that God's love is different from ours—not the kind His creatures understand. Deeply imbedded in our consciousness is the idea that God is primarily interested in our spiritual and moral rectitude; that, therefore, most of what He requires of us will be about as welcome as castor oil.

Of course God is concerned about our growing into mature spirits. And the God I know sometimes asks difficult things of us, it is true. But His will also includes a happiness here on earth abundant enough to float every difficulty.

But when men persist in these mistaken and tragic ideas of the Creator, how can God show us what He is really like? This is the problem that He had with men. And He solved it in the Incarnation. If God were to break into the stream of history—come to earth as a man and demonstrate that He loved people, weep with them when they suffered, rejoice with them in moments of gladness—then there might be a closer relationship between God and His children.

A story that I first read in my late twenties helped me see why the Incarnation had to be:

One day a British scientist discovered a large anthill in his kitchen garden. These were different from any ants he had observed before, so he was eager to study them. But each time his shadow fell across the anthill, the terrified ants scurried off in terror.

"I stepped back," the scientist wrote in his diary, "and sat down on the grass to think out the situation. I had only good will for the ants, did not wish to harm one of them. But how could I make the ants aware of my good will?

"My imagination played with the problem. To those tiny ants, I was an all-powerful creature 'somewhere up there,' whose thoughts they could not guess, whose ways and intentions they could not know.

"If only I could communicate," the scientist wrote. "But even that wouldn't be enough. Even then, I would be a gigantic being to the ants, and they would never believe that I understood their problems—the minute organization of the hill, their struggles for food, their battles with other ants.

"Only one thing could give them complete confidence. That is, if by some alchemy, I could—for a time—become an ant——"

The gap between our understanding of the nature and the

intentions of the Creator is far wider than the gap between that of ant and man. Only as much of God as could be contained in human flesh would suffice to demonstrate to us what the Father is like. That was why the Incarnation was necessary.

That was why Jesus insisted, "I have come down from heaven not to carry out my own will but the will of him who sent me...." [6] and that "He who has seen me has seen the Father." [7]

Then in watching Jesus, what did His disciples learn about God?

The most obvious thing they observed was the daily intimacy of Jesus' relationship with His Father. At first this must have puzzled them. For always He appeared to be listening to a Voice beyond Himself. There is no record of His ever having argued with anyone about the existence of God; this was fact. Also there was no doubt that God was always present to help, to guide, to succor.

Jesus acted as if there was never any question of the Father's willingness to supply all needs—even such material ones as appeasing hunger. God was concerned about men's bodies along with their souls: Divine love delighted in dispelling pain, in restoring sanity, in straightening crooked limbs and opening blind eyes, even in banishing premature death. Jesus said that in heaven there was an instant readiness to forgive and great joy over finding the lost. And are not these the things that ordinary human father-love or mother-love would delight in doing, if it could?

At every turn, Christ Himself made the comparison between human families and the Fatherhood of God. There is the unforgettable story of the universal Father dealing with the prodigal son.[8] And in the Sermon on the Mount, Jesus asked:

> Why, which of you, when asked by his son for a loaf,
>   will hand him a stone?
> Or, if he asks a fish, will you hand him a serpent?

Well, if for all your evil you know to give your
children what is good,
how much more will your Father in heaven give good
to those who ask him? [9]

The gospels make it clear that to Jesus the Father is all-
loving, is of the essence of love, cannot help loving. Moreover,
this love includes the attributes of love known to all of us—
good will, unselfishness, consideration, justice, wanting only
good things for us, desiring our happiness. It is not a love dependent on our earning it. God is "for us" first, last, and
always. By every word and action, by all the force of His
personality, Christ sought to tell us that the Father is always
nearer, mightier, freer to help us than we can imagine.

There were those who said that any man who held such
ideas must be mad. But the disciples who tramped the dusty
roads with Jesus day after day, who witnessed His decisiveness
in dealing with people, His fearlessness of criticism, His sense
of the sacredness of human personality, the realism with which
He faced evil, knew that this One was not mad. Indeed He
was more beautifully sane than anyone they had ever known.

And so the central issue became sharper and sharper. As the
late D. S. Cairns has put it so memorably in his book, *The
Faith That Rebels*, "Either Jesus Christ was a dreamer about
God. . . . or they and all men were dreamers, walking in the
darkness and deeming it to be light. Either He alone was
awake to reality . . . in His incessant summons to faith and the
staking of everything upon God and His purpose of good for
all mankind . . . ," [10] or else Jesus was a liar, a madman, a
charlatan. There was no alternative. And the disciples were
right in concluding that this was the all-important question
which they and all men have to resolve.

The issue is as sharp today as it was then. I have come to
believe that only if we can depend upon the Creator as a God
of love (not an obscure, ethereal love, but love as you and I

know it) shall we have the courage and confidence to turn our life and affairs over to Him. Hannah Smith once wrote this pithy sentence: "Perfect obedience would be perfect happiness, if only we had perfect confidence in the power we were obeying."

What builds trust like that in the Creator? Only knowing Him so well—His motives, His complete good will—being certain that no pressures will make Him change, knowing Him for a long enough time to be sure of these things.

There are many persons who claim that they have broken through to that kind of knowing—from the Apostle Paul down through spiritual adventurers in every century, even to our day. "I know whom [not *what*] I have trusted," is Paul's ringing assertion, "and I am certain that he is able to keep what I have put into his hands. . . ." [11]

And we who long for an equally confident and solid base to life, how do we go about entering into that kind of relationship with God?

3

How to Enter In

SOMETIME BEFORE I was ten, evangelist Gypsy Smith, Junior, came to hold revival services in our town—Canton, Mississippi. A large tent was pitched on a vacant lot near the town limits. It did not prove large enough to hold the crowds that flocked there. On a platform of raw wood, from which the rezin still oozed, sat the massed choirs gathered from all the churches. Their favorite anthem was "Awakening Chorus":

> The Lord Jehovah reigns, and sin is backward hurled!
> Rejoice! Rejoice! Rejoice! . . .

The "Rejoicings" reverberated so shrilly that they always raised goosebumps along my spine. As the congregation sang, the waving arms of the music director would beat out the rhythms of hymns like

> *Stan*-ding on the *prom*-i-ses of *Christ* my *king—*

or

> *Sing* them *o*-ver a-*gain* to me,
> *Won*-der-ful *words* of *Life*. . . .

Each time we collectively took a breath, the pianist would run in scales, chords, and flourishes marvelous to my childish ears.

Then would come the preaching. Gypsy Smith would lean far over the crude pulpit, pausing from time to time to whip out a handkerchief and wipe his flushed, perspiring face or to take a drink of water. His was a sincere testimony. The emotion in his preaching would steadily mount, transferring itself to the congregation. And finally a hush would fall over the tent, as the choir sang almost in a whisper,

> Softly and tenderly Jesus is calling,
> Calling for you and me....

"Believe on the Lord Jesus Christ, and thou shalt be saved," the evangelist would thunder. "That's all you have to do. Accept the Lord Jesus as your personal Saviour."

Soon at the far edge of the tent someone would rise and slowly make his way down the aisle toward the front. Then another person—and another—and another—and another.

From those evangelistic meetings of my childhood, I thought that "believing on the Lord Jesus Christ" simply meant being fully persuaded that what the church believed about Christ's divinity was true.

This did not seem difficult. In fact, it was not long after the revival tent had been packed up and moved to another town that I decided to join the church. One Sunday at the close of the regular morning service in our church, my preacher-father issued "the invitation." On an impulse, I rose, marched down the aisle, and so became a member of the First Presbyterian Church of Canton. Because I had marched spontaneously, I remember my father was so moved that he stood in front of the altar and looked at me through eyes swimming with tears behind his spectacles.

Years passed. Not until my college days did I recognize that something was missing in this inherited Christianity based on an untested assent. By that time I had acquired a parallel King James–Moffatt New Testament. Moffatt's translation brought the ancient words alive for me.

I found that the evangelist of my childhood had been right in insisting that the only way we can really know God is by looking at Jesus Christ. Christ is the center of Christianity. To pretend anything else—that we need think of Him only as a good man who was also a great teacher, for instance—is not Christianity, whatever else it may be.

But I was also astonished to discover that no mere intellectual acceptance of Christ's divinity would have satisfied Jesus as a way of entrance into His kingdom. He will settle for nothing less than making Him the ruler of one's life, with the inevitable result of a practical day-by-day obedience: "Why call ye me Lord, Lord, and do not the things which I say?" [1] No wonder marching down the church aisle had not changed me one whit.

I feel that I have come to a crisis in my life [I wrote in the journal I was keeping during these college years]. It's very easy for me to see how people can lose their so-called religion when they have gotten enough education to make them think at all. That is very likely to happen to anyone whose religion is simply an inheritance or a habit. Unless something intervenes, it could happen to me.

My religion is not on a very firm basis, I'm afraid. I have had no vital experience. God doesn't seem real to me. I believe now—because of people I know who do have something vital and real, like Peter Marshall. But I can't go on like this. What are we here in this world for anyway?

This questioning may have seemed like a prelude to change, but the fact is that I did "go on that way" for many years, even after my graduation and marriage to the young preacher, Peter Marshall.

During those years I was an active, interested minister's wife. In addition to my homemaking, I attended women's meetings, led Bible studies, made talks, called on parishioners, and took part in program-committee meetings. Obviously most of this work was on the organizational level. Even when I led Bible studies for small groups of women or gave a talk or book review, I was still relying mostly on other people's ideas about the Christian life. Those who listened carefully must have missed the authentic note of personal experience.

During all this time, I never stopped struggling to find the way to God for myself. Peter's preaching was a never-ending challenge to me:

> The Christian Church in its early days grew in numbers and in influence because God used the testimonies of men and women who had something to say about Jesus. What they had to say was that this Jesus, who had died on a cross, was alive and spiritually present every day to the disciples.
>
> And they proclaimed everywhere they went, with enthusiasm and conviction, the good news of the gospel. It was to them the thrilling and exciting story of how life had been changed for them,
>   and how they had been changed for life.
> They could no more keep silent than a flower can withhold its fragrance or the sun keep back its light. This power that had made them different, they said, was available to anyone who would believe...
> Sins could be forgiven; Christ could come into human life to change natures and dispositions
>   to change moods and temperaments
>   to banish fear and worry
>   to remove shame and guilt
>   to provide a new dynamic, a new purpose in life,
> a new joy and a peace that nothing could destroy.
> The early disciples were thrown into prison.
> They were persecuted
>   boycotted
>   hounded from place to place.
> Yet thousands joined their fellowship and discovered the truth they were proclaiming, and found life becoming a new and thrilling experience....

Why—under preaching like that, and especially when the preacher was so close at hand to answer my questions and to help—could I not make contact with the Christ whom Peter knew so well? Perhaps I was still not ready. So often this personal encounter with God comes through crisis. Peter's had been a vocational crisis, when he had had to decide whether or not he would leave his native Scotland to enter the ministry. So far my life had been protected, serene, free of urgent need. There was only that deep gnawing ache for Something More that I had known since college days.

Then, in March 1943, came the event that was to change my life. A routine physical check-up brought bad news. Chest X rays showed a soft spotting over both lungs. Specialists were unable to make a conclusive diagnosis, but the trouble appeared to be tuberculosis. *Tuberculosis!* Hated word, hated disease. I was ordered to bed twenty-four hours a day for an indefinite period.

Fifteen months later I had gained some fifteen pounds; otherwise nothing was changed. The area of infection was as widespread as at the beginning. When other specialists were consulted, they rejected the usual pneumothorax treatment, as well as surgery, or even the use of the drugs that were then beginning to be used in TB cases. Their only advice was "More bed rest." When we asked "How long?" they said frankly they had no idea.

Despair settled in. After almost a year and a half in bed, I could see few gains. My husband and four-year-old son needed me. Our household situation was becoming more difficult with every month that passed.

Often during those discouraging days there was a vivid picture in my mind: I was groping my way along a pitch-black tunnel. There were passages, twistings and turnings off the main tunnel. I tried this way and that. Repeatedly I found only dead ends and was forced to grope my way back to the black center shaft. I clung to the hope that somehow, sometime, I would emerge from darkness into the sunlight again. But in order to get there, I had to proceed resolutely straight ahead.

I knew by now that there were no short cuts. Did this mean that I had to deal directly with God, who was insisting through circumstances that He alone knew the shortest way to the sunlight of His presence?

There was in me a desire for an all-out effort to reach Him, born of desperation. Sloughed off now were all the trappings of religion, most of them concerned with the ceremonial or organizational aspects of churches that so often confuse the central issue. I began to see wholeness as more than the search for physical health. As I understood the viewpoint of Jesus, it was that physical soundness is merely part of a more profound wholeness. In this sense, wholeness can only come about as inner cleavages are healed, as man is joined to the Source of his being. Thus, for me, the search for health became the search for a relationship with God. The question was, what was blocking that relationship?

I stood before my Maker starkly, stripped of pretenses. My unworthiness shrieked at me. My tendency to overcriticalness, to harsh, hasty judgments. My little jealousies, the self-centeredness that had made me a poor one for teamwork of any kind. Lying in bed I summoned up the dishonesties of my past. Once in high school I had cheated on an algebra test. Another time, when I had been treasurer of a school organization, I had "borrowed" some money from the fund and then paid it back ten days later.

There were dishonesties of a different sort: I had not always been candid with my husband. I saw in myself a streak of secretiveness, a tendency to bar him from a corner of my mind and heart. I well knew that this was no way to build a solid marriage.

Through agonizing days I made methodical notes on these ignoble traits and deeds. Then I asked Peter to hear me out on the ones that affected him. He listened, looking pained, not so much at what I was confessing as at the spiritual anguish he saw in me.

I then felt it necessary to write two letters—one to the high school principal who had taught algebra, the other to the teacher who had been faculty adviser to the school organization. Since the last thing I wanted was to be considered a religious crackpot, I labored over the wording of the letters. In each case, as matter-of-factly as I could, I told why I felt it necessary to write the letter: that this was one of the steps which would help me to enter into a new and total Christian experience. Three days passed before I could muster enough courage to mail those letters. In the end, I posted them only because I knew that my relationship with God now meant more to me than the reputation that I had once thought all-important.

Both recipients of the letters turned out to be as generous and forgiving as people usually are when confronted with honest confession.

Then Peter, through his preaching, taught me the next step to God. Facing up to ourselves in confession is therapeutic, provided we move on to forgiveness and do not wallow in our wrongdoing. It is possible to overemphasize the self-centeredness, the me-first angle, even in relation to our sins: "Look at me, what a great sinner I've been. My case is worse than most. God is going to have to do a special job on me...*I*...*I*...*I*...."

Having confessed every wrong that had surfaced to my conscious mind, I then specifically claimed God's promise of I John 1:9: "If we confess our sins, He is faithful and just to forgive us our sins, and to cleanse us from all unrighteousness." Then I proceeded to burn the list and the notes I had made as a symbol that everything was, from that moment, forgiven—forgotten—gone forever.

No doubt the burning was a childish procedure. Yet in this way I stumbled on the value of dramatizing and thus making more real—that is, more real for myself—a definite transaction with God.

So now the housecleaning was over—except for one thing. I was aware that a psychiatrist would scarcely regard my amateur self-probing as a thorough enough job of analysis. So I prayed that God would see to it that any residue of debris in the subconscious would eventually come to light, or that He would deal with anything left by pouring His cleansing and healing Spirit into those subterranean levels.

In subsequent months more of the debris did come into my consciousness. For instance, I became aware of a compartment in my being in which I had locked certain persons whom I disliked. They could go their way; I would go mine. But now Christ seemed to be standing by the locked door saying, "That isn't forgiveness. It won't do. No closed doors are allowed. The Kingdom of God is the kingdom of right relationships. Remember what I said—'If ye forgive no men their trespasses, neither will your Father forgive your trespasses?' If you cannot forgive, you cannot enter the kingdom. This unforgiveness grieves me more than any cheating on an algebra test."

By the time I had faced up to this, it was the summer of 1944, time for our annual trek back to the Cape Cod cottage. I got there only by Peter's special arrangements—a compartment on the train and an ambulance to meet me at the station.

Later that June, early one morning I was reading Jesus' parable about the cleansed house:

When an unclean spirit leaves a man, it roams through dry places in search of refreshment and finds none. Then it says "I will go back to the house I left," and when it comes it finds the house vacant, clean and all in order. Then it goes off to find seven other spirits worse than itself; they go in and dwell there, and the last state of that man is worse than the first. . . .[2]

There was danger, then, in my attempts to clean house unless the Spirit of God took over the house. The keys and the management of my house had to be turned over to Christ. For how could I ask Him to heal me until He was completely in charge? Any human physician requires the surrender of a given case into his care; he can do nothing unless the patient agrees to follow his orders. Common sense told me that exactly the same was true of the Great Physician.

So that sunshiny June morning, I got out of bed and stood at the bedroom window looking out at the garden that Peter had so lovingly planted ... Roses and white hollyhocks, yellow day lilies, zinnias, all a riot of color ... A blue, blue sky above ... The sea just over the brow of the hill. There I stood and took the plunge. It amounted to a quiet pledge to God, the promise of a blank check with my life:

"It is ten-twelve A.M. on the twenty-second of June 1944," I said. "From this moment I promise that I'll try to do whatever You tell me for the rest of my life, insofar as You'll make it clear to me what Your wishes are. I'm weak and many times I'll probably want to renege on this. But Lord, You'll have to help me with that too."

I took a deep breath; I was trembling. I had entered in. Yet nothing seemed different. The hollyhock faces still nodded at the window. Fluffy clouds still floated in that blue, blue sky. I turned and noted in my journal the date and the hour of the promise I had just made. There would be moments in the future when this pledge would not seem real to me. But it was real, and writing it down would help to remind me.

I felt no emotion other than the relief of knowing that I had completed my part, so far as I knew it. This brought me a peace of mind I had not known during the tortuous days of self-probing and writing the letters of confession.

The proof of the reality of the pledge I had made began coming during the next six weeks. My physical condition was improving. Each morning I would lie in the yard, soaking up sunshine. Next I tried joining the family for dinner each night. That did not tire me over much. Then I began taking short walks some afternoons with Jeffrey, our cocker spaniel, trotting beside me. It was a joy to stand at the top of the rise in the road and see the sea again, feel the tangy salt air on my cheeks, laugh at the sea-wind blowing back Jeffrey's floppy ears as he stood poised, watching the circling gulls. It was even good to feel sand in my shoes. As of old, I began taking an interest in the garden and the kitchen. Perhaps I could take it as my job to arrange some flowers each day for the house. And would it be possible for the family to gather some beach plums for jelly? I could not help much with the jelly-making, but perhaps a little. It was like coming to life again. And life was good, so good. The speck of light at the other end of the tunnel was becoming a steady beam.

God deals differently with each of us. He knows no "typical" case. He seeks us out at a point in our own need and longing and runs down the road to meet us. This individualized treatment should delight rather than confuse us, because it so clearly reveals the highly personal quality of God's love and concern.

At the same time, there is one central core of the entering-in or commitment experience that is common to everyone who undergoes it. It is the act of putting oneself—past, present, and future—into God's hands to do with as He pleases.

A girl once asked me, "But isn't that a terrible risk?"

Yes, it certainly would be, if we had a God who wanted to deprive us of joy rather than add joy to our lives, if He were not a God who cares supremely for us and our welfare. But what He wants for us is exactly what every thoughtful parent wants for his child—that pure, deep-flowing joy that springs out of maturity and fulfillment.

That God is like this, each of us must discover for ourselves. There is only one difficulty. The discovery comes second, the act of will first. The order of events can never be reversed: action on our part, that is, the decision to hand our life over to God and the promising of obedience; then, and only then, comes understanding and the unfolding knowledge of the character of God.

This decision need not be dramatic nor emotional. It is just as real, though it be but a quiet assent without any emotion whatsoever. This has been vividly demonstrated to me recently by John Sherrill, now a dear friend.

As with most of us, it was personal need that brought John to the point of commitment. My need had been a long illness. John's was a more immediate physical crisis. Three years before he had had a malignant mole removed from his ear which had been diagnosed as melanoma, one of the most vicious killers of all types of cancer. Miraculously—everyone felt—it had been caught in time. But now the doctor had discovered a small lump on John's neck that was suspect.

The details of the physical problems and the prayers for healing are not the point that I want to make here. Suffice it to say that as soon as I heard about the situation, I knew that John's crisis was also my crisis—part of "my bundle" of responsibility, as the Quakers express it so vividly. Then—how were we who were so concerned to pray about John?

A series of thoughts kept pounding at me and would not be put aside: healing is not an end in itself; it is a dividend of the gospel. Physical health is but one part of total wholeness. Then came the inevitable question: had John ever made an act of turning his whole being over to God?

Who was I to ask John a question like that? He was an intellectual—an editor and successful writer. Any emotional approach to Christianity, as well as the usual religious clichés and shibboleths, were repugnant to him. Considering all this, would not any question about his relationship to God be gross presumption on my part and anathema to him?

Still, time was running out. Only twenty-four hours remained until John would enter New York's Memorial Hospital for surgery. After all, what he thought of me did not matter at a time like this. The fact that a life was at stake gave me the courage to telephone John and tell him that I had to see him.

His wife, Tibby, came with him. The three of us found a quiet room and shut ourselves in. There was no attempt at a subtle approach. I explained what had led up to my telephone call, what I had learned about the process of entering in, and why this seemed important as a foundation for any prayer for healing. My heart was in what I was saying, so that several times my voice broke.

When I had finished, John asked wonderingly, "Do you mean that I can just decide that I am willing for God to take over my life, and tell Him so—as blandly and as matter-of-factly as that—and have it work?"

"That's right," was my reply. "Do it as matter-of-factly as you please. You do not have to have all your theological beliefs sorted out either. Nor do you have to understand everything. You just come to Christ as you are—questions, complexes, contradictions, doubts, everything. After all, how else can any of us come? You make a definite movement of your will toward God. After that, the next move is up to Him. The feelings, the proof that He has heard and has taken you on, even the understanding will come later."

At that point John and Tib had to rush away for their last hasty preparations for the hospital. It was not until later that I found out what happened immediately after they left me.

"After we told you good-by and backed out of your driveway," John told me. "I did the simple thing you had suggested —just said 'Yes' to God while driving the car. I can show you the exact spot on Millwood Road where it happened, right by a certain telephone pole.

"Then because it had been such a quiet, interior thing, I felt that I ought to go on record by telling someone. So I said to Tib, I suppose a bit ruefully, 'Well I'm a Christian now.'

"And she asked curiously, 'Do you feel any different?'

" 'Not a bit different,' I told her."

Yet John is different now—so different. The quiet trans-action at that certain spot on Millwood Road was real enough because never have I seen so much action on God's part in the life of one man in one short year. That too, is another story—an exciting one which is his to tell, not mine. Someday I hope he will. But I can at least add that when the famous New York specialist operated, all he could find was a dried-up *nodule*, easy to remove. There was no malignancy.

Church folk often give the impression that there are only two ways of entering into the Christian life: being born into a Christian family or stumbling into a dramatic religious experience as an adult. Either approach to Christianity seems to have two unfortunate factors in common: the initiative was apparently not with the individual and the way to God was clouded in vagueness.

I am convinced that God never meant for anything about the Christian life to be vague, least of all the steps by which we enter into a meaningful relationship with Him. The obscurity must surely be on our side, not God's.

Growing up in a believing family is not to be undervalued. It is still the ideal beginning, because it is the foundation of the happiest possible childhood. Yet I know now that some-thing more is needed: each human being must enter into Life for himself. There is, therefore, no such thing as inheriting Christianity.

David duPlessis, a minister from South Africa and a new friend, recently told me a fascinating story about himself and this matter of an inherited Christianity.

"It happened one cold January night, really cold—in fact five degrees below zero. I had been sleeping soundly, then woke suddenly about four in the morning. I thought that a voice had wakened me. But as I lay there listening, there was no sound except the creak of snow-laden branches outside the bedroom window and the measured breathing of the children in the adjoining room.

"Then the voice came again. This sounds peculiar, I realize, but I don't honestly know whether it was an audible voice or not. At any rate, the words were clear enough, though they seemed nonsensical: 'God has no grandsons.' Just that—nothing more.

"Well, I snapped on my bedside light and reached for a Bible with a concordance in the back. I looked up the word *grandson*. No such reference anywhere in the Scriptures. Then I looked up *grandfather*. Not there.

"Sons? Yes, lots of references. 'Behold what manner of love the Father hath bestowed on us, that we should be called the sons of God. . . .' 'For as many as are led by the Spirit of God, they are the sons of God.' And lots more, a long list of them.

"But," I wondered, "what did these references have to do with God having no grandsons? Yet this one sentence had been clearly imprinted on my consciousness. More puzzled than ever, I finally turned off the light and went back to sleep.

"I didn't find out myself until ten days after the sentence was first given to me," he said. "I was aboard a plane, en route from Milwaukee to Chicago—when suddenly I knew.

"When Christ's apostles first started preaching, they insisted that every individual had to have a personal encounter with Christ and make the decision to accept His way—for himself. Judging from history, there must have been plenty of vitality in that first-century church—enough to shake the sophisticated Roman world to its depths.

"Well, the years passed. After a while those first followers of Christ began to reason, 'These children of ours were born into a Christian family. They have grown up in the church and have been instructed in the faith. They were born Christians. Surely they don't need any special experience of repentance as we did.'

"The church pews were soon filled with the sons and daugh-

ters of those first followers. But since the children had inherited their belief in Christ, they knew Him only secondhand.

"Perhaps it was not surprising that by the second century
the vitality of the church had begun to decline. Proofs of
God's power, like healing through faith, became the exception
rather than the rule.

"Sure, in every century, there are always some who have
had a personal confrontation with Christ. During revival
periods—like the time of Luther in Germany, or the Wesleyan
Revival in England—large numbers have had the personal experience of being truly born again to become sons of God.

"But then in the following generation, the same sad process
starts over. And soon the pews are filled again largely with
secondhand believers—grandsons and granddaughters."

My friend had unintentionally stated what had been my
own case. I understood why my inherited faith had not been
enough. I had been a prime example of a "granddaughter."
And God has no grandsons or granddaughters.

I wonder how many others there are who have thought
of formal church membership as a substitute for that direct
Father-child relationship that God really wants of us? No
wonder much of our religious life today is plagued by vagueness. Let us not mistake it: Entering in does take childlikeness.
The door through which we enter into Life is a low door.
And sometimes it is the humble and the needy who can show
the rest of us the way.

So a group of ministers recently discovered. One of them,
Bruce Larson of *Faith at Work* magazine, told me this story.
They had gathered for a two-day retreat at a church in New
Jersey to discuss mutual problems and to pray about them. As
so often happens, the discussion part predominated. It was
late afternoon of the final day when a startling event occurred.

Suddenly the door of their meeting-room opened and a
stranger walked in. The minister of the host church knew him,
had seen him often around the neighborhood. Self-consciously

the man seated himself at the fringe of the circle. Though there was no more than a momentary pause in the discussion, the experienced eyes of the other clergymen present took in the situation—the watery eyes, the sagging shoulders, the seedy clothing. Obviously the man was an alcoholic.

The discussion continued, while the stranger listened. "It seems to me," a crisp voice said, "that all we have been talking about these two days can be summed up in our need for God's power—the kind of power that changes lives, heals, restores, that——"

He stopped, his attention arrested by the agitated movements of the stranger.

"That's it! That's what I need. I could use some of that."

There was sudden silence. While everyone watched, his bleary eyes filled a bit more and the quavering voice continued.

"My name is Ernie. I drink too much. People have tried to help me ... doctors, hospitals, clinics, missions, and all that. But I ... I can't seem to stop. How do I get this power you're talking about?"

The question hung, quivering in the silence. Despite the fact that these men were experienced in dealing with people in need, the intrusion was embarrassing. There was a time schedule for the meeting, trains and planes to be caught, families to get back to, next Sunday's sermons to think about. Closing time was at hand.

Finally, a white-haired man spoke up. "Ernie, all of us have problems too. It's a problem-filled world...." The voice of the elderly minister was gentle, suave, as he sought to identify with the stranger. All of the men knew that the pastor who was speaking had had professional training in counseling.

"As to how we can get God's help. Well, that isn't always too easy. It takes patience, time. There are many roads to God, many avenues by which—"

"Damn!" The interruption was explosive, passionate.
"Damn ... Damn ... Damn ... Damn!"

The quiet of the room was suddenly being blasted by Ted, a young minister and a former businessman, anger and impatience written clearly on his face. Again and again he beat his fist down on the seat of the empty chair beside him.

"This man doesn't want to hear about our problems," Ted said vehemently. "He's asked us a question—how can he get God's help to stop drinking? We haven't answered him. If we don't know the answer, then let's adjourn this meeting, stop our endless talking, go home and tell our people that the church hasn't any answers for today. In that case, we'd better stop being hypocrites and shut the church doors for good."

There was a shocked silence, but the impassioned words had cleared the air. Almost simultaneously, five or six men—including the angry young preacher and the white-haired minister—rose and walked over to Ernie.

Ted knelt in front of the alcoholic. "Ernie, do you believe that Jesus Christ can come into your life and change it?"

The watery eyes looked down, childlike. "Yes... Yes, I do."

"Then we're going to pray right now, Ernie, that He will do this for you."

The young minister took both of Ernie's hands in his. The white-haired preacher stood behind, placed both hands gently on top of the alcoholic's head. The others stood around in a semicircle, each one with his hands on the stranger.

Ted's prayer was short, hard-hitting, impassioned. He asked for Christ's healing power for Ernie, for the forgiveness of sins, for the beginning of a new life.

"Now, Ernie," Ted said, "you pray too. Just thank God that He has heard you and healed you."

"I hope so," Ernie quavered.

"Not hope so. He *has!*"

"I—— Well, I'd like to believe that."

The answer was gentle, but firm. "Ernie, thank Jesus that He has already come into your life."

The room became completely still. And then in wavery sentences Ernie's voice reached up to God. "God, I'm a tired, weak old man. I don't see what use I am to anyone. But I'd like to find the new life they talk about. Please help me."

It was real. It was vital. Every man in the room knew it, felt it. They had been talking about power. This *was* power.

Forgotten were train schedules, plane reservations, other obligations. For the first time in two days, real contact had been made with God through one of the least likely of persons. The air was charged with emotion. Out from the depths came some of the deep needs of the ministers themselves.

A pastor from New England began it. At first his words seemed unrelated— "I was driving down here several days ago, feeling lonely and apart from God. While crossing over Bear Mountain Bridge, I looked in the ice-clogged river and saw a small boat locked in the ice some distance off shore.

"That boat fascinated me. For my life has been like that. Frozen, isolated, shut within myself. I'm frozen with the fear of other people's opinions, the fear of not being a success, the fear of not pleasing people."

Suddenly his eyes filled with tears. "Would you pray for me, that I'll get thawed out so I can really help people again?"

There was no hesitation now. The men quickly gathered around him. All but Ernie, who hung back, shyly. But the young minister walked over to him.

"Ernie, come on over and pray with the rest of us."

"Oh no! I couldn't do *that*...."

The minister took him by the hand. "Look, Ernie, you've received; now you must give. And *we* need *you* now."

So Ernie knelt beside the minister and prayed with the others. The prayer was very simple. And in this room miraculously filled with power, every one of the ministers made his way back to God with a childlike renewal of commitment.

Later the minister from New England was marveling to the young preacher at the turn of events. "As long as I live, I'll never get over it," he said. "What had happened to Ernie minutes before was the real thing. The proof was that it was Ernie, with his winy breath in my face, who was God's channel for transmitting the power. It was like electricity flowing through him to me." And he added with awe in his voice, "Except ye become as little children, ye shall not enter into the kingdom of heaven...."

And so we enter in, each of us, up our own secret stairs into the most joyous and rewarding relationship of our lives. The good news is that this is no experience meant just for the saints. God welcomes us no matter what our lives have been, no matter what we have done or have failed to do, whether we feel adequate or broken or merely empty.

And the rest of the good news is that the way into the Christian life need not be vague. Sometimes laymen who approach Christianity with few preconceived ideas can be surprisingly specific and helpful. A case in point are the twelve steps toward God outlined by Alcoholics Anonymous. Out of great need and hard experience, the men who were the founders of this movement hammered out the steps. When I first read them, years after my own entering-in experience, I was astonished to find that this path to sobriety was precisely the road I had traveled on my way to a personal commitment to Christ. I have changed only a few words:

1. We admit helplessness in one or more specific areas of our lives.
2. We believe that there is a Power greater than ourselves.
3. We make a decision to turn our lives over to the care of God as we understand Him.
4. We make a searching and fearless inventory of ourselves.
5. We admit to God, to ourselves, and to another human being the exact nature of our wrongs.
6. We are ready for God to change us, to remove these defects of character.

7. Humbly we ask Him to do so.
8. We make a list of all the people we have harmed, and we become willing to make amends to them all.
9. We make direct amends to such people when possible, when to do so would not injure them or others.
10. At intervals we continue to take personal inventory, and when we are wrong, promptly admit it.
11. Through daily prayer and meditation, we seek to improve our conscious contact with God as we understand Him, praying only for the knowledge of His will for us and for the power to carry it out.
12. We try to carry this message to others and to practice these principles in all our affairs.

The way to God is a clearly marked, well-traveled road. Only one question remains to us: Do we really want to find our way down that road?

Do we really want to enter in?

4

The Secret of the Will

Some years before Peter Marshall's death, a man approached him on the sidewalk outside the church following a Sunday-morning service. The stranger introduced himself as a visitor to Washington, a used-car dealer from St. Paul, Minnesota. He had a direct, blunt manner. What he had to say so impressed Peter that he told me about their conversation as we were driving home.

As I remember, the point that the man was making went something like this: "Dr. Marshall, you challenged me this morning to want to apply Jesus' teachings to life. But as a businessman, I'm puzzled by what appears to be a lack of realism in what Christ told us to do—such as in the Sermon On the Mount. Have you ever known anyone who loved his neighbor as much as himself? Or who's willing to turn the other cheek all the time? Or who never has a lustful thought? I'll even make a special trip back to Washington to hear you, if you'll promise to preach a sermon telling *how* we can do what Christ asked."

Like the used-car dealer, many of us are puzzled about the *hows* of Christianity. For some years, I too wondered if there were some principle involved here, some secret that I had somehow missed.

The day that I found the answer—in the book mentioned so often in these pages, *The Christian's Secret of a Happy Life*—I felt like someone who had stumbled on buried treasure. Hannah Smith, in turn, had learned the secret from a book called *Spiritual Progress*, written by the Frenchman, François Fénelon, who lived during the seventeenth century. Fénelon was a cleric with an extraordinary insight into human nature. He was spiritual advisor to the lowly and the great, including Madame de Maintenon and the Duke of Burgandy, heir to the throne of France.

Where Fénelon and others learned the secret, stretching back to the New Testament writers, I do not know. But this I do know: in my life this formula has been the answer to the how.

The secret is simply this: that the Christian life must be lived in the will, not in the emotions; that God regards the decisions and choices of a man's will as the decisions and choices of the man himself—no matter how contrary his emotions may be. Moreover, when this principle is applied, the emotions must always capitulate to the will.

At birth, as I have pointed out, God gives each human being the gift of freedom of will. Under no circumstances will God ever violate this central citadel of man's being. The picture in the book of Revelation of Christ standing, knocking, outside the closed door of the human heart, I believe to be a literal picture:

> ... if any man hear my voice, and open the door,
> I will come in to him, and will sup with him,
> and he with me.[1]

But the latch of the door is on the inside. It is our hand that must open the door. It is our voice that must invite Christ in.

Genuine freedom of will permits no door-crashing, not even from the Lord of glory!

Before the entering-in decision, we have probably thought that we belonged to ourselves, that what we did with ourself was our business. We reasoned that since God gave us intelligence, He intended that we use it for all those decisions that go to make up a life—a career, whom we shall marry, where we will live, how we shall rear our children. Self-interest, what the self thought it wanted, what seemed best to the self —these have been the deciding factors.

But if the man is to enter in, he must decide that while this intelligent self-interest may seem good, there is a better way. A man must will that self abdicate its throne; that henceforth Christ's will determines action. And this movement of the will —that decision-making part of man—must be made without paying any attention to the emotions.

It is important that we not gauge the reality of spiritual experience by our feelings. A sixteen-year-old girl posed this question to me in a letter: "How can one be sure he is a Christian? If a person has asked Christ with sincerity to come into his heart, but still doesn't feel any different, well—how can he know whether He has or not?"

The key to her quandary, it seemed to me, was the word *feel*. We petition, we pray, we wait, but we do not "feel" any different. Feelings are at the bottom of most of our Christian difficulties. Our emotions are often painfully misleading, and at best we have imperfect control over them. This should come as no surprise, for psychology tells us that these emotions often rise up out of the depths of the subconscious, even out of the emotional set of ancestors long dead, out of the race consciousness. Our feelings can be affected by such irrelevant matters as the mood of those around us, by whether we had a good night's sleep, by hunger or indigestion, or by a morning in which the rain blew through the open window, spattered the wallpaper, and the neighborhood dogs turned over the garbage pail. "I don't feel God's presence today," we wail.

What is the remedy? It is simplicity itself: Our emotions are not the real us. The motivating force at the center of our physical being is our will. The dictionary describes *will* as "the power of conscious deliberate action." The will is the governing power in us, the rudder, the spring of all our actions. Before God we are responsible only for the set of that will—whether we decide for God's will or insist on self-will. Our Maker knows that our feelings are unruly, unreliable gauges. So if we see to it that our intentions (our motives) are right, we can trust God to see to the results.

If the girl who is not sure that she is a Christian will make a definite act of giving her will to God, even though she feels nothing at all, in God's eyes that is a real transaction—done, finished. As soon as she accepts the truth of this, God will handle her emotions. Eventually she *will feel* different. Eventually she *will feel* God's presence. The emotions trail behind the will. In the interval, she must not be led astray by ephemeral emotional responses to a date that turns out badly or ants that invade the picnic basket.

Does this sound too simple? Actually, I believe it to be the only principle that makes entering the Christian life possible.

It is a theory that works in real life. I think of what happened in the case of the late Fulton Oursler—for years editor of *Liberty* magazine and senior editor of *Reader's Digest* at the time of his death. Perhaps best known for his *The Greatest Story Ever Told*, Oursler was for years a close friend and associate of my husband Len.

At thirty Mr. Oursler was a self-styled agnostic. He believed in no absolutes of right and wrong, certainly not in anything approaching the supernatural. As he described himself, he was "genially loyal to ethical standards when they did not interfere too much with what I wanted to do. But I sneered at God as an elaborate self-deception and did all that I could to tear down the faith of those close to me." [2]

Then trouble surrounded Fulton Oursler in all phases of his life. *Liberty* went under, so he was out of a job. At the same time there were health and marriage difficulties. There came the day when he realized that he was absolutely helpless to do one thing for himself.

What happened then is vividly described by Oursler himself in a book he later wrote, *Why I Know There Is a God*. On a blustery day with dark clouds lowering, the distraught man wandered down Fifth Avenue in New York City. He stopped in front of a church—self-conscious, filled with conflicting emotions, but knowing that unless he got help he had come to the end of the way. For the first time in years, he ventured inside a church. Let him tell the rest of it in his own words:

"In ten minutes or less I may change my mind," he prayed. "I may scoff at this—and love error again. Pay no attention to me then. For this little time I am in right mind and heart. This is my best. Take it and forget the rest; and if You are really there, help me."

What Mr. Oursler did in the quiet church was what Hannah Smith meant by setting the rudder of the will and disregarding everything else—conflicting thoughts, contrary feelings. And God must have accepted this as the real decision of the real man, exactly as Hannah insisted that He always does. Within two weeks Fulton Oursler's problems began to resolve.

"Only chance would explain it to the unbelieving," he said later, "because nothing either I or anyone else did contrived the events. The complications dissolved... by what the rationalist would call a series of beautiful coincidences God literally took over my life, took it out of my hands."

The more impressive proof that God accepted Fulton Oursler's gift of his will that day in the church is the massive contribution to the religious life of the nation that Mr. Oursler made during the remainder of his life. A knowing, spirited faith replaced his former agnosticism. Lost in emptiness, he found direction. His enthusiasms, his intensity, his insatiable love of a good story that had once poured into murder mysteries, plays, and movie scripts he now dedicated to the building up of faith in others. Since that experience his work includes some eighteen books, an endless succession of articles, and his column "Modern Parables," syndicated in about a hundred newspapers. When he was stricken with a heart attack on May 23, 1952, his *The Greatest Faith Ever Known* was interrupted in mid-sentence.

The principle of the will has the most practical sort of application to numerous everyday difficulties. At the moment we have a home-grown illustration of it with our twelve-year-old daughter, Linda. She is having corrective dentistry to straighten her teeth. After she wore braces for a year, the dentist fitted her with a retainer, a complicated and expensive plastic device to correct the bite. The trouble is that the retainer is removable.

On too many evenings we have had a scene like this:

"Linda, where is your retainer?"

Silence. Then a slightly bewildered expression on her pretty freckled face. "I don't know."

"Did you wear it to school this morning?"

"Yes—but I took it out during lunch."

"And then?"

"Some of the girls started passing it around from hand to hand under the table . . . just in fun, of course."

We give her a glassy stare. "Fun? But not very sanitary! Don't you know that——"

Linda, sensing that a real outburst is coming, adds quickly, "It's in my purse. I'm sure it is. Pretty sure, that is."

"Would you mind looking?"

Linda soon returns, holding the troublesome item aloft. There is a mild note of triumph in her voice. "See—all safe. It wasn't in the purse though. It was in the glove compartment of the car."

We bite our lips helplessly, make no comment. Then— "Linda, how *are* we going to get you to wear it regularly?"

"I don't know" (the stock answer for everything).

More months pass. More hairbreadth rescues of retainer from cars, a doctor's office, the front lawn. Once it had to be mailed back from her grandmother's. Then one day Linda bequeathed it to the Pennsylvania Railroad by leaving it in a ladies' room on one of their trains. She remembered it hours later, after the train was hundreds of miles away. Correspondence with the railroad revealed that my English—even with a thesaurus—was not up to an adequate description of a retainer. Anyway they had not seen it. So back Linda went to the dentist to be fitted for a new one, while her Daddy ground his own teeth thinking about the bill.

The dentist warned Linda that if she kept forgetting, she would undo his two years of work. Neither warnings nor naggings helped. Finally, I decided to try out on her the principle about the will.

One night before her prayers I suggested that because the retainer was clumsy and uncomfortable, something deep inside her had decided "I don't want to wear it, so I won't remember."

"Do you know what it is to have will-power, Linda?" I asked.

"Yes, I think so."

"What does it mean to you?"

"To do something I don't want to do," she answered after some hesitation.

"That's pretty good. You remember that we have told you that all through your life you will have to do certain things that you may not enjoy doing. You can try to make yourself do these hateful things by will-power. But Linda, there's a much better way. If you tell God that you're willing to have Him change you, so that you'll like doing what you must do, then He will. It really works!"

That night Linda added to her bedtime prayers, "God, I hate the old retainer. But I know that if I don't wear it, I won't have pretty teeth. So I'm willing to have You change me on the inside, so that I *want* to wear, want to remember—and then I will."

After praying this way several nights in a row, the problem of the retainer was on its way to being solved. When Linda set the rudder of her will in the right direction, so that God's will became her will, then she no longer had trouble remembering, and she was no longer miserable wearing it.

Remembering a retainer may seem unimportant beside the big issues of life. Yet I have seen this principle of the will operate just as successfully in some of the knottiest, most soul-rending situations life can hand us.

Several years ago a veteran pilot was forced to land a passenger plane in a dense fog in California. The instructions from the tower were apparently not clear to him. To the horror of all who were there to meet the plane—mostly wives and children—the plane crashed at the edge of the landing field and burned. All aboard were killed.

The Civil Aeronautics Board's investigation and findings fixed the blame on the pilot. Many who knew the circumstances felt that this was unfair. In any case, it compounded the widow's grief. It was devastating enough to lose her husband, but it seemed more than she could bear to have him blamed for the death of twenty-three other human beings.

I am acquainted with the pilot's widow and her three daughters. The problem she posed to me was: "How *can* I let go my resentment at the unfairness of this and find peace again?"

Nothing in my experience approached the bitterness of this woman's problem. I pondered it and then wrote her about

what had helped me to handle smaller resentments....
Grudges or resentments are emotions. We cannot get rid of
them by saying, "I will no longer feel that way. I shall now
love this person who harmed me."

Recognizing the principle of the will, I pray something like
this: "Lord, You have plainly told me that all vengeance is
thine, not my business at all. You have said that I must forgive.
I am willing to, but I've tried over and over, and the resentments keep surging back. Now I *will* this bitterness over to
You. Here—I hold it out to You in my open hand. I promise
only that I will not again close my fist and reclaim the resentment. Now I ask You to take it and handle these emotions
that I cannot handle."

There I leave the matter. When thoughts return to it, there
is the quiet inner assertion that it has been turned over to God,
and that He is taking care of it. Always for me, in a matter of
hours or days, I find the resentment has evaporated and in its
place has come peace. The pilot's widow had a long struggle, but she wrote me that eventually she did find a peace of
mind that led her into a creative new life.

I once had success in applying this secret of the will to a
neighbor who invariably irritated me. Ann Sheldon (not her
real name, of course) had not wronged me. Indeed, any reasons I could have given for not liking her were not reasons
at all ... such things as her ceaseless chatter, and that habit of
asking you a direct question and then never pausing to hear
the answer. Her personality affected me like scratching fingernails across a blackboard. My human inclination was to avoid
her. Let Ann Sheldon go her way, and I'd go mine, I told
myself. The world was plenty big enough for the two of us.

But then a curious thing happened. Each time I tried to pray,
the thought of this woman popped into my mind. About the
fourth time it happened, I concluded that God was trying to
tell me something. With a sinking heart, I was afraid I knew
only too well what the message was. "Avoiding Ann will not

do. It is not good enough. Have you forgotten that we are to love one another?"

Love Ann Sheldon? The idea seemed ludicrous. Nevertheless I knew I had to try. First, I recognized that it would have been most unlike Jesus Christ if by "love" He had meant billowing waves of gushing sentimentality. By love He meant something more substantial—respect for another human being, caring about him and his problems, being sensitive to his needs, wanting him to prosper and to be happy.

As soon as I faced up to my defective relationship with Ann, I saw that everything turned on my will. I had to be *willing* to like this woman. Suppose that by some miracle God could replace my irritation with congeniality, even affection? (That *would* be a miracle, I thought glumly.) But all that God was asking of me was a shift in consciousness at the center of my will to include this possibility.

For help I went back to Hannah Smith's illustration in which she compared the will to a wise mother in a nursery and the feelings to clamoring, crying children. "The mother makes up her mind to a certain course of action which she knows to be best. The children rebel, declare they will not obey. But the mother, knowing that she is mistress and not they, pursues her course lovingly, firmly, never giving in for a moment to their contrariness. Eventually the clamoring ceases; the children do what they're told. All is harmony in the nursery."

So, in essence, my prayer was, "Lord, let me admit that my every clamoring emotion rebels at the thought of liking Ann Sheldon! But I put my will over on the side of what is best. So I ask You to handle my feelings."

The first result of my prayer was that I stopped avoiding Ann. On closer contact, I began to realize that her chatter was a camouflage for a desperate unsureness about herself. Ann had always seemed to me a hopeless sentimentalist—witness the way she kept a memory book on the level of a teen-ager.

She even pasted into it paper cocktail napkins and poetry clipped out of women's magazines! Then I saw the reason. She and her husband had always wanted children and had had none. Her affectionate nature had never had enough of an outlet. Soon I had evidence that underneath the sentimentality was a rare capacity for staunch friendship. Then one day I was astonished to realize that Ann Sheldon no longer irritated me.

She never got over her habit of asking questions and interrupting the answer. But there came the time when without malice I could say freely, "Ann, do you want me to answer that—or don't you?" And we would laugh about it together.

Ann died at forty-three—suddenly—of a brain hemorrhage. I had seen her only two days before her death, and we had parted with real affection.

The secret of the will is particularly effective in those areas where emotionally we are divided personalities. We know perfectly well what we should do. We want to do it; at the same time we do not want to.

The tangled emotions of grief often accentuate this divided self. This is the way one widow from a small town in Arkansas analyzed it in a letter to me:

It is five years since my husband died at the age of forty-nine, just half an hour after the doctor told him he would recommend him for insurance any time.

For months, I was so numbed and crushed with grief that I couldn't even realize what had happened to me. Yet in my heart I knew that a big part of this was feeling sorry for myself.

My husband had always praised me for being a sensible person in whatever situation I had to face, and in time I came to know that if I persisted in this self-pity I would be failing him in the worst kind of way. So—how can I handle this?

I think there are several reasons why, in grief, the will is so stubbornly at odds with itself. In the first place, the ego is deeply involved. Love has been wounded, and in the process part of us has died too. Also, like Queen Victoria who made a production of mourning for forty years for her Albert, most of us have a lingering pagan suspicion that those who do not exhibit strong and continuing sorrow are dishonoring the dead.

We take a long time to face up to the fact that no amount of grieving will bring the one we love back to our side. And since life must go on, we are faced with simple alternatives: will it be a good life or a miserable, sniveling existence? At this juncture the secret of the will can take over and steer us down the right road.

After the publication of my book *To Live Again,* which was about my own experience of grief at my husband's death and my subsequent recovery, letters poured in from the bereaved—both men and women. Often the letters were disconcerting, for in effect many of them said, "I have read your book. But let me tell you the peculiarities of *my* case. Do you have something more to say to me?"

Since I had poured myself out in *To Live Again,* I thought I had shared everything that might be helpful. But now I find there is something more. The secret—Hannah Smith's secret —is simple recognition of the fact that sorrow is an emotion and that you have little control over it. You know that God loves your loved one, who is now with Him, and that He loves you. You know that God has a plan for your life. So you admit to God that you are divided. One part of you is clinging to grief almost as an indulgence; another part knows well that until you are willing to let grief go, happiness and a good life cannot be yours again.

The principle of the will can handle this division, though we have to begin farther back. Our prayer here must be, "Lord, I am willing to be made willing."

And there one lets the matter rest for days or weeks, doing no forcing or straining, giving God time to change the emotional climate at deep levels in the personality.

A clergyman friend of mine from St. Louis once told me how he had applied this same principle to a broken marriage. The young woman, Marty, who came to see him at his church office, began by saying that she no longer loved her husband, Bill. He had been unfaithful and had lost her respect.

"Did you love him once?" the minister asked.

"Yes, I did."

"And how does your husband feel now? Is he unchanged, or contrite—or what?"

"We've been separated for a year. Two months ago Bill came to me. He said he'd been a fool, that the affair was all over, and asked my forgiveness. Now he's pleading for a reconciliation."

"Well, can you forgive him?"

The woman hesitated. "I've heard you say often enough from the pulpit that we have to forgive, no matter what. But that isn't my worst problem. When respect goes, love goes. What I really came to ask is: Is it right, even fair to Bill for me to live with him again when I don't love him?"

"Marty, what do you think God's will is for you and Bill?"

She thought for a while. "I suppose that in God's sight Bill *is* my husband. I took him 'for better or for worse.' Then it must be God's will for me to love my husband."

The counselor smiled at her. "But your difficulty, Marty, is that love can't be summoned like whistling for one's dog. Is that it?"

"Yes, that's it."

"There is an answer, Marty. If you are willing to do what you deeply feel God wants you to do, then He will attend to your emotions, give you back your love for Bill."

"How can you be so sure of that?"

"I can guarantee it, if you'll fulfill certain conditions." Then the minister explained to the young woman the principle of the will. As he talked, he shoved across his desk a crude diagram.

"This is not original with me," he explained. "I got the idea from Dr. Glenn Clark."

I will ... to will ... the will of God.
　　↓　　　　　↓　　　　　　↓
Man's will　the will　　　God's will
　　　　　　　in
　　　　　　action

Marty studied the diagram. When she finally looked up, her eyes were hopeful. "I begin to see a way out of my box! You mean that love is an emotion, and I can't control *that*, but I can control my will. And if I set my will right, then the emotions *have* to come right too. Is that it?"

"That's it."

"Then," Marty continued, "my part is to decide to go back to him."

"A little more than that," the clergyman corrected. "You have to go back, not reluctantly or half-heartedly, but willing to find joy and a new love for Bill. You can supply the willingness; God will do the rest."

That was five years ago. The marriage has not only lasted, but according to this minister Bill and Marty—now more mature and tested—are happier than they ever were before.

Surely we have misunderstood Christianity if we think God wants us to obey Him reluctantly—resisting, bucking, hating every step of the way. In fact the New Testament tells us that this reluctant obedience growing out of fear of punishment was the old way, the Old Covenant. Jesus came to show us a new way by which God promises to work in us "both to will and to do of His good pleasure." [3] This means that God will bring about such a change in us that His plans and desires for us will be our delight.

God's will gets written in our hearts by the simple application of the principle of the will to each life situation as we meet it. Christ would indeed be unrealistic if He asked us to do the impossible. He does not. His "secret" not only tells us how, but speeds us on our way with joy.

5

Dare to Trust God

Now DON'T PUSH the term *faith* at me," a lawyer told me bluntly at a dinner party recently. "The word is like a red flag."

"Why such a violent reaction?" I asked.

"Well, because I object to the way Christianity uses faith as a theological gimmick to duck all rational problems. At every point where a man wants to understand, they say, 'You just have to have faith,' or 'Reason can only go so far.' I resent it! I see nothing wrong with 'Prove it to me first, then I'll believe.'"

As we talked, I realized that it had never occurred to this intelligent, well-educated man that in his everyday life he often follows the reverse order—belief and acceptance first, then action. Every day he lives, he acts on faith many times with little proof or none at all, and he does not feel that he is being impractical.

He demonstrates an act of faith each time he boards a plane. He believes that it will take him to his destination, but he has no proof of it. He entrusts life itself to several unknown mechanics who have serviced the plane, as well as to a pilot about whom he knows nothing.

Each time he eats a meal in a restaurant he trusts some unknown cook behind the scenes and eats the food on faith, faith that it is not contaminated. He enters a hospital for an operation and signs a release giving permission for surgery. This is an act of faith in an anesthetist whose name he may not even know and a surgeon who holds in his hands the power of life or death.

He accepts a prescription from a doctor and takes it to a druggist, thus acting his faith that the pharmacist will fill the prescription accurately. The use of the wrong drug might be deadly, but he is not equipped to analyze the contents before swallowing the pill.

It is obvious that were we to insist on the "proof first, then faith" order in our daily lives, organized life as we know it would grind to a screeching halt. And since life together among men is possible only by faith, as we act our trust in other people, it should not seem odd that the same law applies to our life with God.

The New Testament makes it clear that in the spiritual realm, when for some reason or other we refuse to act by faith, all activity stops just as completely as it does in the secular realm. There is no way for us even to take the first steps toward the Christian life except by faith, any more than a baby can get launched on his earthly life without blind baby-trust in his parents and other adults. We have to accept the fact of a personal relationship with Jesus Christ by faith, even as our young children accept the fact of parental love. For the child, as for the new Christian, understanding and proof come later.

In the same way, every step in our Christian walk has to be by faith.

In Jesus' ministry of healing the spirit, the mind, and the body, faith seems to have been necessary before the divine act, not (as logic would have it) afterward. The gospels are studded with statements of this:

And he said to the woman, Thy faith hath saved thee, go in peace.[1]

Then touched he their eyes, saying, According to your faith be it unto you.[2]

... Jesus said ... all things are possible to him that believeth.[3]

All that ever you ask in prayer, you shall have, if you believe.[4]

Much of my own problem with faith arose from an early misunderstanding of what faith is. First of all, I used to believe that faith had something to do with feeling. For example, when I had messed up some situation and had asked God for forgiveness, then I would peer inside myself to see if I *felt* forgiven. If I could locate such feelings, then I was sure that God had heard and had forgiven me. Now I know that this is an altogether false test of faith.

We would not be so foolish as to go to a railroad station, board the first car we saw, then sit down and try to feel whether or not this was the train that would take us where we wanted to go. Our feeling would obviously have no bearing on the facts. Yet I know now that at times my actions in the spiritual realm have been just that foolish.

Another misconception I once had was that faith is trying to believe something one is fairly certain is not true. But faith is not hocus-pocus, opposed to knowledge and reality. In fact, faith does not go against experience at all; rather it appeals to experience, just as science does. The difference is that it appeals to experience in a realm where our five senses are not supreme rulers.

Nor is faith a kind of spiritual coin which you and I can exchange for heaven's blessings. Nor is it simply believing doggedly in some particular doctrine. One can believe in the divinity of Jesus Christ and feel no personal loyalty to Him at all; indeed, pay no attention whatever to His commandments and His will for one's life. One can believe intellectually in the efficacy of prayer and never do any praying.

Perhaps one reason that the real meaning of faith eluded me

personally for so many years was that it is so surprisingly simple, so practical. Faith in God is simply trusting Him enough to step out on that trust.

My first lesson in stepping out on trust came in connection with the problem of financing a college education. We were then living in a little railroad town in the eastern Panhandle of West Virginia. By the time I reached my senior year in high school, the town had for some years been struggling through the long aftermath of the 1929 crash. Its only industry —the Baltimore and Ohio railroad shops—were all but shut down. The church my father served as minister was suffering along with everything else. Father had voluntarily taken several cuts in his already meager salary. Even grocery money was scarce. It was fortunate that Mother knew how to prepare fried mush in a way that made it seem like a rare delicacy.

Something I had dreamed of as far back as I could remember—a college education—now seemed out of the question. The dream even included a particular college—Agnes Scott in Decatur, Georgia.

Agnes Scott accepted me. Although the school was accustomed to ministers' and missionaries' daughters whose ambitions outstripped their pocketbooks, the financial burden nevertheless looked hopelessly heavy. Even with the promise of a small work scholarship and the $125 I had saved from high school essay and debating prizes, we were several hundred dollars short.

It was frightening to see that my parents were helpless in this situation. It was in their faces, in their voices. Through all my growing-up years, in every childish emergency they had been equal to anything. What now? Did this mean that I was going to have to relinquish my heart's desire?

One evening Mother found me lying across my bed, sobbing. She sat down beside me, put her cool hand on my forehead. No words were needed. She knew what the trouble was.

Presently she said quietly, "You and I are going to pray

about this. Let's go into the guest room where we won't be disturbed." And she took me firmly by the hand.

We sat down on the old-fashioned golden-oak bed, the one that Mother and Father had bought for their first home. "Let's talk about this a minute before we pray," Mother said slowly. "I believe that it is God's will for you to go to college, or else He would not have given you the mental equipment. Furthermore, all resources are at God's disposal. Do you believe that, Catherine?"

"Yes—yes—I think I do."

"All right. Now here's another fact I want you to think about. Everybody has faith. We're born with it. Much of what happens to us in life depends on where we place our faith. If we deposit it in God, then we're on sure ground. If we place our trust in poverty or failure or fear, then we're investing it poorly. So keep that in mind while I read something to you." She opened a Moffatt Bible to I John 5:14, 15:

Now the confidence we have in him is this,
that he listens to us whenever we ask anything
in accordance with His will; and if we know that he
listens to whatever we ask, we know that we obtain the
requests we have made to him.

"Note how the thought goes in that promise, Catherine. Whenever we ask God for something that is His will, He hears us. If He hears us, then He grants the request we have made. So you and I can rest on that promise. Let's claim it right now for the resources for your college." And so we knelt by the bed and prayed about it.

I shall never forget that evening. During those quiet moments in the bedroom, I was learning what faith is and how it works. It is true that my faith was immature and weak, but the strength of Mother's was contagious. She had helped me take my first step in faith. The answer would come. We knew it would, though neither of us had any idea how.

When it came, it was the offer of a job for Mother with the

Federal Writer's Project. Would she be willing to write the history of the county? Would she! Her salary would cover the amount needed for my college expenses with a little to spare. Since history has always been one of Mother's loves, no job could have been more to her liking. Moreover, she could work at home and, along with her writing, keep a hand on all of the family projects.

That was the way I learned that we must have faith *before* the fact, not after, if we are to function as human beings at all. The only question is—faith in whom? Faith in what?

God challenges us to place it in Him rather than in fallible human beings: "Taste and see that the Lord is good." [5] In my experience this is not an ivory-tower approach. It is the only effectual one.

I have seen faith in God vindicated many times in stirring ways. No story ever captured my imagination so much as George Müller's. My children will read it and—if I have anything to say about it—my grandchildren.

In the year 1828 a man sat in a room in Teignmouth, England, struggling with a problem. A German, George Müller was then twenty-three years old. His father was a collector of excise taxes in Prussia, and the son had inherited the father's preoccupation with figures, his adding-machine mind, his astute business sense. During this period in England the Industrial Revolution was well under way. George Müller felt he could become a successful industrialist. Yet he hesitated.

Only three years out of the University at Halle, George had been mostly preoccupied with taverns, women, cards, and occasional study. He certainly had not been at all interested in religion. Then there had come a turning point. It had come through Müller's unexpected discovery one night at a friend's party that he could have fun in a Christian group—a different, deeper kind of pleasure than he found in his favorite tavern.

To his own surprise, George Müller began to think about

the meaning of life. Often he pondered the fact that all through the Gospels there kept recurring Jesus' plea for us to have faith, to ask . . . ask . . . ask:

> Hitherto you have asked nothing in my name;
> ask and you will receive, that your joy may be full.[6]

> If for all your evil you know to give your
> children what is good, how much more will
> your Father in heaven give good to
> those who ask him? [7]

Had Christ meant those words literally? If so, then why—generation after generation—did mankind continue to ignore them or water them down?

Müller thought of several individuals he had recently met. One was a man who had to work at his trade fourteen to sixteen hours a day. He had no time for his family, no time to enjoy life. Concerned, Müller had spoken to him only a week before: "Henry, you simply have to work less. Your family needs something more of you than your pay. Your body's suffering and your soul is starving."

But the reply had been, "But if I work less, I won't earn enough for the support of my family."

When Müller had quoted him the promise, "Seek ye first the Kingdom of God, and His righteousness, and all these things shall be added unto you," [8] Henry had said with a wry grimace, "I wish I could believe that applies to my situation, George. Guess I just need more faith."

Müller now sat chin in hand, staring out the second-story window over the chimney pots of the town to the sea in the distance, foaming and curling at the base of the red cliffs of Parson Rock. But he was not seeing the beauty of a sunset on Teignmouth's coast now. Instead he was thinking of an old woman, Marie, so frightened of old age without a pension, so terrified of the poorhouse waiting for her at the end of the road. Where was her faith in God's ability to take care of her?

And then he was thinking of Lawrence, a man now in his early thirties and in a business he hated. But he dared not switch to where his heart was—medicine. "How would I take care of my family while I complete my studies?" He too had merely shrugged when Müller had mentioned faith in God as the solution.

So what could he—George Müller—do about it? How could he define this matter of faith and prove to these people that Jesus had meant it when He bade us *ask*.

At that moment he saw out the window two ragged little girls on the cobblestone walk. He had seen them before. Their father was a merchant seaman whose ship had been lost last year off Desolation Island in the Magellan Straits. Two weeks ago their mother had died of tuberculosis. Müller recalled the pathetic funeral, the raw pine casket, the lost look on the faces of the children. He knew that the eleven- and thirteen-year-old girls were trying to take care of three younger children. And these were not the only destitute children in the town, either. There seemed to be no institutions for needy children in England. He wondered why not.

The thoughts went round and round. And then he noticed his Bible open on the table beside him. It was open to the Psalms: suddenly he was reading a verse he had never noticed before: "Open thy mouth wide, and I will fill it." [9] Müller suddenly found himself quietly praying, "All right, I'm opening my mouth to ask. If You want me to do something about all this, you'll have to show me how and where to begin."

George Müller began by offering his services to a local mission. His drive and imagination soon revitalized it. The records show that he met and married Mary Groves in 1830. The two of them consecrated their marriage vows with a rather remarkable demonstration of Jesus' words... "Sell what you possess and give it away in alms...." [10] Just so, did George and Mary part with their household goods. Like many daring experimenters, Müller wanted to go all the way. His desire was to make himself and his wife dependent for everything on God alone. Their motive was sincere, above all suspicion. At the time he and his wife kept the act of giving away their possessions a secret from all who knew them.

The next step was even more daring. Müller refused all regular salary from the people of the small mission he had been serving. He and his wife would henceforth tell their needs to God alone in prayer. Theirs would be a test case for the world to see.

Then George found his thoughts centering on the idea of founding an orphan's home. It would not be just a place to care for a few homeless children, but a vast institution—built and operated on faith. He would make it too a pure example of trust in God.

On April 21, 1836, the first Orphan Home was dedicated in a rented building. Within a matter of days there were forty-three children to be cared for. Müller and his co-workers decided that the controlled experiment would be set up along these lines:

1. No funds would ever be solicited. No facts or figures concerning needs were to be revealed by the workers in the orphanage to anyone, except to God in prayer.
2. No debts would ever be incurred. The burden of experiment would therefore not be on local shopkeepers or suppliers.
3. No money contributed for a specific purpose could ever be used for any other purpose.
4. All accounts would be audited annually by professional auditors.
5. No ego-pandering by publication of donors' names with the amount of their gifts; each donor would be thanked privately.
6. No "names" of prominent or titled persons would be sought for the board or to advertise the institution.

7. The success of the institution would be measured not by the numbers served or by the amounts of money taken in, but by God's blessing on the work, which Müller expected to be in proportion to the time spent in prayer.

When the first building was opened, George Müller and his associates stuck to their principles, spending time in prayer that ordinarily would have gone to fund-raising. An unbelieving public was amazed when a second building was opened six months after the first. Müller concentrated on prayer, and the money kept coming in. Eventually, there were five new buildings, with 110 helpers taking care of 2050 orphans.

Before opening his first orphanage Müller had said that he would consider the experiment a failure if ever the orphans had to go for a single day without food. They never did. Nor were these children taken care of in minimal fashion. Part of George Müller's conviction was that God not only provides, but that He provides bountifully. For their time, his orphanage buildings were constructed with remarkable details—built-in cupboards with a large pigeonhole for each child's clothes; sunny playrooms with shelves and cupboards for the toys that were not yet there. Each child must always have not one but three pairs of shoes. Each boy, three suits; each girl, five dresses. There must always be white tablecloths for the evening meal and flowers whenever possible. Behind the scenes were the latest laborsaving devices available: one of the first American washing machines in England and an early type of centrifugal dryer.

After each year's audit a detailed report was made public showing how the Lord had provided for that year. Soon it became apparent that all around the world people were watching this experiment with fascination. Businessmen were particularly interested. One executive traveled a considerable distance for an interview with Müller. His firm was threatened with bankruptcy. In his methodical manner, Müller wrote out for his visitor a prescription of five parts—advice as applicable today as it was then:

1. Each day you and your wife are to spread your business difficulties before the Lord.
2. You are then to watch for answers to prayer and expect them.
3. Absolute honesty necessary; avoid all business trickeries.
4. Beginning immediately, a certain proportion of your income must be given to God.
5. Keep a record—month by month—how the Lord is dealing with you, what's happening.

The man did keep a record; in fact he sent a monthly report to Müller, and in his journal Müller recorded that during the first year the man's business came out of the red and up some three thousand pounds over the previous year. For as long as George Müller recorded the figures, the businessman's profits continued to mount.

The results of his amazing orphanage experiment have been published in detail in the four volumes of George Müller's *Journals*. For more than sixty years he recorded every specific prayer request and the result. His mathematical mind kept meticulous books on every penny received and all money expended.

So great did public interest in the orphanage become that when Müller was seventy, he felt that the time had come to tell the story himself. So over a number of years he traveled 200,000 miles, lecturing in forty-two countries. For hundreds of thousands of people he became a living demonstration of the fact that faith is nothing more or less than believing God, not just intellectually but actually.

Faith is only worthy of the name when it erupts into action. Unlike George Müller, most of us can show few trophies won through faith. Were we to use the muscles of our legs as little as we do the muscles of our faith, most of us would be unable to stand.

Then what can we do to strengthen them?

First, we cannot trust God until we know something about Him. The way to begin is by reading His word and thinking about it. The Bible acquaints us with the nature and character of God: His power; His unselfish, unchangeable love; His infinite wisdom. We read instance after instance in which God has exercised His power and wisdom in helping and delivering His people.

Second, faith is strengthened only as we ourselves exercise it. We have to apply it to our problems: poverty, bodily ills, bereavement, job troubles, tangled human relationships.

Third, faith has to be in the present tense—now. A vague prospect that what we want will transpire in the future is not faith, but hope.

Fourth, absolute honesty is necessary. We cannot have faith and a guilty conscience at the same time. Every time faith will fade away.

Fifth, the strengthening of faith comes through staying with it in the hour of trial. We should not shrink from tests of our faith. Only when we are depending on God alone are we in a position to see God's help and deliverance, and thus have our faith strengthened for the next time.

This means that we must let Him do the work. Almost always it takes longer than we think it should. When we grow impatient and try a deliverance of our own, through friends or circumstances, we are taking God's work out of His hands.

George Müller was faithfully reflecting the New Testament in his blunt, realistic insistence in depending on God alone. The Epistle of James declared that "faith, unless it has deeds, is dead in itself." [11] And John added more bluntly still, "He who will not believe God, has made God a liar...." [12]

Believe what? Believe the consistent testimony in Scripture of the unfailing love and good will of our God, of His ability to help us, and of His willingness—indeed eagerness—to do so.

The adventure of living has not really begun until we begin to stand on our faith legs and claim—for ourselves, for our homes, for the rearing of our children, for our health problems, for our business affairs, and for our world—the resources of our God.

6

The Prayer of Relinquishment

AFTER THE DISCOVERY that faith in God can make life an adventure, comes the desire to experiment with prayer. Like most people, I was full of questions, such as why are some agonizingly sincere prayers granted while others are not?

Many years later I still have questions. Mysteries about prayer are always out ahead of present knowledge—luring, beckoning on to further experimentation.

But one thing I do know; I learned it through hard experience. It is a way of prayer that has consistently resulted in a glorious answer, glorious because each time power beyond human reckoning has been released. This is the Prayer of Relinquishment.

I got my first glimpse of it in the fall of 1943. The illness that I have mentioned before in these pages had kept me in bed for many months. A bevy of specialists seemed unable to help. Persistent prayer, using all the faith I could muster, had resulted in—nothing.

One afternoon a pamphlet was put in my hand. It was the story of a missionary who had been an invalid for eight years. Constantly she had prayed that God would make her well, so that she might do His work. Finally, worn out with futile petition, she prayed, "All right. I give up. If You want me to be an invalid for the rest of my days, that's Your business. Anyway, I've discovered that I want You even more than I want health. You decide." The pamphlet said that within two weeks the woman was out of bed, completely well.

This made no sense to me. It seemed too pat. Yet I could not forget the story. On the morning of September fourteenth (how can I ever forget the date?) I came to the same point of abject acceptance. "I'm tired of asking" was the burden of my prayer. "I'm beaten, finished. God, You decide what you want for me for the rest of my life...." Tears flowed. I had no faith as I understood faith. I expected nothing. The gift of my sick self was made with no trace of graciousness.

The result was as if windows had opened in heaven; as if some dynamo of heavenly power had begun flowing, flowing into me. From that moment my recovery began.

Through this incident and others that followed, some of which I want to tell later, God was trying to teach me something important about prayer. Still I got only part of the message. I saw that the demanding spirit—"God, I must have thus and so; God, this is what I want you to do for me—" is not real prayer and hence receives no answer. I understood that the reason for this is that God absolutely refuses to violate our free will and that therefore, unless self-will is voluntarily given up, even God cannot move to answer prayer. But it was going to take more time and more experience for me to begin to understand the Prayer of Relinquishment.

Part of that understanding has come through learning of other people's experiences with this type of prayer. It has been exciting to uncover in contemporary life, in the Bible, and scattered through the writings of men in other centuries the infallible power of this prayer technique.

Some years ago, I stumbled across one example in the life of the New England writer, Nathaniel Hawthorne. In 1853

Hawthorne had decided to take his family abroad for an extended stay. He wanted a broadening of his horizons, contact with other writers in England and Italy. By then he was already recognized as a master of the craft of the short story through his *Twice-Told Tales* and was famous as the author of the successful novel *The Scarlet Letter*.

In late 1858, the Hawthornes were settled in a villa in Rome. February 1860 found them in the midst of a grave crisis. Una, their eldest daughter, was dying of a virulent form of malaria. The attending physician, Dr. Franco, had that afternoon warned the distraught parents that unless the young girl's fever abated before morning she would die.

As Sophia Hawthorne sat by her daughter's bed, her thoughts went to her handsome husband in the adjoining room. She could picture him—his troubled blue eyes, that splendid head with its mop of dark hair, bowed in grief. She recalled what he had said earlier that day, "I cannot endure the alternations of hope and fear, and therefore I have settled with myself not to hope at all."

But Sophia could not share Nathaniel's hopelessness. Una could not, must not die. This daughter strongly resembled her father, had the finest mind, the most complex character of all the Hawthorne children. Why should a capricious Providence demand that they give her up?

Moreover, Una had been delirious for several days and had recognized no one. Were she to die this night, there would not even be the solace of farewells.

As the night deepened, the young girl ceased her incoherent mutterings and lay so still that she seemed to be in the anteroom of death. The mother went to the window and looked out on the piazza. There was no moonlight; heavy clouds scudded across a dark and silent sky.

"I cannot bear this loss—cannot—cannot." Then suddenly, unaccountably, another thought took over. "Why should I doubt the goodness of God? Let Him take Una, if He sees best. I can give her to Him. No, I won't fight against Him any more."

Then an even stranger thing happened. Having made the great sacrifice in her mind, Sophia expected to feel sadder. Instead she felt lighter, happier than at any time since Una's long illness had begun.

Some minutes later she walked back to the girl's bedside and felt her daughter's forehead. It was moist and cool. The pulse was slow and regular. Una was sleeping naturally. Sophia rushed into the next room to tell her husband that the crisis seemed to be past. She was right. Though Una was months getting the malaria out of her system, she did recover completely.

A contemporary answer to prayer reminiscent of the Hawthornes' experience was related to me by a friend in a letter:

... Three years ago our son was born. At first he seemed a normal, healthy baby. But when he was not quite twelve hours old, while I was holding him in my arms, he had a convulsion. More convulsions followed the next few days.

The only explanation the doctors had was that he must have suffered a brain injury of some kind at birth. This only added to my terror.... If he lived, perhaps he would be blind, deaf, dumb, or a cripple, or with his mind affected.

I've never felt so alone as during the time that followed. I prayed, but I couldn't feel that God cared about me any more. Why had this had to happen to my baby?

I know now that my prayers were not prayers at all, but accusations. I was demanding that God heal my child.

Then out of sheer exhaustion of body and soul, I stopped commanding God and gave in to Him completely. I just said, "Take him if that's what You want. Anything You decide will be all right with me. Even if You want him to be a cripple or deaf, then I will just have to learn to accept it and live with it." I put myself and the baby entirely in His hands.

From that instant, not only did Larry begin to improve, but suddenly my tears left, and my fears went with them. An inex-

*plicable peace filled my heart, and I knew, just knew that Larry
would not only live but would have a normal, useful life....*

*Well, the end of the story is that Larry is now as normal and
healthy as any little boy. He's very very intelligent, and if he were
any more active, well I'd be the one to be a cripple.*

Larry's story and Una's have several points in common. In
each case, the mother wanted the same thing desperately—life
and health for her child. Each mother commanded God to
answer her prayer. While the demanding spirit had the upper
hand, God seemed remote, unapproachable.

Then, through a combination of the obvious futility of the
demanding prayer plus weariness of body and spirit, the
mother surrendered to the possibility of what she feared most.
At that instant there came a turning point. Suddenly and in-
explicably fear left and the feeling of soul-strain with it.
Peace crept into the heart. There followed a feeling of light-
ness and joy that had nothing to do with outer circumstances.
This marked the turning point. From that moment the prayer
began to be answered.

The intriguing question is: What is the spiritual law implicit in this Prayer of Relinquishment? I think I know at
least part of it.... We know that fear blocks prayer. Fear is
a barrier erected between us and God, so that His power
cannot get through to us. So—how does one get rid of fear?

This is not easy when the life of someone dear hangs in
the balance, or when what we want most in all the world
seems to be slipping away. At such times, every emotion,
every passion, is tied up in the dread that what we fear most is
about to come upon us. Obviously only strong measures can
deal with such a powerful fear. My experience has been that
trying to overcome it by turning one's thoughts to the positive
or by repeating affirmations is not potent enough.

It is then that we are squarely up against the law of relinquishment. Was Jesus showing us how to use this law when
He said, "Resist not evil?" In God's eyes, fear is evil because

it is acting out of lack of trust in Him. So Jesus is advising "Resist not fear."

In other words, Jesus is saying: "Admit the possibility of what you fear most. And lo, as you stop fleeing, as you force yourself to walk up to the fear, as you look it full in the face, never forgetting that God and His power are still the supreme reality, the fear evaporates." Drastic? Yes. But effective.

One point about the Prayer of Relinquishment puzzled me for many years. There seemed to be a contradiction between the Prayer of Faith and that of relinquishment. If relinquishment is real, the one praying must be willing to receive or not receive his heart's desire. But that state of mind scarcely seems to exhibit the faith that knows that one's request will be granted. And as I read the gospels, Jesus placed far greater stress on the Prayer of Faith than on the Prayer of Relinquishment.

Now I believe I have the explanation. The fact is that I went through a period of misunderstanding faith. Once I thought that faith was believing this or that specific thing in my mind with never a doubt. Now I know that faith is nothing more or less than actively trusting God.

Peter Marshall liked to illustrate what such active trust means by a homely example:

> Suppose a child has a broken toy.
> He brings the toy to his father, saying that he
>   himself has tried to fix it and has failed.
> He asks his father to do it for him.
>
> The father gladly agrees...
>   takes the toy...
> and begins to work.
>
> Now obviously the father can do his work most quickly and easily if the child makes no attempt to interfere, simply sits quietly watching, or even goes about other business, with never a doubt that the toy is being successfully mended.

But what do most of God's children do in such a
situation?
Often we stand by offering a lot of meaningless advice
and some rather silly criticism.

We even get impatient and try to help,
and so get our hands in the Father's way,
generally hindering the work . . .

Finally, in our desperation, we may even grab the toy
out of the Father's hands entirely, saying rather bitterly that we hadn't really thought He could fix it
anyway . . . that we'd given Him a chance and He had
failed us.

Grabbing the toy away is certainly not trust. But what
does demonstrate trust is to put the thing or the person one
loves best into the Father's hands to do with as He pleases.
Thus faith is by no means absent in the Prayer of Relinquishment. In fact this prayer is faith in action.

And that is why this prayer is answered, even when the one
making the relinquishment has little hope that what he fears
most can be avoided. For I have always felt that God is not
half so concerned about our having a few negative thoughts
as He is concerned with what we do. And the act of placing
what we cherish most in His hands is to Him the sweet music
of the essence of faith.

This kind of faith can be used to solve any type of problem.
I remember an attractive young girl, Sara Bradford, who sat
in my living room and shared with me her doubts about her
engagement.

"I love Jeb," she said, and there was deep feeling in her
words. "And Jeb loves me. But there are problems. He had
an unhappy childhood. His mother and father were divorced
when he was ten. His mother was a great beauty. She's still a
beautiful woman at sixty-two. She married again, and that
marriage was unhappy too. Jeb is most defensive of her."

"Does this make you feel that Jeb is a poor risk for marriage?"

Sara hesitated. "Well, it's left a lot of marks. There are other problems too. At twenty-four, Jeb is still restless——"

"You mean he hasn't settled on a career?"

"No, he hasn't. Then too, it bothers me that religion doesn't mean much to him. Oh, a few times he's gone to church with me. But his heart isn't in it. I don't really want to establish the kind of a home in which God will be left out. And then there is his drinking . . . What should I do? Do all these doubts mean that God is trying to tell me to give Jeb up?"

As she talked on and on, Sara reached her own conclusion. It was that she would lose something infinitely precious if she did not follow the highest and the best that she knew. Her voice broke as she said, "I'm going to have to break the engagement. Then if God wants me to marry Jeb, He will find some way of showing me."

Right then, simply and poignantly, she told God her decision. Her prayer was a true relinquishment. She was putting her broken dreams and her now-unknown future into God's hands.

I remained interested in Sara and in knowing how her future turned out. Jeb did not change, so Sara did not marry him. But a year later Sara wrote me an ecstatic letter. "Something wonderful happened that afternoon in your living room. It nearly killed me to give Jeb up. Yet God knew that he wasn't the one for me. Now I've met The Man. He's terrific and we're to be married in October. Now I *really* have something to say about trusting God."

The Prayer of Relinquishment also helps us in small matters. A friend confided that she had been suffering from insomnia. Her doctor had prescribed sleeping pills.

"I've been reading so much lately about how the sales of sleeping pills rise and rise. Are we becoming a nation of addicts?"

"Not you, certainly," I reassured her.

"Thanks. But the principle of this bothers me. I'm not sure I want this crutch."

Later we met again and she told me what happened.

"I decided nix on the pills. So that night I lay and prayed, 'All right, God, I put myself and my sleep into Your hands. If You want me to stay awake most of the night, fine. You decide'."

"And did you stay awake?"

There was a sheepish look on her face. "No, I slept like a baby."

No doubt psychologists, as well as the sleep experts, could comment knowingly on this incident. But I relate it here only because it illustrates the Law of Relinquishment not in a dramatic crisis but in an ordinary situation.

My own latest adventure with the Prayer of Relinquishment came in connection with the mundane problem of household help. In the weeks prior to my marriage to Leonard LeSourd, I was happily excited but at the same time panicky at the thought of taking on three young children. After all, I had thought myself finished with child-rearing. Peter John had then been out of the home nest for three years, away at school. At the same time I wanted to keep on with my writing. What if I was not adequate to the situation?

In his efforts to reassure me, Len made solemn promises of household help. But after our marriage, the help was slow in materializing. Three months passed, four. One maid stayed for three weeks, then decided to go back to her home in North Carolina. Then a cleaning woman who was helping me one day a week had to stop when she fell and injured her leg.

Many a morning Len and I prayed about it. Soon after our marriage, we had hit upon a pleasant way to begin our day with quietness and prayer. An automatic coffee pot attached to a clock would waken us with the fragrance of percolating coffee. Then we would sit propped up in bed, sipping coffee, reading a portion of Scripture together, thinking through the day ahead.

One morning I was particularly discouraged. I was caught between all my blessings—a wonderful husband, three lovely children at home and a fourth in and out, a big new house, and my daily writing. I was, quite frankly, exhausted. We had tried everything we knew: agencies, the suggestions of friends and relatives, the Help Wanted columns in the local and New York newspapers. Just the evening before a promising candidate from Boston with whom we had been corresponding had telephoned that she could not come.

So once more we took the situation to God.... "Lord, we've tried everything we can think of. Every road has seemed a dead end. Doors have been so consistently shut in our faces that You must be trying to teach us something. Tell us what it is——"

There followed the illumination that prayer often brings. In this case, it was not pleasant. I had been trying to dictate the terms of my life to God—what I wanted: help in the home so that I could get on with my writing. A thought stabbed me. What if—for this period of my life—I was supposed to give up the writing? Immediately this possibility brought tears. Why should I have to relinquish something which I had from the beginning dedicated to God—and something from which I also got such intense satisfaction? Still it was obvious that our home and the children had to come first. So, knowing that I would get no answer from God until I was willing to surrender the writing, I set myself to the task.

At that point, Hannah Whitall Smith's practicable principle of the will came to my rescue. Resolutely I set my will to accept what had to be accepted. Though my emotions were in stark rebellion, I knew that sooner or later they would fall into line.

I plunged into homemaking, completing the furnishing and decorating of the house...meals...laundry...groceries...

creating an atmosphere of security for children who badly needed it.

Then I realized that, beyond the writing, there had been another reason why I had wanted help. It was the haunting fear that I would be physically and emotionally unable to handle all the housework, take care of the children, be a good wife to my husband—all at one time. But now I was learning that I could cope with it. With that knowledge came the self-assurance that washed away all fears. And I would never have had this sense of security and confidence if we had started our marriage with domestic help.

When the relinquishment was complete, the breakthrough occurred. Unexpectedly a letter came from Boston. The woman who had refused us before said that she was now available. Lucy Arsenault came to us. Lucy—settled, reliable, a superb cook, a rare person. As always, a loving God had planned so much better than we ever could have.

The morning mail frequently holds surprises for me. On one particular morning a few months ago I noticed that the tissue-thin air mail letter was postmarked Quito, Ecuador. After glancing over the first two paragraphs, I turned to the second sheet to see the signature—and gasped. Betty Elliot! Only a few days before I had been reading about her in *Life* magazine. Her husband had been one of the five missionaries brutally massacred by the Auca Indians on January 8, 1956. I was curious to know why she should be writing to me.

I have just spent Christmas alone here in an Auca Indian settle-ment reading your book, To Live Again. *Though my present circumstances could hardly be more remote from those you describe, I responded deeply to much of your message, and I felt I wanted to thank you....*

Then she went on to tell me what her circumstances were. Betty and her small blonde daughter, Valerie, together with Rachel, the sister of Nate Saint (another of the murdered men) are now living in the midst of the South American Auca tribe. The two women and the tiny girl are altogether at the mercy of the same men who killed their husband and brother. They have no weapons; there are no other white people within miles of jungle, inaccessible except on foot or by air-lift. How did such circumstances come about? "God led us here, opened the way through Dayuma, an escaped Auca woman. . . ." Betty explains simply.

Yet Betty Elliot is a realist. "It is possible for us to lose our lives any day. The Aucas are still savages, who do not even think of killing as wrong. Fear can drive them to kill in a twinkling. What the future holds for Rachel and Valerie and me is God's business. . . ."

I found my imagination straining as I thought of how the pages I held in my hand had been written. She had penned them seated in the doorway of the palm-thatched hut that Betty calls home. The muddy Tewaenon River flows nearby. Her husband's body, a broken spear still imbedded in it, had been found three years before floating face down in the same river. And closer, the lush green jungle forever impinges on the natives' clearing.

All around her as she wrote those words were the short savages with their tea-colored skins and straight black hair. Both men and women go naked except for the vines tied tightly around waists, ankles, and wrists. Valerie nearby chattered animatedly with a pet parrot. . . .

I was awed at the evidence of such a love for God as these two women were demonstrating. Then my eye fell on the last paragraph of the letter:

Your solution to grief is just another way of giving the same answer that God gave me in the first empty days—Accept this. Only in acceptance lies peace—not in forgetting nor in resignation nor in busy-ness. His will is good and acceptable and perfect. . . .

So this woman, in the midst of such cruel events, had dis-covered the secret too: there is a difference between acceptance and resignation. One is positive; the other negative. Acceptance is creative, resignation sterile.

Resignation is barren of faith in the love of God. It says, "Grievous circumstances have come to me. There is no escaping them. I am only one creature, an alien in a vast unknowable creation. I have no heart left even to rebel. So I'll just resign myself to what apparently is the will of God; I'll even try to make a virtue out of patient submission." So resignation lies down quietly in the dust of a universe from which God seems to have fled, and the door of Hope swings shut.

But turn the coin over. Acceptance says, "I trust the good will, the love of my God. I'll open my arms and my understanding to what He has allowed to come to me. Since I know that He means to make all things work together for good, I consent to this present situation with hope for what the future will bring." Thus acceptance leaves the door of Hope wide open to God's creative plan. This difference between acceptance and resignation is the key to an understanding of the Prayer of Relinquishment.

Obviously Betty Elliot's acceptance left the door open to a creative plan daring enough that only God could have conceived it. Can two women and a tiny girl succeed in taking Christianity to Stone-age savages where many men have failed? For other white men died violently at the hands of the Aucas before the five missionaries. In 1942 the Shell Oil Company lost three men by Auca spears, in 1943 eight more. Since then the tribe has repaid with death any invasion of their territory by white men.

So now the world watches while an adventure story unfolds. In the plan that God gave Betty Elliot, I have never seen a better example of the "foolishness" of God being wiser than men, and the "weakness" of God being stronger than men.[1]

To the disciples of Jesus Christ, His actions during the last week of His life on earth must have seemed equally nonsensical. Their Master had a great following among the common people. His disciples were hoping that He would use this following to overthrow the Roman grip on their little country and move, at last, to establish His earthly kingdom. Instead He deliberately set His feet on the path that would lead inescapably to the cross. For let us not mistake it. Christ could have avoided that cross. He did not have to go up to Jerusalem that last time. He could have compromised with the priests, bargained with Caiaphas. The disciples were probably right in thinking that He could have capitalized on His following, appeased Judas, and set up the beginning of an earthly empire. Later Pilate would all but beg Him to say the right words so that he might release Him.[2] Even in the Garden of Gethsamane on the night of betrayal, Christ had plenty of time and opportunity to flee.

But He would not flee. Instead He knelt to pray in the shadowy Garden under the gray-green leaves of the olive trees. And in His prayer that night, Jesus gave us, for all time, the perfect pattern for the Prayer of Relinquishment.

Jesus had been given genuine humanity, as well as divinity. Part of that humanity was His free will. He chose to use His free will to leave the decision to His Father as to whether He must die by execution.

It was agony, such agony that as He knelt there He could not have been aware of the beauty all around Him. The valley under the brow of the hill was washed in moonlight. Below Him the brook Kedron rippled and sang over stones and through rushes. Around Him were the myrtle trees, palms, and fig trees that melted into the olive groves. And in the enclosed Garden of Gethsemane, all around His prostrate figure were the leaves and trunks of the olive trees silvered by filtering moonlight. . . . This was not a world that Christ, the man, wanted to leave.

Was there a moment when He wondered *how* to pray about the terrible alternatives before Him? If so, in the end

He knew that only one prayer could release the power that was needed to lift a sin-ridden world:

"Dear Father, all things are possible to You. Please—let me not have to drink this cup. Yet it is not what I want, but what You want." [3]

In these words Jesus deliberately set himself to make His will and God's will the same. The prayer was not answered as the human Jesus wished. Yet power has been flowing from His cross ever since.

God has given you and me free will too. And the voluntary giving up of our self-will always has a cross at the center of it. It is the hardest thing human beings are called on to do.

When we come right down to it, how can we make obedience real, except as we give over that self-will in reference to each of life's episodes as they unfold? That is why it should not surprise us that at the center of answered prayer lies the Law of Relinquishment.

7

Forgive Us Our Sins...

At the heart of the Christian gospel lies forgiveness, the greatest miracle of all. Only as each of us opens himself to receive this most wondrous of gifts, can the inner self deep within us be freed to become the happier, finer person we are meant to be. Whenever I think of our desperate need for forgiveness and of how difficult it is for some of us to accept it, my thoughts go back to Margaret Stanley—Meg, as some of us call her.

It is a long story covering some four years. It begins in the drab living room in a government housing project called Lillypond in Washington, D.C. Meg was musing, letting her mind roam over the previous evening. Every detail remained vivid. From the street the building had looked like a Victorian stone mansion. Only the polished brass plate beside the door had revealed that this was a church. Meg had not been near a church in years. She had let her sister, Alice, talk her into going this Wednesday night only because she had been assured that she would meet some interesting people.

She recalled the moment when they had pushed open the green door and a turbulence of voices, humming and buzzing, rising and falling, had beat upon them. She shut her eyes to recapture her first impression of the large entrance hall. There were stairs, with curving arches above them forming a backdrop. The bare parquet floor had been polished to mirror brightness. A square, old-fashioned grand piano stood to one side. People had been clustered in little groups talking animatedly. Alice had linked an arm through hers and had taken her from group to group. Names . . . so many names. There had been an obvious affection for Alice, a warmth that had flowed from her and back to her. Meg thought of that now with envy. She wondered if anyone had ever really loved *her?*

Then there had been dinner at small candlelit tables, with music in the background; afterward they had assembled in the little chapel to the left of the hallway. The chapel must have been made, Meg thought, by forming together two rooms of the old mansion.

Alice had tried to reassure her that this was not a church service. "Just a class," she had said lightly. "Meets every Wednesday. Arnold teaches it. He's the minister."

But he had not been Meg's idea of what a minister should look like. He was young, with a crew cut. His clear blue eyes had laughter crinkles at the corners. His clothes were preposterously casual. He even wore loafers.

If Meg had known that the class was called "What Christians Believe and Do" she probably would have fled before it started. As it was, the young minister had startled her into listening. "Christ requires a toughness to follow Him that frightens us," he began. "He asks that we deal decisively with all the things that keep us petty and make us ineffective.

"This is not just 'religious stuff.' It is practical. It works. In fact, if you are willing to try Christ for even six months, I'll guarantee that your life will be changed."

Back in her drab housing-project living room, Meg grimaced as she thought back to those words. Then she lifted one foot, kicked disgustedly at the ridiculous-looking coal stove in the center of the living room. Changed? Maybe some people, but not *her*. If those people at the church knew about her past, they would never let her set foot in the place!

She and her sister had come from a broken home. After years of dissension, their parents had been divorced. As a little girl Meg had been so unhappy that she had been unable to adjust to any school. There had been eighteen of them in all. After her second year in high school, she quit school and found a job.

Her need for affection drew her to friendships with men. Many of them were nice enough fellows and they had needs too. If she could give them a little pleasure, why not? Then she discovered that liquor helped to dull the feelings of guilt that always went with the affairs. There were a succession of men, then an illegitimate baby.

The Florence Crittenton home placed the baby for adoption, and a few months later she met Maynard. He seemed even nicer than the other men she had known. So she married him, because she thought marriage would change her. It had not.

Maynard had gone into the service and was sent to the West Coast. For Meg back home there began again the round of parties, heavy drinking, and now extra-marital affairs. A psychiatrist later analyzed her behavior not so much as wanton depravity but as a type of "sloppy kindness" brought on by her desire to please. Without a spiritual morality it quickly got out of hand.

Eventually Meg began spending every Saturday night at a down-at-the-heel dance hall. She found the young men there quick to take advantage of her weakness. Almost always there would be a drunken brawl; most Saturday nights the patrol wagon had to be called. Though Meg was disgusted by the brawls and managed to stay out of them, the police in the vicinity came to know her well.

Tales of what was going on at home got to Maynard. By this time, 1944, he was in a psychiatric ward in a veteran's hospital in Texas. There he tried to commit suicide. Hearing of

this, Meg had been jolted enough to try and pull herself together. Eventually Maynard came home and fourteen months
later a daughter was born to the couple. But their marriage
was in no better shape. Finally Maynard asked Meg for a
divorce.

The young minister's words rang now in her mind: "If you
are willing to try Christ for six months, I'll guarantee that
your life will be changed." Gurantee! How could he guarantee? One part of Meg's mind said, "Better not go near that
group again, if you want to hang on to the old life." But another part of her wanted to see those people again. There were
things she wanted to figure out. For instance, what was the
vitality that flowed from them? Why did they get so excited
about ideas? Why did she feel a warmth—yes, that was
it, warmth—in their presence? Suddenly Meg realized how
starved she was for love. Love! All her affairs and her attempts
at love had not touched the aching need that gnawed at her.

So on other Wednesday nights Meg did go back to "the
church in the house," as she came to call it. After several din-
ners with the group, she decided that hypocrisy must be lurk-
ing somewhere: nobody could be *that* nice. But how could
she accuse the folks at the church of hypocrisy when they kept
saying that the church was meant for sinners, that those who
thought themselves good were not yet ready for a church.

Moreover, there was a closeness in their relationships that
Meg had never seen before. It was more than friendship. For
instance, she marveled at the way Steve, once a seemingly
hopeless alcoholic and now a successful piano salesman, was
helping Phil, a painfully shy man who worked in the Interior
Department. Ben, who drove a bread truck, would at times
minister to Betts, an interior decorator. There was Martha, a
secretary; Sam, an oceanographer; Jane, a beautician; Bill, a
former Harvard professor; Estelle, a publicity girl; Karl, who
had spent forty years as a sailor—drunk most of the time.
All saw a great deal of one another and shared each other's

problems. Their lives were transparently open to the fellow-ship. In this transparency it seemed the natural thing to reveal their faults freely and to ask for help.

Nevertheless Meg was sure that she had a margin on all of them when it came to sin. She went through a period of trying to shock them. Over the years she had developed a hard line of talk. Increasingly she tried it out at the church. Once she let out some oaths in the chapel. No one batted an eyelash.

Then she had a conference with the minister, Arnold, and tried out on him raw statements of disbelief liberally sprinkled with profanity. She was dismayed to find him shockproof. He seemed neither surprised nor impressed by anything she said.

"Why should any of us be startled," he commented to her one afternoon, "to find out that human nature is capable of anything? There aren't any new sins, Meg. Just variations on old ones. Besides, the sort of thing you've been telling me is pale stuff compared to the adventure that Christ brings into life." He grinned at her discomfiture, and it was a disarming grin.

"Christ doesn't want to condemn you. He didn't come to earth to deepen our sense of moral defeat. He came to deliver us from what defeats us. All He wants, Meg, is to lift the weight of your past from you, so that you'll be free—really free. It's His love that makes that possible, Meg, His love——"

Meg burst into tears and fled from the office.

There were times when Meg was sure that Arnold and all the people at the church were crazy. Then there was a period when she thought they were rich—how else could they give so much money to the church? Finally there came the time when Meg did not care what they were. She knew only that she wanted what they had. She needed their love, needed to know that she belonged. Still—how could they love *her?*

Meanwhile Meg had asked Maynard to delay the divorce. She was now actively enrolled in a course called "Christian

Growth" and there was the outside chance that she might get some help toward saving their marriage. Maynard was distant and unimpressed, but agreed to postpone divorce action for a few weeks. He even began dropping in at the church to see what it was all about.

One evening Arnold was talking about sin. "Sin is not simply the violation of a code," he told the class. "Sin is an affront by one spirit against another—an outrage of love.

"That's bad enough, but it's even worse when we try to deny our sin to God and ourselves. Because that shuts off forgiveness and the peace that comes with a reconciliation with the God of love.

"Why does the Bible tell us that sin is so deadly?" As Arnold talked on, Meg began taking notes:

1. Our sins come between us and God and make it difficult to feel His presence. They are like mud and dirt thrown up on a window pane, shutting out the sunlight.
2. Even small sins narrow down the channel by which life and vitality flow to us, thus choking off creativity. But often we don't understand the connection between our lack of productivity and sin.
3. Sin divides us on the inside, splits us asunder. It separates conscious mind from subconscious, so that we are a personality in conflict with ourselves.
4. Our wrongdoings cut us off from other human beings. God reaches down to hold my hand. With my other hand I touch the lives of fellow human beings. Only as both connections are made can the power flow. And sin will break the connection every time. Isn't that why Jesus warned us that if we want forgiveness for ourselves, we'd better forgive others?

Outside the classroom a bell rang. The young minister picked up his notes, put them in the pocket of his coat. "Now that we are all aware, I hope, of our need for forgiveness, next Wednesday we'll try to answer the question how can we go about getting it."

Meg sat there for a moment staring at him. That was what she most wanted to know.

The following Wednesday, Meg had her notebook out and her attention riveted on getting down the steps in forgiveness as Arnold outlined them:

1. We have to be honest—candid and above board with God about all our sins and failures.
   Drop all excuses and explanations; these are not important.
   Be as specific as possible in confession.
2. We claim for ourselves one of God's promises of forgiveness. Here are some to choose among:
   "If we confess our sins, he is faithful and just to forgive us our sins, and to cleanse us from all unrighteousness." [1]
   "Him that cometh to me I will in no wise cast out." [2]
   "Come now, and let us reason together, saith the Lord: though your sins be as scarlet, they shall be as white as snow; though they be like crimson, they shall be as wool." [3]
   "For Thou, Lord, art good, and ready to forgive; and plenteous in mercy unto all them that call upon thee." [4]
3. We accept Christ's forgiveness *right now*, by faith—even though we feel no different yet.
   We also accept an initial entering into a personal relationship with Him, or an instantaneous return to fellowship with Him, as the case may be.
4. God may ask you to make some restitution. (This is not always possible. Some wrongs can never be righted by us.) If He does ask restitution, obey—no matter what the cost to your pride.
5. Now turn from the past to face the future. No more wallowing in remorse. God has forgiven you and wiped out your sins. Now you must forgive yourself. "Forgetting those things that are behind" is the only healthy way.

"When you've gone through these five steps," Arnold continued, "you're ready to begin living. Remember that it's everyday life that Christ wants to sanctify. Sometimes a new Christian makes the mistake of thinking he ought to be mystical, of wanting a sort of ivory-tower faith. Believe me, when you let Christ order your days, you won't spend your time reading spiritual books while your children are on the street and your house in disorder——"

Meg raised her hand. Her face was flushed, her voice trembling a little. "I've taken notes on all this, but there's still something I don't understand."

"Ask any question you'd like," Arnold encouraged.

"Well, Maynard and I have a coal stove in our living room. It's the bane of my life. Shake it down once and coal dust covers the whole house. Talk about disorder! I hate it almost as much as I hate myself." Meg hesitated, then blurted out, "How in th' hell can you sanctify a coal stove?"

When the friendly laughter had subsided, Arnold's answer seemed inspired: "In other words, the hated stove has become a sort of symbol to you. Think of it like this, Meg. When the coal is placed in the stove to come in contact with the flames, there's always an initial burning off of surface dust, gases, the superficial debris. The coal is not yet united with the flame. We are the coal. The flame is God's love.

"Once the superficial things are burned off, then a more fundamental change takes place. The coal itself catches fire. Finally it glows red-hot, even at its heart. This is a depth transmutation in which the coal and the flame are fused——"

"What about all the ashes which I have to dust and which Maynard has to keep carting away?" Meg asked.

"The ashes, Meg? All during your lifetime ashes will be sifting off...."

On Good Friday of that year Meg and Maynard slipped into the back of the chapel to find a play going on. During their drive to the church, Meg had been talking about how stupid Good Friday seemed to her. Why did the churches make such a commotion about it? What did Jesus' death and resurrection have to do with them?

There was little space at the front of the chapel, so the

stage set had to be simple. The play had been written by Elizabeth Ann Campagna, one of the group. It consisted of a conversation between two middle-aged women about their sons, their hopes for them, the trials and joys of raising children. In the end it turned out that one woman was the mother of Judas, the other the mother of Christ. It was direct and powerful. And something profound got through to Meg. When she left the chapel an hour and a quarter later, for her Jesus Christ had passed from a historic figure who had lived and died long ago to a Person alive now.

Meg described later how she felt after that performance. She saw that she had a choice. She could say to Him, "Yes I will let You live in my heart." This would be disturbing, unsettling to her existence. Or she could say, "No, I will not let You into my life." In that case, she felt she would be a part of the mass of people who crucified Him. She would, in effect, be pounding in some nails herself. And far as she was concerned, Christ's agony would have been for nothing.

As she walked down the stone steps into the Washington spring, she whispered an interior "Yes" to this Christ of whom she was now acutely aware. All along Massachusetts Avenue the trees were a delicate chartreuse lacework of green. Azaleas flamed here and there in the yards—fuchsia and coral and magenta. She sniffed the fragrant air. Soon all across Haines Point and the Tidal Basin the Japanese cherry trees would be budding—rose and pink, flesh and white. Meg tried to let the spring seep into her spirit.

But something was wrong. Even the "Yes" she had whispered had left her no feeling of relief—only the dead weight of wrong, so much wrong.

Late that spring Meg became pregnant again. During the previous two years she had had two miscarriages. The doctors at the George Washington University Hospital could find no physical cause for her problem.

After talking with Meg at length and after several examinations, one of the gynecologists summed up their findings for her: "Our conclusions will probably surprise you. We believe that on occasion a deep-seated sense of guilt can bring about a spontaneous abortion. Let me explain that a woman's emotions are a powerful factor, especially in the first months of pregnancy.

"You've been amazingly frank with us about your past. Because of certain actions resulting in guilt, your subconscious mind has persuaded you that you aren't fit to be a mother. Understand, I'm not saying that is true. That's your verdict about yourself. But the result is that each time you become pregnant, you abort the fetus."

Meg, abrupt as usual, merely asked, "So what can I do about it?"

"This is where medicine has to join hands with psychiatry or religion—maybe both. There are several possible approaches," the doctor answered cautiously. "I'm going to stick my neck out here a bit because your situation is unusual. Psychoanalysis might help. Or if you're a Catholic, the confessional might do it. If you're a Protestant, you could seek out a minister. But if you are intent on bringing this baby to term, we do urge something in addition to the drugs and the help we're going to give you."

The doctor stood up and held out his hand. "Good luck. You know we will do everything we can here at the clinic."

Now that it was imperative that she find the way to accept forgiveness, Meg felt desperate. The baby's life depended on it. Apparently guilt could kill. But she and Arnold had talked so often about getting rid of guilt. What more could he tell her? Nevertheless she set up a conference with him for the first afternoon he had some free time.

"The problem as the doctor analyzed it," Arnold reflected, "is how to persuade yourself at deep levels of consciousness that God has forgiven you. This may take time, Meg. What

I suggest now is that you try the game of 'acting as if——' "

"I don't understand—"

Arnold rose and stood in front of the fireplace, his hands behind his back. "Meg, do you believe that God is so eager to have us as His children that He accepts us the minute we come asking for forgiveness?"

"Yes, I think I can believe that."

"All right, then. You have asked, and He has forgiven. But there is something in you that dies hard, that refuses to feel clean. So from now on, try disregarding that soiled feeling. Act the truth—that the past is wiped out. And if that sometimes seems like hypocrisy, like acting a lie, tell yourself you're playing the game of 'acting as if.' "

"All right, I'll do it. I'll try anything. I've got to have this baby! I've got to!"

In the days that followed Meg found a technique that helped her with the 'act as if' game. Each time a self-despising thought assaulted her, she would counter by reading over one of the Scripture verses she had typed on cards. Some of the friends at the church who were more familiar with the Bible than she had helped her cull them:

Now ye are clean through the word which I have spoken unto you.[5]

We know that we belong to God. . . . We reassure ourselves whenever our heart may condemn us; for God is greater than our heart, and he knows all.[6]

We do know, we have believed, the love God has for us. . . .

Love has no dread in it. . . .

So you must consider yourselves dead to sin and alive to God. . . .

Let us enjoy the peace we have with God through our Lord Jesus Christ.

There were more verses. Meg found them living words, weapons against the still-lurking shadows. After a time she scarcely had to glance at the cards. Her hope was that as she memorized the words, spoke them over and over, that stubborn core inside would finally yield to the love of Christ.

The nine months of her pregnancy seemed endless. On two occasions when self-loathing rose strongly to haunt her, she came close to losing the baby. Each time she took a firmer grip on 'acting as if' and on the healing words of Scripture. Even so, final victory was to come only after the baby's birth.

It happened in the hospital, three nights after Jacqueline was born. Meg awoke about midnight. The room looked as it had a few minutes before—pale moonlight streaming across the polished linoleum floor. Scrim curtains billowed gently into the room on an evening breeze. Three pink roses drooped in a vase on the dresser, yet there was a Presence in the room. Meg felt it, knew it. This was Christ, and He had come to take her on a journey.

The journey took her back to her childhood. All that long night Christ helped her emotionally to relive episode after episode from her past. Through part of this she appeared to be dreaming. Then she would emerge into consciousness and would cringe and weep over the vivid pictures that had risen to haunt her, the faces of those whose lives she had soiled —no detail too tiny to recall.

Yet she was aware that something wonderful was happening. Into each painful memory there was flowing the healing of the Spirit of God. Then she would sink again into the dreaming state, and she and Christ would move on to the next episode —and the next. It was a falling and rising, a falling and rising, and in the process the recalcitrant subconscious was being healed and made of one piece with the conscious.

She knew now that Christ did not minimize her sins. He loathed the deeds that had soiled and betrayed her. Yet how tenderly He loved her!

As light flooded the hospital room Meg knew that she would never again see a sunrise so beautiful. She wept once more, this time not from shame, but to think that Christ had cared enough about her—after all she had done and been—to seek her out and to make complete the forgiveness she and Arnold had begun by faith. For the first time in her life Meg felt clean.

One of the fascinating sidelights of her experience was that although on that memorable night the name and face of every man with whom she had been sexually involved were vividly remembered, she was to discover a few years later that she could not recall a single name. Thus it was literally true that her transgressions were wiped out, removed from her.

Almost immediately her friends saw the transformation. Meg's hardness and profanity died in her. The expression on her face was different; her manner altered. Even her taste in clothes changed.

And how she looked forward to seeing her friends at church and to listening to Arnold's teaching! Step by step she moved ahead. "If we don't keep our window panes clean," Arnold told her and the others one night, "the excitement that we feel when we first enter the Christian life will fade. Even an accumulation of small sins can make life seem like a bottle of ginger ale from which all the fizz is gone. So here are some hints.

"Discouragement about our failures and stumblings is never the way to handle them. In an old book I found this statement, 'All discouragement is from the devil.' Whether you believe in the devil as a personality of evil in the world or not, ponder that one.

"Some kind of methodical cleaning out at intervals is necessary if we are to have an uninterrupted fellowship with God. We in the Protestant churches don't make enough provision for this, though certain high Episcopal churches do offer the Confessional.

"In trying to keep cleaned out, beware of things that you have an instinctive desire to keep hidden—no matter how insignificant these may seem to you.

"In this connection, I want to read to you a paragraph from Carl Jung's *Modern Man in Search of a Soul:*

"To cherish secrets and to restrain emotions are psychic misdemeanours for which nature finally visits us with sickness. . . . It is as if man had an inalienable right to behold all that is dark, imperfect, stupid and guilty in his fellow beings—for such of course are the things that we keep private to protect ourselves. It seems to be a sin in the eyes of nature to hide our insufficiency—just as much as to live entirely on our inferior side. There appears to be a conscience in mankind which severely punishes the man who does not somehow and at some time, whatever cost to his pride, cease to defend and assert himself, and instead confess himself fallible and human. Until he can do this, an impenetrable wall shuts him out from the living experience of feeling himself a man amongst men. . . ." [7]

For Meg came the final step toward forgiveness that Christ sometimes requires—restitution. She knew that she could never undo all the wrong she had wrought. Yet now that Christ had offered her the love that would never let go, He was making it clear to her that neither would that love let her off.

"Christ told me," Meg said later, "to go back to the spot where I'd shared degradation with so many youngsters and show them some real fun. It was a case of 'Go home to thy friends.' "

So each Saturday night she went. About the fifth week a burly Irish cop met her at the door of the dance hall. "Lady, it's wonderful what you're doing for these kids," he confided. "You know, there used to be the most awful woman down here——"

"My head went down and I stared at my shoes," she recalls. "I breathed a quick little prayer, 'God, when you gave me a new life, I hope that you gave me a new face. Please don't let him recognize me. I couldn't take that—yet!'

"I guess that there wasn't much danger that the cop would

recognize me. Already God had done a pretty thorough job. The man just patted my hand in a fatherly way and said, 'Lady, the police force is sure glad you're here!' "

The new person that is Meg became an integral part of the small church that had lured her away from the old life. It was there that I came to know her. Of course, Margaret Stanley is not her real name. I have cherished her friendship for something over ten years. I have marveled at her ceaseless striving for growth in her new life, have been astonished at the flashes of insight that come to her.

Often as I have witnessed her unwavering compassion for the failures and foibles of all human beings, I have remembered that nameless woman of long ago. Out of her shame a group of Scribes and Pharisees had dragged her before Christ. For me, the scene is forever etched as Peter Marshall's words painted it:

> ... The woman lies before Christ in a huddled heap,
>   sobbing bitterly.....
>   shivering as she listens to the indictment.
> The penalty for adultery is stoning.
>
> Jesus' steady eyes take in the situation at a glance.
> He sees what they try to hide from Him—
>   the hard faces that have no mercy or pity.
> Every hand holds a stone and clutching fingers run
> along the sharp edges with malicious satisfaction.
>
> They have brought the woman to Christ as a vindictive
> afterthought, not for formal trial,
>   (for they have already tried her)
> but in a bold effort to trap Him.
> Either He will have to set aside the plain commandment
> of the law, or tacitly consent to a public execution.....
> And has He not said often, "Be ye therefore merciful"
> How can He condemn the woman and still be merciful?
> The circle of bearded men wait impatiently for His
> answer....

Christ looks into the faces of the men before Him, and steadily—with eyes that never blink—he speaks to them:

"He that is without sin among you,
let him first cast a stone at her."

His keen glance rests upon the woman's accusers one by one....

There is the thud of stone after stone falling on the pavement.

Not many of the Pharisees are left now.

Looking into their faces Christ sees into the yesterdays that lie deep in the pools of memory and conscience.

He sees into their very hearts...

Idolater...

Liar...

Drunkard...

Murderer...

Adulterer...

One by one, they creep away—like animals—slinking into the shadows...

Shuffling off into the crowded streets to lose themselves in the multitudes.

"He that is without sin among you, let him cast the first stone at her."

But no stones have been thrown.

They lie around the woman on the pavement.

She alone is left at the feet of Christ.

The stillness is broken only by her sobbing.

She still has not lifted her head....

And now Christ looks at her.

He does not speak for a long moment.

Then, with eyes full of understanding, He says softly:

"Woman, where are those thine accusers?
Hath no man condemned thee?"

And she answers,

"No man, Lord."

That is all the woman says from beginning to end.
She has no excuse for her conduct.
She makes no attempt to justify what she has done.
And Christ looking at her, seeing the tear-stained cheeks,
                    seeing further into her heart,
                    seeing the contrition there,
says to her, "Neither do I condemn thee:
                    go, and sin no more...."

And His voice is like a candle at twilight,
    like a soft angelus at the close of the day....
        like the singing of a bird after the storm....
It is healing music for the sin-sick heart.

All is quiet for a while.
If she breathes her gratitude, it is so soft that only
He hears it.
Perhaps He smiles upon her, as she slowly raises her
eyes,
    a slow, sad smile of one who knows that He Himself
    has to pay the price for that absolution.....

She has looked into the eyes of Christ.
She has seen God.
She has been accused
            convicted
        judged but not condemned.
She has been forgiven!

And now her head is up.
Her eyes are shining like stars, for has she not seen
the greatest miracle of all?

It is more wonderful than the miracles of creation....
    more mysterious than the stars....
        more melodious than any symphony....
            more wonderful than life itself.....
that God is willing, for Christ's sake, to forgive sinners
like you and me....[8]

And that is the miracle that came to Meg.

8

...As We Forgive Those Who
Sin Against Us

Forgiveness has two sides that are inseparably joined: the forgiveness each of us needs from God, and the forgiveness we owe to other human beings. Most of us prefer not to face up to the fact that God's forgiveness and man's are forever linked.

Jesus warned us that if we want the Father's forgiveness, there is only one way to get it: Start the flow of forgiveness between heaven to earth by forgiving our brother from the heart. The story of Harvey Smith, a friend of my husband Len, is an extraordinary example of man's need to forgive those who have wronged him.

This young minister recently wrote Len that he would soon be passing through New York. "I'm resigning my pastorate in Danielsville, Georgia, to move to Boston for some graduate work. With a wife and four children, you can imagine that this has been a hard decision. I could come out to Chappaqua to see you late Saturday afternoon." So it was arranged.

When our guest arrived, I found him as curious about me as I was about him. At first, I put this down to his interest in how I might be adjusting to my new situation: a husband, a new household, and three young children in addition to Peter John. But as Harvey Smith shook my hand firmly and looked me straight in the eyes searchingly, he said, "Before I leave, I want to tell you the main reason that I've been so eager to meet you."

"Then that makes two stories for me to hear," I told him.

Harvey and Len had been friends in 1950 when they were both attending the Marble Collegiate Church in New York. Len had told me the bare outlines of Harvey Smith's story—his experience with forgiveness—but I wanted to hear it directly from him.

Our guest settled himself in a lounge chair and crossed his long legs. He had an easy manner and soft speech of the southerner. "Forgiveness? I used to think I knew a lot about that subject." Suddenly Harvey Smith's thoughts seemed far away.

"Every time my congregation repeats that one sentence in the Lord's Prayer, I stand there in the pulpit wondering if they realize the terrible condition of forgiveness that they are acknowledging."

"How do you mean?" I asked.

"The sentence 'Forgive us our trespasses as—that is, in proportion as—we forgive those who trespass against us.' "

"Christ was even more specific after He had finished teaching them the prayer," Len added, "when He says that if we do not forgive other men, God will not forgive us.[1] That seems rugged."

"I've had good reason to ponder that teaching," Harvey continued. "It certainly doesn't mean that God is threatening to punish us by paying us back in kind."

"But Jesus must have meant what He said," I added. "He could not have been more clear-cut or emphatic about it."

As the three of us discussed the sentence in the Lord's Prayer, we came to the conclusion that the terrible condition is there, not because Jesus willed it but because it states an inescapable fact, a law. When we hold unforgiveness or malice in our hearts, then we cannot possibly have our hearts open to the love of God. We are the ones who have shut the door, not God.

And then Harvey Smith spoke several memorable sentences which I hope I can quote accurately:

"In forgiveness, there has to be a flow. It is the law of the tides; the law of seedtime and harvest. No receiving without giving; no dead-sea hearts are possible. As we give, it is given unto us—in money, in health, in love, in forgiveness. We just cannot have forgiveness in any other way, because that is the way life works."

And then Harvey told us his story.

In the autumn of 1950 Harvey Smith had come to New York City from La Grange, Georgia, to attend Columbia University. Soon after arriving, he had met a boy named Jack in one of his classes. Jack was a young man with an unhappy background, reared in a broken home. He had just done a miserable stint in the Navy, and now was confused about his future. He seemed to need a friend, so Harvey let him share his apartment. It was a basement apartment in the shadow of the Cathedral of St. John the Divine.

What the Southerner did not know was that Jack had always been an emotionally disturbed person. This unhappy truth came out soon enough. Periods of seeming normalcy would be followed by uncontrollable temper tantrums. As these became more frequent and Jack's drinking bouts grew heavier, Harvey realized that he was in a situation he could not handle. Moreover, his unhappy friend refused to go to a counselor.

Finally Harvey knew what he had to do. He would move out and leave the apartment to Jack. His plan was to find a room nearby, so that they could still be friends. Perhaps then he could be more objective and so be of more help.

It was on a Thursday morning just as he was about to leave for school that Harvey told his apartment-mate of his decision. It was only later that he realized how shattering this was to the distraught man. Apparently he had become Jack's only security. Now love was being withdrawn, and his whole world was collapsing.

The agitated Jack pleaded at first. Then rage took over. He struck out at Harvey, who protected himself from the flailing arms and held them until the other boy quieted down.

When the anger seemed to be spent, Harvey went over to the mirror to tend to a cut on his nose. At that moment he heard a noise like a snarl behind him. As he wheeled, Jack shoved the door to with one foot. In one hand he was brandishing a hammer.

Harvey was not frightened. He was a larger man than his apartment-mate; he was sure he could disarm him easily. But as he grabbed for the hammer and kicked it under the dresser, he felt a heavy blow in the back. Then as the two men grappled, there were two more sharp thrusts in Harvey's back.

This was the worst tantrum yet. He must get Jack out of the room. He shoved his antagonist back to the door, then held him with one hand, while with the other he turned the latch. Suddenly there were two more lunges at him, one to the abdomen and one to the chest. And at that moment Harvey's eyes caught the flash of a knife.

Summoning all his strength, he shoved Jack into the hall, threw the latch, and stood leaning against the door, trying to understand why he could not get his breath.

Through the closed door, he called for help. Mr. Rogers, the building superintendent, had a workshop just down the hall. Perhaps he would hear. Then Harvey realized that his voice did not sound right. Feeling something sticky on his sweater, he looked down. Red-tinged bubbles were seeping through the sweater from his chest. A sickening realization swept him. "I've been stabbed. My lungs are punctured." He swayed, then steadied himself against the door.

Immediately there was a knock. *Must be Mr. Rogers.* The wounded man managed to open the door, then collapsed in a heap on the floor.

The superintendent took one horrified look. Blood-specks had spattered the young man's face and sweater. A red stain was spreading across his chest. Color was draining from Harvey's face, his eyes were glazing.

Fear gripped Mr. Rogers. Without realizing what he was doing, he left Harvey where he was and ran to get the police, leaving the apartment door open.

Jack appeared again in the doorway. He stood over his helpless victim, the bloody knife still in his hand. Lying there, Harvey knew that there was nothing he could do to prevent Jack from finishing the job. One more stab would probably be enough.

Instead, Jack half-lifted, half-dragged Harvey to the bed. From far away, his assailant's voice came to him, "Harvey, can you forgive me?"

Harvey tried to open his eyes. Jack's face swam hazily above him. *Jack was sorry.* The haze cleared a bit. He saw Jack raise the knife to plunge it into his own chest. *Must stop him— must.* With his last strength, Harvey half-raised himself, grabbed the knife, and dropped it behind the bed.

Now the blackness began to close in. But Jack's request for forgiveness lay like a stone on Harvey's mind. He heard his own voice from a great distance, "Yes, Jack, I forgive you."

Mind and spirit seemed to be separating from body. *That's not me, the natural man speaking. That came as a response from all the things I've ever learned in my Christian faith....* There were no more thoughts.

In the operating theatre of Knickerbocker Hospital on New York's West Side, Dr. Ruth Selznick was examining Harvey Smith's multiple chest wounds. This skilled physician, a specialist in chest surgery, had never seen a worse case. Five deep knife wounds...lungs rapidly filling with blood...patient in a state of deep shock...

She set to work. Hours went by. Then suddenly there was a new crisis. The patient's breathing stopped. A split-second decision required a new incision, then alternate pressure and suction on the lungs. No response from the inert form on the table. Minutes passed...four...six. Suddenly a tremor went through the patient's body. Harvey began to breathe again.

Seven hours and fifty minutes after having been placed on the table, Harvey was wheeled from the operating room. But the struggle to live had only begun. The doctor sat by his bed and labored over him all that night.

For a week Harvey hung between life and death. Most of the time he was conscious and thinking clearly, but he had to lie still. With both lungs punctured and collapsed, the least movement might cause hemorrhaging.

There was pain too—much pain, and at moments, self-pity. *Do I really know the meaning of forgiveness? I told Jack I had forgiven him. I gave it all I had. And it wasn't enough, because I still feel resentful.*

Harvey lay very still, thinking. His thoughts roamed over the weeks prior to the stabbing. Then an idea came to him. Are any of us ever blameless? Maybe it had been out of pride and not a little self-righteousness that he had been trying to help Jack. Perhaps his "goodness" had actually been a stumbling block to Jack.

Then the pain would come back again. Harvey would gasp for a breath that was slow in coming. Nothing but a gurgling sound deep in his chest. And in his heart, fear.

This isn't easy. Forgiveness is costly. Am I really willing to pay the price? Do I really forgive him?

It seemed even more costly that day when Harvey heard that Jack was building his testimony on the basis of self-defence. Harvey's fingerprints were on the hammer. Of course they were! So Jack had decided to plead that he had been attacked first, had struck with the knife only to protect himself. Grimly Harvey pondered the irony of it. *Forgiveness is costly....*

He thought back to that moment when he had lain on the bed with Jack standing over him brandishing the bloody knife. "Yes, Jack, I forgive you...." The instinct that had told him that this was not really him speaking had been right.

He had not the ability to get rid of the surging resentments, the bitterness, the self-pity, the temptation to compare Jack's conduct to his. He could not cleanse himself of those emotions, but the One who had spoken those words of forgiveness for him that day in the apartment could complete the job for him now. All he had to do was to be willing to let the resentment go and to set his will toward forgiveness. Christ would do the rest. *But forgiveness is costly: it cost Christ a great deal.*

As he lay in his hospital bed, near death, Harvey found the meaning of life. Out of new understanding, once more from the depths of his being, came the words "Jack, I forgive you." And at last there was peace in his heart.

Meanwhile, during those weeks in the hospital, Harvey's friends at the Young Adult Group of the Marble Collegiate Church were donating blood—a great deal of it. Over and over they met to pray for Harvey and for Jack. One member of the group was Ann Hougasian, whom Harvey had met some months before.

Quietly the young people raised the money to pay all of Harvey's hospital expenses. Daily they inquired about him, sent flowers, fruit, showered small kindnesses on him. Through them Christ's love was flowing to him. He dared not dam up any of that love and prevent it from flowing to the one who needed it most—Jack.

Then Harvey learned something else about forgiveness. It was his red-haired doctor who taught him.

"You're going to get well," she told him one morning.

The patient smiled at her. "I've known that for several days. It's mostly thanks to you, too."

"No—o. There's another reason. Your condition has been so precarious that anything could have tipped the scales."

"What do you mean?"

"I've watched you closely. You've been at peace with yourself, especially the last ten days. If you had held on to any hate at all, that negative emotion would have sapped so much of your energy that you probably would not have pulled through."

Throughout the rest of the day, Harvey pondered the doctor's words. In this case, hateful unforgiving thoughts would literally have destroyed him.

The doctor was right. Her patient eventually did make a complete recovery. And Harvey, convinced that his life had been spared for some purpose, became intent on finding that purpose.

It was more than three years before he knew. In the meantime, he had taken a full-time job with the Boy Scouts of America. On Christmas Day 1952 he and Ann Hougasian were married in a quiet ceremony in La Grange, Georgia.

Len and I had listened to this gripping story through part of the morning and during lunch. Immediately after lunch our twelve-year-old Linda appeared in the doorway. "Daddy, I've spilled something on the rug by my bed and need to use the vacuum sweeper. But it won't work. Something's wrong. Will you——?"

"I'll have a look at it," Len said. Soon he and Harvey were down on hands and knees taking the plug apart. In the end, it was Harvey who found the loose wire and reconnected it. I remember this little incident because what to some might have been an annoying interruption was to Harvey Smith a pleasure: he was helping someone.

After that, Harvey told us the second part of his story. "This is the part I really came here to tell you," he said to me. "It happened one Saturday night in mid-April 1955. I was then completing my third year as a district Boy Scout executive in New York City. Ann and I and another couple had gone to the Roxy to see the movie of your book, *A Man Called Peter*.

"I sat there completely absorbed in the story. There came that scene at the Naval Academy in Annapolis where Dr. Marshall had decided at the last minute to change his sermon and preach about death. He didn't know why; it seemed an odd topic for the young cadets. But that same afternoon he discovered why. Over the car radio came the news that Pearl Harbor had been bombed. We were at war.

"In that scene God got through to me. Nothing spectacular —no visions, mind you. Just a simple message to heart and brain, 'Harvey, I want you to give up Boy Scout work. I led Peter Marshall. I can lead you. You're to go back to school and prepare for the ministry.'

"My response was immediate. No struggle, in spite of the fact that I loved Scout work. No indecision, though going back to school would mean a financial struggle. By then, Ann and I had a year-old son.

"I just said to myself, 'All right, Lord, if that's what you want for me.' I remember trying to hold back the tears. Ann sensed my emotion because she reached for my hand.

"The rest of the movie was lost to me. I had to go back a few weeks later to see how it ended.

"Later that evening, when I told Ann what had happened in the theatre and asked her how she would feel about being the wife of a minister, she was jubilant. 'Why, darling, now I can tell you. I thought you were studying to be a preacher when I first met you. Be a minister's wife? Nothing could please me more.'

"The decision had to go through a time-testing period to make certain that this was no ephemeral emotionalism. But months later I was as sure as ever, the call as clear, my enthusiasm just as great. So I entered seminary in the fall. You know the rest of the story."

The three of us marveled at the events that had dovetailed and conspired to bring Harvey to the place where God wanted him.

Then I asked, "But what happened to Jack?"

"He was sentenced to several years' treatment in a corrective institution. I understand that now he is out again." Harvey was silent a moment. "There is so much to learn the hard way about forgiveness."

Then he repeated again the steps.

"First, came the realization that I was not without blame, that none of us ever are. Second, that forgiveness isn't easy—it's costly. And then I learned that from God's point of view, forgiveness isn't complete until a severed relationship has been mended. It took me a while to see that this is the point of that Scripture verse, 'If thou bring thy gift to the altar, and there rememberest that thy brother hath aught against thee; Leave there thy gift before the altar .... first be reconciled to thy brother, and then come and offer thy gift.' [2]

"This means that we won't feel that our prayers are getting through, or our gifts being accepted, until we have done something to try to heal the broken relationship. So you see, actually the forgiveness process between Jack and me is not finished yet."

"But Harvey," Len interrupted, "after all that has happened and considering Jack's emotional situation, do you really think a constructive relationship could be established now?"

"It takes faith to think so," Harvey answered slowly. "I can't honestly say I relish trying it. But it's unfinished business, so only God can tell me how to finish it."

I have a feeling that Harvey will get back to Jack. Someday I shall learn the final chapter of this extraordinary story.

Jesus had a great deal to say about forgiveness. Take the scene recorded by Matthew in which the subject is under discussion: The disciples know that according to old Jewish law, one must forgive three times. After that, a man can be as hostile to another as he wishes.

But impetuous Peter is feeling expansive. He draws his striped robe about him and asks, "Lord, how oft shall my brother sin against me and I forgive him?" A smug look creeps across the disciple's face. He will be overly generous in answering his own question and so win a word of approval from the Master: "Until *seven* times?"

Christ looks at His disciple, His eyes showing amusement. Peter is so transparent, always ready to talk. "Your arithmetic is all wrong, Simon, as wrong as that of the scribes and Pharisees. Forgive seven times? Nay—seventy times seven."

Then seeing Peter's face screwed up, obviously working on the sum in his head, the Master says, "Let me tell you a story:

"A certain King had a servant who owed him ten thousand talents—"

Immediately Matthew, the former customs collector with the mathematician's brain, exclaimed, "Ten thousand talents! Why, the total annual taxes of all five provinces of our land are but eight hundred talents. That's—that's twelve and a half times that much!" *

Jesus continued. "Of course the king knew that a debt like that was impossible of repayment, so he ordered the servant, his wife, and children sold into slavery.

"But the miserable servant prostrated himself, bowing his head in the dust before the king. 'Lord, have patience with me. I will pay thee all.'

---

* About two million dollars in our money; the purchasing power of that sum was many times what it would be today.

"It was so preposterous as to be touching. The King's amusement was tinged with pity. This servant had many lovable qualities. With sudden compassion, he said, 'All right, I release you from the debt. Rise up. Be gone!'

"The servant leapt to his feet, rejoicing. He would have kissed his master, had he dared. He was free—free!

"Later on the same day, the servant went to the bazaar to purchase fresh pike for the master's household. Suddenly down the street, opposite the linen draper's shop, he spied Nahum's retreating back. Nahum had owed him a hundred shillings for half a moon. Was the rascal trying to avoid him?

"The servant drew his robe about him and ran down the cobblestone street, ducking women with baskets and pails, sidestepping donkeys and asses. He caught up with Nahum at the dove stall. Roughly he reached for his throat. 'You've been running from me long enough! You'll pay what you owe me right now.'

"Nahum fell at his feet. 'Look, I'll pay. I promise. Just have patience. If you'll give me till the sun goes down tomorrow——'

"'Patience, indeed! I will not! I've caught you now, and I'm not going to let you go again or else it will be another moon. A few days in jail may sharpen your conscience.' And he summoned the magistrate, who had no choice but to throw the debtor into jail.

"Soon word of the episode got back to the King. His own generous forgiveness had wrought no gratitude after all! He summoned his servant to him. 'Thou wicked servant! I forgave thee all that great debt. Could you not have had like mercy on your fellow servant? Your heart is hard, incapable of receiving forgiveness. Torment is always the end of the hard heart. Torment will be yours until you learn that only as you forgive, shall it be forgiven you.'"

The Master finished. His penetrating eyes circled the group, looked into each man's face in turn. For once even Peter was

silent. The message of the story was sinking into their hearts:
Our debt to the Heavenly Father is inordinate, unpayable, so
we are at the mercy of the Father's compassion. In comparison with our debt to Him, the most any human being can owe
another is trifling.

Every one of us is guilty before God. There are sins of the
mind and the spirit as well as of the body. There are unworthy
motives. There are all the opportunities that have gone begging away. There are all the times we have chosen second
best. Yet God is willing freely to forgive us, no matter what
we have done, *provided* we are willing to be "kind one to
another, tenderhearted, forgiving one another, even as God for
Christ's sake hath forgiven you." [3]

Today our civilization cries out for forgiveness. Husbands
and wives need it...Parents and children...Friends...
Statesmen. Businessmen and labor leaders need it.

Yes, and nations. Jesus would tell us that we Americans
must forgive the Japanese for Pearl Harbor, just as the Japanese must forgive us for Hiroshima. The Jews have so much
for which to forgive the Germans. And the Germans have
much to forgive the Russians; and the Russians the Germans.
Have the Ethiopians forgiven the Italians? And what about the
Israelis and the Arabs with so much bitterness on both sides.
If the wounds of millions are to be healed, what other way is
there except through forgiveness?

Jesus, at least, gives us no alternative. The command is
stern. The terms are set. "But if ye forgive not men their
trespasses, neither will your Father forgive your trespasses." [4]

God's forgiveness and man's are one.

9

How to Find God's Guidance

IN A POPULAR MAGAZINE some years ago, I read a story whose broad outlines have haunted me ever since. The author followed a man through one day of his life. First we saw him on a May morning, walking down the tree-shaded Main Street of his home town. He passed children on their way to school. Already some of the housewives were busy with their spring cleaning.

Up ahead on the left was the white frame cottage of a girl he knew well. All at once, he longed to push open the iron gate and stroll up the uneven brick walk for a chat with her.

For a moment he hesitated. The upstairs shades had been raised; she must be up. But no—he really should get on down to the bank. So he walked on.

Then the author interrupted his own story to show us how different the rest of this man's life would have been had he followed that impulse to push open the iron gate and walk through.

Ah—but that was not the way he decided it. And so the story went on through the trivia of the rest of the man's day.

It is a parable of our lives. At the time of each choice, we stand at one of life's crossroads. How many examples each of us could cite of seemingly insignificant decisions that changed the course of a life! The plane reservation canceled a few hours before the plane crashed.... The strange timing that led to meeting the man one later married...and so on.

Then, if decisions—large and small—can be so important, on what basis shall we make them? Without God, most of us muddle through somehow, often with better hindsight than foresight, and sometimes with poor to disastrous consequences. To make decisions, we employ a potpourri of common sense, what we have learned through past experience, immediate circumstances, the weighing of factors for and against, the advice of others—all with a dash of emotion and another of prejudice.

Christianity from the first has taught that a better way for making decisions is available: the direct guidance of God to the individual. The promise that God can guide us is the clear teaching of Scripture, both in its total sweep and in its specific promises.

This Scriptural teaching rests on three pillars: (1) that God has all wisdom, hence knows the past and the future and what is best for His children; (2) that He is a God of love who cares about the individual enough to want to direct him right; (3) that He can communicate with men. As Abraham Lincoln once commented, "I am satisfied that when the Almighty wants me to do, or not to do any particular thing, He finds a way of letting me know it."

As for specific promises, there are many in the Bible, among them:

In all thy ways acknowledge Him and He shall direct thy paths.[1]

He calleth his own sheep by name, and leadeth them out.... He goeth before them, and the sheep follow him: for they know his voice.[2]

If any of you lack wisdom, let him ask of God, that giveth to all men liberally, and upbraideth not; and it shall be given him.[3]

Howbeit when he, the Spirit of truth is come, he will guide you into all truth . . . and he will show you things to come.[4]

Then the Bible goes on to show us how these promises were fulfilled in the lives of men and women. Take, for example, the incident concerning Paul and Ananias, as told in the ninth chapter of Acts. Let me put the story in modern language. . . .

One morning in the city of Damascus about the year A.D. 34, God spoke to a man named Ananias. "I want you to get up and go to number 38 Straight Street. That is the home of one Judas. There you are to ask for a man named Saul—"

"But Lord——"

"This Saul has lost his sight. You will know why later. I want you to lay your hands on him, and he will recover his sight."

Suddenly a thought stabbed Ananias. "Lord, you can't be sending me to Saul of Tarsus! Appalling reports are abroad about that man. He's a murderer! He stood by and watched Stephen's death and did not lift a finger to save him. He's even had men and women who claim to be Your disciples put in chains. Why Lord, he's one of your worst enemies——"

So Ananias, wondering if he had heard God aright, tortured with the thought that his mind might be playing tricks on him, started out for Straight Street. He found that number 38 was indeed the home of Judas and that a man named Saul was there.

But the moment he walked into the room where Saul sat, all doubts and fears left him. Whatever this Saul had been before, he was now a broken man—stunned, bewildered, lost. In a wave of compassion and confidence which Ananias scarcely understood himself, he heard himself saying, "Saul, my brother, I have been sent by the Lord to let you regain your sight and to tell you the next step——"

What if Ananias had refused to follow God's directions that day? Was this one of those hinges upon which history turns? For Saul was to become Paul, saying "I have been wrong," one of the most dramatic turnabouts any man has ever made. He was to become Paul of the towering mind, of the blazing convictions, giant of an apostle to the Roman empire, impelling advocate of Christianity to the Western world.

There are many such instances of direct guidance in Scripture. Apparently the first-century Christians expected to receive their marching orders from God, regarded this kind of inner guidance as the rule rather than the exception.

But what about today? Can we expect the same sort of direct word from God?

It would seem so, for the New Testament attaches no time tags to its promises of guidance. When I first became interested in this subject, I could not ignore Peter Marshall's oft-reiterated conviction that God can and does communicate His will to modern men and women just as He did to those in Biblical times. In his life, Peter had not often had the guidance of the inner Voice. More frequently his direction had come through providential circumstances plus a strong inner feeling of rightness about a particular decision. He had thus been led from Scotland to the United States to enter the ministry when he had thought he wanted to go to China. When the door to China had been shut in his face, he had tried for home-mission work in Scotland. That door closed too. Through a series of remarkable circumstances, the way to the United States then opened. Certainly this was God's guidance to an extraordinarily fruitful life.

I too knew more of this type of guidance by circumstance than that of the inner Voice. But it was of inner guidance that Peter and I both longed to know more.

About two years after we moved to Washington, the matter was further brought to our attention by a certain group of friends in the old Oxford Group, which was the forerunner of Moral Rearmament. They believed that quietness, a receptive mind, and a pad and pencil would result in God's Voice speaking to the inner man. Since this technique was obviously meaningful to some people, I decided to try it.

Each morning after Peter left for the church office, I would shut the bedroom door and sit quietly, trying to still my churning thoughts. My thoughts were usually unruly: those two thank-you notes that should be written ... Don't forget to telephone for the pick-up of the dry cleaning ... What are we going to have for dinner tonight?

Impatiently I would break away from such trivialities, trying to make my mind a blank again. No use! Morning after morning no mighty inspiration came, no inner Voice made itself heard. The notebook on my lap had little written on it other than lists of household tasks.

Peter and I had close friends, however, who often experienced inner direction. Sometimes the guidance they received was of quite a dramatic nature.

For instance, we had two women friends who customarily spent their winters together in Florida. On Sunday they went to separate churches, because Tay is a Catholic and Fern is an Episcopalian. On one particular Sunday, after Mass in Palm Beach was over, Tay picked up Fern on the corner nearest her church. As Fern got in the car, Tay said, "I've got news for you. We're going to run down to see Grace." Whereupon she started backing into a driveway to turn around.

"You mean now? Before lunch?" They both knew that Grace's home was in Delray Beach, twenty-two miles away.

Tay nodded. "I know it's an odd time to go visiting. I may as well tell you the truth, Fern. During Mass it came to me strongly that Grace needs us desperately, right away."

"I—see. Well I'm not going to argue with that." Fern sensed an authority behind her friend's words. There had been a long series of similar guidances in the past, most of them uncannily correct. And Fern herself had often experienced a similar sort of inner direction.

As the women drove into their friend's yard, the screen door of the house burst open, and Grace came to meet them. "Am I glad to see you! I've been trying to reach you for hours by phone."

Then she told them of the emergency. During the night her husband had suffered a stroke. Already the doctor had warned her that the sick man could not possibly recover. His distraught wife was anxious to get him home to Akron, Ohio, where their married children and their families were. If the doctor's prediction was correct, then above all else her husband would want this final reunion with his family. But it was now a race against time. Tay and Fern spent the rest of the day making the arrangements.

Not until a month later, after Grace and her husband had gotten safely home and the dying man had had six days of joyful reunion with his children and grandchildren before the end, did Grace think to ask Fern how it was that she and Tay had driven by her house that Sunday.

At the time I wondered how to analyze such a dramatic happening. Some might call the direction Tay received in church that Sunday an example of extrasensory perception. I suspected that the first Christians would have said, "There is more to it than that."

It is true, of course, that as the church grew and spread across the centuries, some of the ideas that had meant most to those first-century disciples were almost forgotten—sturdy practical beliefs like the communion of the saints, healing, and God's direct leading. As often in the history of Christendom, it is the rebellion of small segments or fringe groups that points unerringly to the dead spots in the organized church.

Thus it was in the England of 1647 that George Fox, the son of a weaver of Drayton-in-the-Clay, conceived some strong convictions about the formalism and deadness of the churches of his day. Fox had no thought of forming a separate religious sect; he simply wanted to see the church revivified. He and his cohorts called themselves the society of friends (not even with capital letters) and among other convictions they held strongly to the "perceptible guidance of the Holy Spirit," "the inward light," meaning the distinct and conscious voice of God in the heart and mind.

During this period of my searching out the question of guidance I became especially interested in the experiences of the Society of Friends, since this is one of their strongest teachings. One memorable story of a visiting Friend, a woman who was talking to a weekday meeting in a suburb of Philadelphia, appeared in one of Hannah Whitall Smith's books.[5] The visitor knew no one in the room except those to whom she had been introduced a few minutes before.

Suddenly she interrupted her talk to say, "A young man has come into this room who has in his pocket some papers by which he's about to commit a great sin. If he will come and see me this afternoon (and she told where she was staying) I have a message from the Lord for him that will show him a way out of his trouble." Then the woman resumed her sermon.

Hannah Smith, who was present that day, followed up this case. A strange young man did call that afternoon at the house where the woman preacher was stopping. He had a forged check in his pocket. He was on his way to cash it when something made him stop and slip into a seat in the back of the meeting house. His name was not asked for nor given, but he tore up the check in the presence of the woman. Later it was discovered that he had been so impressed with this message from God that, from that hour, he determined never to attempt such a dishonesty again.

On another occasion the same woman preacher was staying with a cousin of Mrs. Smith. The guest came down to breakfast one morning saying that during the night God had told her to take a message to a man living some miles away. She had been given neither name nor directions. Yet her faith was such that she asked the cousin to get out his carriage and take her. "God will show us the way," she insisted.

At each crossroad the woman would point the direction they were to go. Finally, after about six miles in countryside which neither of them knew, she pointed to a farmhouse in the distance. "That is the house, and when we get there, I'll find the man in the garden. Thee may wait for me at the gate."

It was as she said. She delivered her message to the man in the garden: "Thee art contemplating a wrong action that will bring great trouble on thee and thy family. The Lord so wants to deliver thee that He told me to come and try to open thy eyes to the danger."

At first the man was too startled to reply. Then he haltingly admitted that what his strange guest had said was true. This was the day on which the plan was to have been carried out. Now he dared not go on with it. If God had cared that much about him, then surely He could be trusted to work out the problem. And subsequently this man's problem was resolved in a much simpler way than he had thought possible.

I could have no reasonable doubt as to the authenticity of these stories because I appreciated Hannah Smith's Yankee hard-headedness. In fact, so clear-eyed was she that throughout her work, she warns against the dangers of delusion and fanaticism if one does not apply certain commonsense checks to these inner impressions.

It was not until after my entering-in experience in 1944 that the inner Voice became a reality to me. Apparently this surrender of self is necessary groundwork, since not even God can lead us until we want to be led. It is as if we are given an inner receiving set at birth, but the set is not tuned in until we actively turn our lives over to God.

Then too, most of us think of our lives in compartmentalized fashion—home life, business life, social life. Actually the various aspects of a truly creative life must dovetail. God will not direct a man's business life, for example, when the man insists on running his family life his own way. Any such partial surrender or halfway commitment will not work.

Next I discovered that for a beginner like me, it was important that I concentrate on one or two questions on which I needed light, and ask God for directions on those. This selectivity proved more effective than trying to make my mind blank, ready to receive any message on any subject.

Also, I found that I had to be willing to obey—no matter what. Otherwise no directions would be forthcoming. Receiving guidance is definitely not a matter of telling God what we want and hoping that He will approve.

A further finding was that the inner Voice was more likely to speak to me at the first moment of consciousness upon awakening, or during some odd moment of the day as I went about routine tasks, than while I waited expectantly with pad and pencil in hand.

I experienced this one day when I was working on a curtain for our kitchen door. In a woman's magazine I had seen a picture of an hourglass-shape curtain, so attractive that I decided to copy it. It looked easy, but I soon discovered that when I pulled the curtain together in the middle, the rods bowed at top and bottom.

I worked and struggled, trying without any success to figure it out. Some sort of mathematical problem seemed to be involved, and I am not good at mathematics! I grew more and more exasperated at my own stupidity. How silly to be nonplused by such a small problem!

Then I called a friend in, but she could not solve it either. Finally, in great disgust, I gave up, went upstairs and flopped down on a bed. After I had been lying there a few minutes, the inner Voice said very quietly, "You do it this way." There followed a set of simple directions involving graduated tucks. The directions worked easily, perfectly.

Does this seem trivial? Of course it is. Moreover, it might be argued that it is not unusual for a solution to be served up *in toto* from the subconscious when the mind is relaxed. People experience this constantly. Then how can I justify connecting God with it?

In the first place, I think it a mistake to think of God's intervention only in terms of great events and dramatic circumstances—a sudden healing, or the saving of a life in jeopardy. After all, most of our days are full of ordinary events and common experiences. Are we to believe that God has no interest in these?

Secondly, who knows what the subconscious, or the unconscious, really is? Psychologists admit that they do not. For example, here is what the late Carl Gustav Jung had to say on the subject:

.... in so far as anything is unconscious it is not definable. Since we cannot possibly know the limitations of something unknown to us, it follows that we are not in a position to set any limits to the self....

Since a scientific man like Jung admits that we cannot set limits to the self, the Christian may be permitted to wonder whether somewhere in the deeps of personality—still beyond the reach of our scientific probing and measuring—there is not a place where the Spirit that is God can impress upon the spirit that is man a thought, a direction, a solution. Certainly it is neither plausible nor scientific to say that such things "just happen." Or if so, then many things have "just happened" to me during the course of my ordinary days.

One Sunday, our whole family (including a small guest of Peter John's), went to a Washington Hotel for Sunday dinner. After dinner, Dr. Marshall lingered in the lobby of the hotel to talk to an acquaintance. Since the grown-up talk went on for some time and the two little boys got restless, they asked to go out and play. The hotel was set safely back from the street in wide lawns, so I let them go.

Minutes passed. Then, gently but clearly, that still small Voice gave me a message, "The boys need you. Better go out to them immediately."

I excused myself and went. The two boys were standing hand in hand on the curbing just ready to try to cross 16th Street—one of Washington's busiest and most dangerous thoroughfares.

Such happenings make me wonder whether God does not try more often than we know to save His children from the accidents and disasters of our lives on this earth. But many of us do not practice the art of listening to the inner Voice with regard to small everyday matters. Because we are not tuned in, He cannot get His message through to us even in emergencies.

Sometimes these emergencies are a matter of life and death. On the evening of December 7, 1946, a businessman, Stuart Luhan (he prefers that his real name not be used), checked into the Winecoff Hotel in Atlanta, Georgia. He asked for and got a room on the tenth floor above the city's traffic.

Sometime after retiring, Mr. Luhan was wakened by noise in the corridor. A strange red glow was reflected in the sky outside his window. *Fire!* Heart pounding, he opened his bedroom door into the corridor only to have billowing clouds of suffocating smoke all but engulf him. Backing into the room, he hastily shut the door and the transom and rushed to the window to fill his lungs with air.

What he saw there was even more terrifying. Ten stories below a crowd was gathering, milling around fire trucks. Behind him, he could hear screams and cries for help.

Fear so consumed him that it was like a weight on his chest. But years before he had formed the habit of setting aside a time each morning for prayer and practice in listening to the Voice inside. From long experience, he knew that he could rely on God in any emergency, even in a burning building.

He retreated to the center of the room and forced himself to begin speaking slowly the Ninety-first Psalm: "Because thou hast made the Lord, which is my refuge, even the most High, thy habitation, there shall no evil befall thee...."

No evil befall thee? In this situation? How could he claim that for himself?

As he repeated this verse, suddenly his thoughts cleared. God is my very life, he reasoned. Therefore that life is eternal. "I hereby put myself in Your care and keeping," he prayed. "Let Your presence be my fortress. I await Your instructions as to the way out of this crisis."

"The first sure sign that God was with me in that fire-surrounded room was that after this prayer my fear just left me, siphoned off like poison," Mr. Luhan wrote me later. "Judging from the sounds around me and the increasing heat in the room, the situation was getting worse by the minute. Yet on the inside was a center of calm, such calmness that I really could hear that inner Voice."

The first instruction was that he should pull on his clothes. The next clear suggestion was to make a rope of the sheets, all blankets, even the bedspread. As he tied the knots, he knew that the rope would not reach more than a third of the way to the street. But he followed instructions, sure he would be told what to do next.

As he put the rope out the window, he heard the Voice say, "No—not yet, Trust Me——"

It seemed as if the delay might be fatal. Again the man started to throw the rope out the window. Again the clear order came, "Not yet.... Wait."

It took will power to obey, because now black smoke was seeping into the room. But long ago he had learned to trust the Voice of God; it had led him out of other predicaments.

Finally the Voice said, "Now is the time. Put the rope out the window. Tie it around the center part of the window frame and climb out."

As Mr. Luhan climbed over the sill, the wood was getting hot. In his mind rang the words, "God is my life and my salvation. . . . I shall not fear. . . . God is my life———"

Down the twenty feet he slid, but his rope reached only to the eighth-floor level. What could he do now? Once again he deliberately turned his thought to God, his fortress. "God is my life. . . . My life. . . . God is my life. . . ."

Across the face of the building he saw a fireman extending a ladder to the eighth floor. That was as far as the ladder would reach. Even so it was still too far away, one room to the right.

Suddenly the fireman saw Mr. Luhan hanging there. He signaled him and swung a rope hanging from a window above toward him. The first time the rope came close; the next time not so close. How could he grasp the swinging rope and still cling to the knotted bedclothes? Once again the rope hurtled through the air. This time Mr. Luhan caught it.

He took a deep breath, twisted the rope around his right hand, let go the knotted bedclothes, and swung in a wide arc across the burning wall. The fireman at the top of the ladder leaned over as far as he dared, caught the end of the rope on which the man dangled, pulled it over. For a moment both men balanced precariously on the slender ladder. Then Stuart Luhan climbed down to safety.

He looked up. His improvised rope was already burning. Flames billowed from the window of the room he had just left. Yet here he was, safe on the ground with no injuries except some rope burns on the palms of his hands. God's timing had been perfect.

The next day the nation's newspapers carried ghastly pictures of the disaster and its victims, calling it one of the nation's worst fires. One hundred twenty-seven people lost their lives; many more were injured. The details that I have put down here have been checked in correspondence with Mr. Luhan.

Why was one man saved by such split-second timing when so many others died? Did God love them less? Not at all. A loving God plays no favorites, is "no respecter of persons." Could it not be that God was unable to get through, to make His voice heard and His help tangible to those who lost their lives? On the other hand, Mr. Luhan was one of those rare individuals who was not only aware of the inner Voice, but had practiced using his "receiving set" in tranquil days—before crisis struck.

The guidance Stuart Luhan received, as well as most of the other instances I have mentioned, came to the individual concerned at the psychic level. Or, expressed in theological terms, these people are what the New Testament calls "the sons of God . . . . who are guided by the Spirit of God." [*]

There is, however, a warning or corollary teaching to be seen in the New Testament. I have already mentioned it in passing: the guidance or inspiration that reaches us via the unconscious should be subjected to certain tests.

The reason that guidance must be tested is one that many find difficult to believe. The writers of Scripture insist that at the unconscious level, we are open to influences not alone from the Holy Spirit but also from perverse and evil spirits. Even those who cannot credit this in the Bible have no trouble accepting the same point when a psychological interpretation is put on it. Every one has experienced thoughts and impulses rising out of the subconscious that are selfish rationalizations or so wrongly motivated as to be evil. The end result is the same, to whatever source we credit the evil.

What are these tests to which we should subject inner messages? There are at least four of them: that of Scripture, the advice of trusted friends who are also seeking God's leading, providential circumstances, and the application of our judgment and what we might call sanctified common sense.

Testing our inner impressions by Scripture is important. Our generation is rediscovering the Bible. Modern translations, many making use of newly discovered ancient manuscripts, have made the Scriptures more readable and understandable. Anyone who means business about God's leading will need to turn again and again to the Bible as a textbook. There are several reasons why this is important. We cannot really know what God is like until we know how God incarnate in human flesh acted, what Jesus' attitude was and is with regard to every facet of the human experience—sin, sickness, disasters, and so on. For this we have to study the Bible intelligently, not as if the Scriptures were a sort of holy rabbit's foot, but for its wisdom in the broad sweep of its teaching about the nature of God and of man.

Then too the Bible has more explicit guidance for us than most of us are willing to obey. It gives clear directions about money, lawsuits, racial prejudice and social snobbery, marriage and divorce, the discipline of children, how to treat servants, advice about avenging injuries, about scruples, and much more.

Especially important, God's voice will never contradict itself. That is, He will not give us a direction through the inner Voice that will ever contradict His voice in the Scriptures.

Hannah Smith once cited a humorous example of this. A Quaker, actually a woman of integrity, stole some money because she had opened her Bible at random and put her finger on I Corinthians 3:21: "... For all things are yours. ..." Obviously the woman would have done better to have considered the consistent voice of Scripture on the side of total honesty, and its thundering "Thou shalt not steal."

The point is that, in the main, the Bible deals in principles —not disjointed aphorisms or superficial rules of conduct.

These principles are valid checks: God is love, so He will not tell us to do anything unloving. God cares about other people as much as about us, so He will not tell us to do something selfish or harmful to others. His true guidance works for the benefit of all persons concerned. God is righteous, so He will not guide us to any impure act or dishonest act.

The check of a close fellowship is the next most important one. Christianity was never meant to be a lone-sheep experience. One reason the first Christians received so much guidance was that they had the *koinonia*, a corporate fellowship which made them "of one heart and soul." It was in this setting that illumination, inspiration, and guidance flourished.

Every one of us needs as much of the *koinonia* as he can find. We must seek out mature Christian friends with whom we can share questions, problems, and the joys of discovery. Ideas will often come to our corporate mind that would not come to us in isolation. And sometimes God does speak directly through these friends. At the very least, their love, perspective, and common sense will help to steer us clear of wild tangents.

Then there is the check of providential circumstances. We are most fortunate in having this test. When we have asked God to guide us, we have to accept by faith the fact that He is doing so. This means that when He closes a door in our faces (as when Peter Marshall wanted to go to China and was turned down by the London Missionary Society), then we do well not to try to crash that door.

Sensitivity is needed here. When God is guiding us, we need not ride roughshod over other people's viewpoints, lives, and affairs. The promise is that the Shepherd will go ahead of the sheep; His method is to clear the way for us.

Fourth, there is the check of our judgment and common sense. It is true that sometimes God asks us to do something the reason for which we cannot understand at the time—as in the case of Ananias in the Bible or my friend in Florida.

On the other hand, neither individual was being asked to do anything that violated basic principles of right and wrong, or indeed that violated anything except personal convenience. God does not ask us to cancel out the minds or ignore the common sense He has given us, except in most unusual circumstances.

In relation to the matter of inner judgment, the Quakers were fond of saying, "Mind the checks." They meant that when we feel a strong doubt that a particular course is right, then wait. Don't move on it. Or to put it positively, we should always move forward in faith—never out of fear.

If a strong inner suggestion is from God, it will strengthen with the passing of time. If it is not from Him, in a few days or weeks it will fade or disappear entirely.

In addition to these four checks, there are other truths about guidance that have accumulated through the centuries. Here are a few time-tested suggestions I have found useful:

Obey one step at a time, then the next step will come into view. God will not give us a blueprint of the future; He still insists that our walk be step by step in faith.

As we practice obedience, the Voice becomes clearer, the instructions more definite. Perhaps it should not surprise us that with guidance, as with anything else, we learn through practice.

That is why it is wise to give God a chance to speak to us each day, perhaps the first thing in the morning when the mind is freshest. A few minutes of quietness helps us focus on the areas where we most need God's help. And we need to remember that even God cannot get His word through to us when our prayers are limited to self-centered monologues.

Do not rule out God's help with the small details of life. After all, details make up the totality of life. If we do not let God into our everyday lives, He may not be able to intervene in the crises.

Finally, if you are one of those individuals who does not believe that the Creator can possibly be interested in your little affairs, then you are just the person to experiment with guidance. A few personal experiences of finding God's wisdom (a wisdom easily recognized as beyond your own), a few proofs of His personal solicitude; and your doubts too will melt away.

But you will never know until you try.

10

The Power of Helplessness

Wʜᴇɴ ɪ ʟɪᴠᴇᴅ in the nation's capital, I used to notice how often the Washington papers reported suicide leaps from the Calvert Street Bridge over Rock Creek Park. In fact, this happens so repeatedly that the site is often called "suicide bridge."

It was easy to sense the human tragedy behind these brief notices—the plunge of the young wife of an Air Force major who had learned that she had an inoperable cancer, or that of the elderly man whose wife had just died. These were people in the grip of circumstances which they felt helpless to change. They saw no way out of their predicaments except the way that lay over the bridge.

Helplessness is a terrifying thing to most of us. We resist it, deny it, and when we are finally face to face with it, a few of us find that we are unable to endure it.

Yet I often thought that if I could speak with such persons at the zero hour, I would use one thought to try to stop them in their mad race toward death. That thought would be that helplessness is actually one of the greatest assets a human being can have. In clichés like "God helps those who help themselves" there is but half truth. Of course, if there were no God and if we could expect no help outside ourselves, then naturally we would do well to work up all the self-confidence and self-sufficiency possible. When we could no longer muster it, we would react as did those people who took their last walk to the Calvert Street Bridge.

But since God does exist, then the cult of self-sufficiency is mistaken—tragically so in some instances, misleading in all. In my case, the most spectacular answers to prayer have come following a period when I could do nothing for myself at all.

The Psalmist says, "When I was hemmed in, thou hast freed me often." [1] Gradually I have come to recognize this hemming-in process as one of God's most loving and effective devices for teaching us that He is gloriously adequate for our problems.

This was first brought home to me at the time of Peter Marshall's death. On that chilly January morning in 1949—as I looked at my husband's face for the last time, then turned to leave the bare little hospital room—it seemed like whistling in the dark to believe that God could bring good out of such tragic loss. For to me and others in Washington and across the nation, the stilling of this effective, prophetic voice at forty-six seemed tragic waste indeed.

Here was the ultimate in helplessness—death. Sometimes life finds us powerless before facts that cannot be changed. Then we can only stand still at the bottom of the pit and claim for our particular trouble that best of all promises, that God will make even this to "work together for good to them that love God." [2] So that is what I did, and the Great Alchemist set to work.

I, who was a novice at writing and editing, put some of Peter's sermons together to form the book, *Mr. Jones, Meet the Master*. From the work I got immense satisfaction and some assuagement for my sore heart. Then there came the thought of a book I might write myself. Bit by bit my childhood dream of becoming a writer seemed to be coming true. This only began to happen after God had underscored for me again—so that I would never forget it—the creative power that can begin at the point of helplessness.

It happened about halfway through the writing of *A Man Called Peter*. While I had always had a penchant for writing, I had had no training except in college English courses. I knew nothing about the technique of putting a book together. I was also on shaky economic ground because I had resigned a teaching position in order to give full time to the book.

Events reached a climax on the day that I received devastating criticism from a man whose judgment I trusted: "The manuscript lacks warmth, emotion. The facts are here—" my critic thumped the pile of pages in his lap "—but not the heart. You haven't even begun to get inside the man Peter Marshall."

Back in the apartment Peter John and I shared in Washington, the gravity of this criticism shattered what little self-confidence I had. Yet I knew that my friend had spoken the unvarnished truth. I remember standing at the bedroom window looking out through a blur of tears at a group of children playing in the courtyard, then throwing myself across the bed to cry it out.

What I did not realize then was that this was the crucial point at which the book and my future could have gone either way. Every human inclination was pulling me toward the trap of self-pity.

And why not? It is easy to rationalize self-pity. How much can one person take? My husband was gone at the prime of his career, leaving me with a small boy to rear alone. There was no overabundance of money. And what made me think that I could write anyway? I had no training except as a preacher's wife.

My thoughts went back to lines from one of Edna St. Vincent Millay's poems that I had been fond of in college:

> My spirit sore from marching
> Toward that receding west
> Where Pity shall be governor....

What does one do when the spirit is sore from marching? Give up? Let Pity be governor? Yet I knew that this kind of thinking was self-indulgence. It was settling down to a self-centeredness that shuts God out, blocks His power, cuts the nerve of creativity.

And so I faced my crossroads. Perhaps I should put the manuscript aside for a while. That would give my thoughts time to jell, I would tell myself. Meanwhile, the practical solution was a job that would provide a steady income for Peter John and me. Looking back now I wonder whether, if I had yielded to this urge, I would ever have gotten back to the writing.

Sometime during the next hour, out of some dusty pigeon-hole of my mind, rose words to haunt me from Brother Lawrence, a seventeenth-century French Carmelite monk. I had read his tiny *Practice of the Presence of God* so often that many of the archaic sentences were forever mine.

.... When an occasion of practising some virtue offered, he addressed himself to God saying, "Lord, I cannot do this unless Thou enablest me."

.... When he had failed in his duty, he simply confessed his fault, saying to God, "I shall never do otherwise if Thou leavest me to myself; it is Thou who must hinder my falling, and mend what is amiss."

"It is Thou who must mend what is amiss...." For me, a great deal was amiss. Odd that I should think of those words now! Yet not so odd, because it was Brother Lawrence who had first called my attention to the power of helplessness. He, like so many other seekers through the centuries, had finally seen his human helplessness as the crucible out of which victory could rise.

And so I was able to turn from my sense of failure enough to put the writing project into God's hands. I was inadequate, but God was adequate. He knew the secret of successful creative effort. I did not. Without realizing what I was doing, I prayed the Prayer of Helplessness. I asked that God should guide the creation of *A Man Called Peter* and that the results should be His too.

And they were. I still regard as incredible the fact that from time to time I hear of lives changed by that book, of men entering the ministry because of the inspiration of Peter Marshall's life, and of Peter's voice reaching now to a world-wide audience. And significantly, in the years since, no one has ever commented to me about *A Man Called Peter* without mentioning—often ruefully, referring to their own involuntary tears—a quality in the book that irresistibly reached in to touch their emotions.

Out of this experience I learned that when achievement has come because of our helplessness linked to God's power, it has a rightness about it that no amount of self-inspired striving can have. Furthermore, when achievement comes this way, it does not bear in it the seeds of increasing egocentricity that success sometimes brings. Because we know that ideas and the ability to implement them flowed into us from somewhere beyond our selves, we can be objective about our good fortune. We know, too, that if, in the future, the connection with the Source of creativity is broken, there will not be success the next time.

Since then God has never allowed me the fulfillment of a soul's sincere desire without first putting me through an acute realization of my inadequacy and my need for help.

It should not surprise us that creativity arises out of the pit of life rather than the high places. For creativity is the ability to put old material into new form. And it is only when old molds and old ways of doing things are forcibly broken up by need or suffering, compelling us to regroup, to rethink, to begin again, that the creative process starts to flow.

Fritz Künkel, German physician-psychiatrist noted among other things for his attempts to unify the findings of Freud, Adler, and Jung, puts it this way: "The way to real creativeness is through danger and suffering. Thus we see that each creative act must be preceded by a certain time of need, distress, or even despair. . . . Nor should anyone say, 'I am clever enough to overcome all the difficulties of my crises. I can bring myself through all their changes.' Such statements reflect egocentric thinking. . . . He who relies upon his own small private consciousness must fail, for the source of creativity is not the individual but the We, or to state it another way, not the individual but God who manifests Himself in the We, of which the Self is a part. . . ." [3]

Crisis brings us face to face with our inadequacy and our inadequacy in turn leads us to the inexhaustible sufficiency of God. This is the power of helplessness, a principle written into the fabric of life.

At this point some realist will surely say, "I cannot accept this helplessness theory. It goes against everything I have been taught about rugged individualism. Where would our nation be now, if it were not for the pioneer spirit of our forefathers who refused to admit defeat in the face of tremendous odds? America was built by men who scorned weakness and helplessness."

It is precisely here that the realist misses the point about this principle. For the realization of helplessness in no sense precludes a courageous pioneer independence. Being adventuresome does not mean that we cannot admit our need for God. To be sure, if by a rugged individualist one means a man who says, "I can by myself do all things," then he violates the principle. But as I read American history, our nation was not built by men who denied their dependence on their Creator.

Preachers and patriotic speakers mention glibly "the faith of the Founding Fathers." How much do most of us really know about their faith? Anyone who has stood on the deck of the *Mayflower II* (the modern replica of the tiny original) has some inkling of what a terrifying voyage it was to America in the seventeenth century. Those who sailed on the first *May-*

flower, or any other sailing ship, had to want to come in the most ardent way. Powerful motives beyond self-gain must have been involved. The settlers' trepidation and awe, along with their spirit of adventure, are reflected in such documents as the Mayflower Compact, the Fundamental Orders of Connecticut (1639), the Rhode Island Colonial Charter, the Articles agreed on at Jamestown in 1651, and other ringing statements of purpose.

In the summer of 1787 in Philadelphia, the Constitutional Convention was in full swing. The sessions were long and wearying. May and a part of June had come and gone. There were marked differences and long debates. At a critical point, Benjamin Franklin, the oldest delegate in the assembly, rose and made a daring and impassioned speech:

Mr. President: The small progress we have made after four or five weeks close attendance ... is, methinks a melancholy proof of the imperfection of human understanding. We indeed seem to feel our want of political wisdom, since we have been running about in search of it. ...

In this situation ... how has it happened, Sir, that we have not hitherto once thought of humbly applying to the Father of Lights to illumine our understanding? In the beginning of the contest with Great Britain, when we were sensible of danger, we had daily prayer in this room. Our prayers, Sir ... were graciously answered. ... And have we now forgotten that powerful Friend? Or do we imagine we no longer need His assistance?

Thereupon the Constitutional Convention waited upon God in prayer—with results that have stood the test of time.

It was George Washington's habit to begin and close each day with a time of prayer, alone in his room. How important this was to him is reflected in statement after statement of his public speeches: "No people can be bound to knowledge and adore the Invisible Hand which conducts the affairs of men more than those of the United States. Every step by which they have advanced to the character of an independent nation seems to have been distinguished by some token of providential agency...."

Abraham Lincoln is considered the classic example of the rugged individualist, the frontiersman, the rail-splitter who went from log cabin to the White House by the most prodigious feats of energy and application.

Yet this is the same man who prowled the White House corridors at night, pleading for direction from God for a nation in mortal struggle. This is the same man who went on record as saying, "I should be the veriest shallow and conceited blockhead...if I should hope to get along without the wisdom that comes from God and not from man."

Thus through hard experience Americans have learned the truth of that towering Biblical statement, "Apart from me, ye can do nothing." [4]

Nothing? That seems a trifle sweeping. Perhaps Jesus meant simply that we shall be more effective with His help than without it.

But when we go back to the context in which the statement is made, we find that Jesus meant precisely what He said. This is the allegory of the vine and the branches: "I am the vine, you are the branches." The point is not that the branches will do better when they are attached to the vine. Unless attached, the branches must wither and die.

Dr. Arthur Gossip, famous Scottish theologian who wrote the exposition on John for the *Interpreter's Bible*, calls the statement "Apart from me, ye can do nothing" the *most hopeful words in Scripture*. "For it is on the basis of that frank recognition of our utter fecklessness apart from Him that Christ enters into His covenant with us, and gives us His tremendous promises...." [5]

In the complex world of today, just how self-sufficient are we? We had nothing to do with our being born—no control over whether we were male or female, Japanese, or Russian, or

British, or American, white or yellow or black. We did not control our ancestry or the basic mental or physical equipment with which we started life.

Even after birth an autonomic nervous system controls the vital processes of life. A power that no one understands keeps our hearts beating, our lungs taking in air, our blood circulating, our body temperature up.

A surgeon can cut human tissue, but he is helpless to make the severed tissue heal. We grow old relentlessly and automatically. In the end, despite all the so-called miracles of modern medicine, every one of us must die.

Self-sufficient? Hardly!

The planet on which we live rotates on an axis tipped at the angle of 23½ degrees, the necessary angle for the climatic conditions that support life. Were the earth not tilted, continents of ice would lie at the poles and probably deserts between them. Moreover, the earth is exactly the right distance, some ninety-two million miles, from the sun. Any nearer, we would be consumed with solar radiation; any farther away, we would be frozen to death. Were this angle and this distance somehow to change, we would all be instantly destroyed.

The natural balance of oxygen and nitrogen in the air we breathe is exactly right for men and animals. The law of gravity which holds the world together operates independently of us. And is man—little man who struts and fumes upon the earth—self-sufficient? Not at all . . .

The Scriptures say that you and I are helpless even in relation to our own spiritual lives. We want to feel that God is real. We think that we are reaching out for Him. This is an illusion. "No one," Jesus said, "is able to come to me unless he is drawn by the Father." [6] "Ye have not chosen me, but I have chosen you." [7]

We want salvation from our sins and we yearn for eternal life. We think that we can earn these things; Saul of Tarsus thought so too. Then we find out, as Paul did, that we cannot pile up enough good marks and merits to earn anything from God. No, salvation "is the *gift* of God: not of works, lest any man should boast." [8]

Indeed, not a single spiritual quality—faith, peace of mind, joy, patience, the ability to love the wretched and the unlovely —can we work up by self-effort. Anyone who has tried, knows that he cannot.

Moreover, Christ tells us that the same human dependence applied equally to Him while He wore His human flesh. "I can of mine own self do nothing," He told His apostles. [9]

I came across a dramatic example of this human helplessness of God several years ago in the writings of Dr. A. B. Simpson, a famous New York City clergyman. While in his twenties, Dr. Simpson had developed serious heart trouble. His preaching and pastoral work were done at great physical expense. Usually it took him until Wednesday to get over the effects of his Sunday sermons. Climbing stairs or even a slight elevation was suffocating agony.

Dr. Simpson was only thirty-seven when he was told by his physician that he might not have long to live. On his doctor's advice, he went for a long rest to the resort town of Old Orchard Beach, Maine. There he happened into an unusual religious meeting conducted by a Boston physician, Dr. Charles Cullis. Dr. Cullis was then having much success with treating tubercular patients through prayer and common sense health measures alone.

Several statements made in the meeting about healing through prayer sent Dr. Simpson back to the Bible to find out what Jesus had to say on the subject. He soon became convinced that Jesus had always meant for His gospel to include healing of the body along with healing of the mind and the spirit.

In the quiet of his room, Dr. Simpson reviewed his life. He was always struggling desperately for even his minimal needs —for enough health to keep going, for enough ideas and intellectual resources to write talks and sermons, for enough caring about other people. It was almost as if his creed was "Of myself I must do everything." But somehow he always fell short of his objectives. Was God now trying to reach him with a new idea? Had he ever really given God a chance to run his life?

One Friday afternoon shortly after that, Dr. Simpson went for a walk. Since he was always out of breath, he was forced to walk slowly. The path led into a pine wood, and he sat down on a fallen log to rest. All around him was that thick carpet of moss so often seen in the Maine woods. Sunlight filtered through the tall pines, laying striped patterns across the emerald green floor. Simpson pulled out his watch and saw that it was three o'clock.

"All things in my life looked dark and withered," Simpson wrote afterward. "The doctors had made it clear that they could do nothing for me. Intellectual life and spiritual life were also at a low ebb. So there in the woods I asked God to become my life for me, including physical life for all the needs of my body until my life work was done. And I solemnly promised to use His spiritual and physical strength in me for the good of others. God was there all right, because every fiber of my body was tingling with His Presence. He had come to meet me at the point of my helplessness."

A few days later, Simpson took a long hike and climbed a mountain three thousand feet high. "When I reached the mountaintop," he related joyously, "the world of weakness and fear was lying at my feet. From that time I literally had a new heart in my breast." [10]

He also had a new source of creativity. For the first three years after his heart was healed, he kept count and found that he had preached more than a thousand sermons, had held sometimes as many as twenty meetings in a week—and without exhaustion. Simpson's output of literary work was equally prodigious. He lived as vigorously as any man could and died at seventy-six. To this day much of his work, including the Christian and Missionary Alliance, is still a vital force.

An experience like Dr. Simpson's points up the other half of the Prayer of Helplessness. For in helplessness alone there would be no value, our situation would be intolerable if Jesus had left us there. But He went on to add, "With God all things are possible."

"All things!" This is as audacious a statement as the opposite was, "Apart from me, ye can do nothing." Jesus must be saying that there is nothing in heaven or in earth over which God does not have control.

Most of us can believe that God can control us, provided we are willing. Thus if we are in the hole because of our own foolishness, misjudgment, or sin, we can concede God's ability to help.

But there is another type of life situation at which faith often staggers. This is when heartbreak has come to us because of other peoples' sins and failures—what might be called "second causes."

The tragedies most difficult to take are those that come through the failures, ignorance, carelessness, or hatred of other human beings. These are times when men seem to be working havoc with God's plans. I had a friend, for instance, a well-known man in the District of Columbia, who died because of an error made by a pharmacist in filling a prescription. Another friend's husband is an alcoholic. No amount of institutional or religious help can seem to cure him. But it is my friend and the children who are the real victims.

It is important that we believe that God is adequate even for these situations. Otherwise the Prayer of Helplessness will fall to the ground. In order to fly, the bird must have two wings. One wing is the realization of our human helplessness, the other is the realization of God's power. Our faith in God's ability to handle our particular situation is the connecting link.

What the Bible says about this is worth listening to, if we are to find a creative way out of the holes into which life so often throws us. For if we cannot believe that God can help us recover from troubles shaped by human beings as well as those we bring upon ourselves, then we have a narrow basis indeed for our faith in Him.

The Old Testament story of Joseph illustrates perfectly how God can operate in and around and in spite of the sins and shortcomings of men. When Joseph was a seventeen-year-old boy, he was literally at the bottom of a pit. He had been thrown there by his own brothers. Their act was the climax of years of hostility arising out of envy.

Joseph was the favorite child of their father's old age. To his brothers, the boy seemed overprotected and spoiled, a threat to their futures. So they bargained with some Ishmaelite traders and sold him into slavery for twenty pieces of silver.

A bewildered boy found himself being carried to the slave market of Egypt's capital. He was forced to stand, stripped, on the slave block, while he was measured and scrutinized. He was finally bought by Potiphar, one of the Pharoah's officials.

The years went by swiftly. Transplanted from his simple nomad world, the boy adjusted to the sophistication of Egypt. For him it was a new world of city streets and chariots, of pleasure barges on the Nile, of elaborate tombs and great granaries, of clean-shaven men in white pleated garments and women with painted eyes and heavy jewels.

The boy made the adjustment by coming to terms with himself. Since his fate was to be a slave and he was helpless to change it, he determined to be the best slave Potiphar had ever had. Thus the Israelite soon found himself chief steward, in charge of his master's house.

Adversity had changed a spoiled boy into a mature man. And Potiphar's wife found the man attractive. Undoubtedly a sensualist and a woman with too much leisure and too much luxury, she propositioned the slave.

Joseph could have reasoned that when in Egypt, he might as well do as the Egyptians. Their flexible standards knew few scruples and little morality. But since his master had trusted him so completely, the Israelite could not bring himself to betray that trust. Day after day he turned away from her allurements so brazenly displayed.

Joseph did not reckon with the fury of a woman scorned. Unable to seduce the handsome young slave, Potiphar's wife turned violently against him. One day she caught and tore a piece of the slave's garment, made a scene, and then cried out to her husband, "The Hebrew servant . . . came in to mock me: and . . . as I lifted up my voice and cried, he left his garment with me, and fled out."

Potiphar believed his wife and promptly had Joseph thrown into prison. Egypt's prisons were terrible beyond belief. In the midst of filth and despair, Joseph must have faced his supreme moment of truth.

He had lived up to the best he knew. He had resisted temptation when giving in to it would have been easy. Goodness had not been rewarded. Bitterness and self-pity must have clamored for possession of him. Betrayed by his own kinsmen, now he languished in prison, not through any sin he had committed, but because he had refused to commit one. He remained in prison for more than two years.

How many times during those years Joseph must have prayed the Prayer of Helplessness and by so doing, overcame the bitterness and self-pity. The captain of the guard found something about the young man's spirit so appealing that he put Joseph in charge of some of the other prisoners.

When the answer to Joseph's prayer finally came, it was marvelous beyond belief. Through a talent he had possessed from childhood—the gift of dream-interpretation—he caught the attention of the Pharoah. Then through a series of remarkable events, Joseph at thirty suddenly found himself prime minister of Egypt.

The suffering through which he had passed reaped its harvest in a burst of creativity. Joseph conceived a workable plan by which the Land of the Nile piled up a crop surplus while neighboring countries run by less imaginative men were in the grip of famine.

The final testing of Joseph's character came when his own brothers came from the land of Canaan and stood before him, begging to buy grain. They could not possibly have recognized the strong-jawed, bronzed Egyptian as their kinsman.

But the fires of despair had done their work well. Joseph had no thought of vengeance. When he finally revealed his identity, it was in words that could only have been spoken by one whose eyes had so often been washed with tears that now they saw clearly. "Now therefore be not grieved, nor angry with yourselves, that ye sold me hither: for God did send me before you to preserve life. So now it was not you that sent me hither, but God...." [11] And a little later he reassured them with the unforgettable words, "But as for you, ye thought evil against me; but God meant it unto good...." [12]

Joseph was saying that his brothers had only *thought* that they were in control of the situation. As long as Joseph maintained his dependence on God, He was able to take all these evils that had befallen Joseph and weave them into His master plan. Thus an omnipotent God could make even "the wrath of man to praise Him." He can take any sins, any evil, any calamity—no matter where it originated—and make it "work together for good to them that love God." This practical omnipotence of God is the consistent cry of all of Scripture, written by a variety of men over a period of some thirteen hundred years.

It was also the viewpoint of Jesus. That black moment in the Garden under the olive trees when Judas betrayed his Master with a kiss appeared to be the opening scene in a drama written, staged, and directed by the powers of evil. It would seem to us that if ever the free will of wicked men— sundered from and at cross-purpose with the will of God—

was in control, it was at the execution of Jesus Christ by crucifixion.

"Not so," was Jesus' assertion. Never for an instant during the acting out of that drama did God abdicate as sovereign ruler. Christ made this point over and over. In the Garden, when impetuous Peter whipped out his sword, Jesus ordered, "Put your sword back into its place. . . . Do you think I cannot appeal to my Father to furnish me at this moment with over twelve legions of angels?" [13]

To Pilate, as the Roman governor boasted to the Nazarene of his power of life and death over Him, Christ retorted bluntly, "You would have no power over me, unless it had been granted you from above." [14]

The powers of darkness in control? It only appeared so. Long before Passion week, Jesus was explaining, "Therefore doth my Father love me, because I lay down my life, that I might take it again. *No man taketh it from me,* but I lay it down of myself." [15]

Thus even the events that swept Christ toward the cross had been woven into a plan for the greatest good of mankind.

Ever afterward there would be men who would glory in that cross "towering o'er the wrecks of time"—the wrecks that we always manage to make in every century. They would glory because the cross stands as the final symbol that no evil exists that God cannot turn into a blessing. He is the living Alchemist who can take the dregs from the slag-heaps of life —disappointment, frustration, sorrow, disease, death, economic loss, heartache—and transform the dregs into gold.

This is the hope and the promise that I claimed for myself that long-ago day and that I yearn to pass on to everyone whom life has hemmed in; to the would-be suicide, and to the merely discouraged who do not consider suicide but who also will not consider God.

So sure am I of this alchemy by which all things can be made to "work together for good to them that love God" that

I would stake my life on it. This means that no sinner is hopeless; no situation is irretrievable. No case is past redeeming. That is why Jesus' insistence on our helplessness is the most hopeful note in Scripture. That is why every one of us—imperfect as we are—can take heart and thank God for the power of helplessness.

11

The Prayer That Makes Dreams
Come True

ONE OF THE MOST provocative facts I know is that every man-made object, as well as every event in anyone's life, starts with an idea or a picture in the mind. It was my mother who first taught me this, as over and over she demonstrated to me the prayer that helps our dreams come true.

Mother always believed in action; she was certain that idle children—hers or anyone else's—were headed for trouble. It was she who suggested that my brother and sister and I make a collection of butterflies and moths, plant a wild-flower garden, build a treehouse in the cherry tree.

Mother also headed the Girl Scout program for our West Virginia town—all six troops of us. She persuaded my good-natured father to go on camping expeditions (which he loathed), made him sleep on canvas cots in tents that often leaked, wade through mud, endure mosquitoes, warmed-over hot dogs and canned beans, and (what was worst of all to him) breathe the fumes of citronella. Father made endless jokes through it all.

Idle? Not a chance for any of us. Beyond all our family

projects and the Scout program, Mother devoted even more energy to her one-woman crusade for the individual and civic rehabilitation of Radical Hill.

This slum district was located in what should have been the town's most beautiful residential section on the side farthest removed from the railroad tracks. There unbelievable filth was surrounded by gently rolling hills, and beyond them, towering mountains.

Mother stood one day in the midst of it and envisioned what Radical Hill would be like with clean, newly painted houses, with tidy yards filled with flowers, with running water, plumbing, garbage disposal. And there would be a small white church. Her first move in the direction of her dream was to rename the district "Potomac Heights."

Next she started taking a personal census of the area. This involved calling on every shack. Some of the young people from our church helped. I have already described how awed we children were when Mother came back from her first afternoon of visiting and wept at what she had seen.

She and her young helpers found that, of some five hundred families in Potomac Heights, only eighty had even a nebulous connection with any church. So Mother and her group rented a building, cleaned it, painted it, crudely furnished it, and began holding a Sunday school on Sunday afternoons.

There Mother met a boy, Raymond Thomas, who had no idea who his real parents were. He lived with foster parents in a small, clean house set in the midst of the dirt.

Dressed in working clothes and clodhoppers that seemed to reach up to his knees, Raymond came often to our home to talk with Mother. He was always clean, but he did not even own a suit of clothes. Despite a slight speech impediment that made him self-conscious, he would sit on the top step of our vine-shaded front porch on a summer afternoon talking ... talking ... while Mother sat in a wooden rocker shelling peas or stringing beans or darning socks. Mother soon saw that this boy had boundless energy and a fine mind.

During one of these talks there emerged one clear-cut idea—the dream of Raymond going to college. Once the dream was out in the open, standing there shimmering, poised in the air, Mother was delighted to see the wistfulness in Ray's brown eyes replaced by kindling hope.

"But how can I manage it?" the boy asked. "I've been working on the state roads, but I've been turning over my paycheck to my folks. I've nothing saved."

There was another obstacle, too: His foster parents had not gone to college; why should Ray? They thought the idea so foolish that they actively opposed it.

Mother quietly encouraged and prodded. "Raymond, whatever you need, God has a supply of it ready for you, provided you're ready to receive it. What seems impossible for you is entirely possible for God. Ours is still a land of opportunity, Ray. The sky is the limit! Money—what's money? Money should be the slave, not the master, of every dream that's right for you, every dream for which you're willing to work."

For a preacher's wife who had little enough herself, this was a doughty philosophy, but Mother believed it and had often proved it so. And these ideas took root in Raymond.

There came the day when Ray accepted Mother's philosophy so completely that she could lead him in the prayer that releases dreams to make them come true. On so many occasions in my own life has she prayed the dreaming prayer for me that I can easily imagine how it was for Ray: "Father, you've given Ray a fine mind. We believe You want that mind to be developed, sharpened, to know some of the wisdom of other men through the ages. You want Ray's potential to be used to help You lift and lighten some portion of our world. All resources are Yours. So will You please make it possible for Ray to receive what he needs for an education?

"And, Father, I believe that You have big plans for Ray. Unshackle him from all thoughts of lack. Let him know that there are no limitations to what You can do. Plant in his mind and heart the vivid pictures, the specific dreams that reflect Your plans for him. And, oh, give him joy in dreaming—great joy."

Raymond never forgot that prayer. A decade later he was recalling to me the fragrance of the clematis vines on the porch that afternoon, a fragrance that even now can recreate the moment for him. Long afterward he would be saying with awe in his voice, "To one woman I owe the key to life."

Even while Mother was praying the dreaming prayer with Ray, the name of a certain wealthy woman friend had slipped into her mind. So without telling Ray, she wrote the friend about him and his yearning for more education: "All this boy needs is a chance. If it should seem right to you to help him, you will find that every dollar invested in his education will pay big dividends."

The reply came within a week. It would give her real pleasure to help a young man like this one. She agreed to underwrite a portion of Ray's expenses for the first year.

When Raymond read this letter, he stood speechless, looking at Mother, shaking his head. Finally he said, "Pinch me...I can't believe this is really happening to me."

When Ray's friends at our church heard what was going on, they wanted to have a part too. A group of men bought him a suit and some other clothes. The women bought luggage and even packed for him. They thought of everything—even items like buttons, needles, thread. And Ray, his dream brighter than ever, climbed on a bus and went off to college at Davidson, North Carolina.

He insisted on repaying the woman who wanted to be his benefactress and who lived in the college community by mowing her lawn, scrubbing her floors, firing her furnace—anything she would let him do.

Soon Ray was sending Mother the schedule he had worked out. She was astonished at how he was budgeting his time as well as his money: a certain number of hours for study, for classes, for work, for church services, for recreation.

At Christmas he hitch-hiked home. His foster parents had softened and were glad to see him. The following summer he worked for the Celanese Corporation in Cumberland, Maryland. That enabled him to return to college in the fall with enough money saved for the first semester. From then on he made ends meet through some twelve jobs—waiting on tables, baby-sitting for the faculty, repairing typewriters, typing papers for other students. It was hard going sometimes, but Mother kept encouraging him with a letter a week. It was as proud a day for her as for Ray when he received his Bachelor of Science degree, *cum laude*.

Then during the second world war and afterward, I lost touch with Raymond. I had heard that his ship had been sunk under him in the South Pacific, and that in the explosion he had lost all but five per cent of his hearing. Sometime after that mother told me that he was living in Vienna.

In the summer of 1958, I was in Europe and wrote Raymond that Vienna was on my itinerary. His response was immediate and enthusiastic.

In Rome, I found a glowing letter from him, listing for me the sights that I should see. Then when I checked into the hotel in Florence, the mail clerk handed me another letter from Ray:

When you see the high dome of the Duomo, remember that it took Brunelleschi fourteen years to build it. Last winter I climbed to the highest balcony right at the top of the dome and crawled all around it....

The letters kept coming: Venice... "I've written to my friend at the Salviati Glass works and asked him to send a gondola for you. You must see the master glass-blowers at work...."

Bad Gastein... "You'll find it rugged. I've skied quite a lot near there...."

By now I was very curious. This man bore no resemblance to the underprivileged boy from Radical Hill. Obviously he knew Europe as few Americans do. And the drive and indefatigable zeal in his letters intrigued me.

Ray met me at the airport, a bouquet of flowers in hand. "Flowers and music are a part of Vienna," he explained. He had changed little, except that his hairline had receded. He was tall and spare and still had the trace of the speech impediment.

Later, over *Sachertorte* and coffee, I asked Ray about his life since graduating from college. He had absorbed European ways and would not be rushed. "After I learned from experience that what your mother had said was true—and had graduated from college, I knew that any right dream can be realized. Material resources *are* at the beck and call of the dream. There are no ceilings to dreaming."

Then he described his war experience. He was one of a handful of survivors of a torpedoed destroyer. During convalescence he had dreamed up a plan for the rest of his life.

"At that time my dreams were three," he went on. "I wanted to be a world citizen. That meant traveling extensively. I put no limits on that. But I knew I couldn't be a world citizen without mastering several languages. Tied with that, I wanted to get my Ph.D. preferably from a fine European university. After all, why stop with a B.S.? Then out of gratitude for all that America means to me, I wanted to serve my country somehow in peacetime."

"I'm amazed that your dreams were that specific," I interposed.

He seemed lost in thought as he stared out the window at the lights of Vienna. "I've come to feel that this dreaming process won't work unless we are specific. That's because a big part of the power to make the dream come true arises from a mental picture. And for a mental image, you need specifics."

"Ray, you astonish me! From Radical Hill—excuse me, Potomac Heights—to Vienna. Who would have thought it? Now tell me how these three dreams have come out."

"Well, so far I've traveled in sixty countries. I still haven't gotten to Australia, New Zealand, South America, or the southern half of Africa. I'm working on that! Every vacation I strike out for some new spot."

"And your studies?"

"I got my Ph.D. in physics from the University of Vienna."

"But Ray, how did you manage the lectures with your hearing problem?" I asked.

"I found a girl who would take the lectures down in shorthand. That meant that I had to learn shorthand too. Work on the Ph.D. also meant mastering German. I can speak Spanish now, passable French, some Italian, Dutch, and Swedish, a little Russian."

And the dream of serving his country was coming true through his job with the United States Atomic Energy Agency here in Europe. "Ray, what does your foster mother back in West Virginia think of all this?"

"She couldn't be more proud. To hear her brag you'd think it was all her idea. I manage to fly home to see her once a year."

"So now you've achieved all these dreams, what next?"

Ray laughed. "One of the pitfalls of middle age is that we stop dreaming—especially dreaming big. But I'm working on one——"

In the spring of 1946 a friend, Anita Ritter, asked me to join her for a few days rest at a little inn in the Valley of Virginia. Her invitation came at a welcome time. Peter and I had then been living in the city of Washington for nine years. The upheaval of the second world war was over. Both in church life and in private life, we were feeling the need of rethinking our situation to chart a clear course.

I took with me to the inn a religious book which someone had sent me.[1] One section charted a procedure aimed at helping an individual discover himself and what he wanted out of life. I decided to take this program seriously—a minimum of an hour a day at the task. I took along a notebook and a dozen pencils, ignoring no technique that the author suggested as too infantile.

One of the first suggestions was that the reader retrace his steps to childhood to remember what his ambitions were then. Of what did the child dream before the adult world muddied the waters with its false values?

Thinking back to my childhood immediately conjured up two pictures. The setting for both was the same West Virginia town in which Raymond had grown up. First, I saw a girl sitting with her back against an ancient locust tree, gazing dreamily out over a panorama of valley and mountains.

The grove of locust trees—grotesquely stark in the winter, fragrant with white blossoms in the spring—was at the back of our large manse yard. Out beyond the locusts were granite ledges which we children called "The Rocks." They formed a sheer drop of some two hundred feet from the back of our yard to a dirt road winding around the base of the cliff. Ferns and rare Scottish bluebells grew out of the rock crevices.

From atop The Rocks we could see for miles up the narrow green valley hemmed in on two sides by the rugged Appalachians. This world of far horizons fed imagination and spirit and was the scene for much of my adolescent daydreaming. There I conceived the idea of being a writer, in fact made first attempts at putting ideas, conversations, and descriptions on paper.

The second remembered scene was that of a girl sitting at the kitchen table by a window. Sheets of paper were spread out all over the oilcloth cover. One day I was writing a story with the unimaginative title, "Virginia Dare and What Happened to Her." On another occasion I began a "novel". It never progressed beyond the second chapter.

So definitely did the flavor of those childhood moments return to me that I could recollect the exact form of the little-girl ambitions I had put alongside the writing. ... I had wanted to be "a pretty lady with plenty of perfume—and also a writer!" At age—what? I've no idea. Remembering that the perfume had been just as important to me then as the writing, I laughed at myself. Still, deeply entrenched desires were there.

The self-analysis went on. There were areas other than the childhood one to search out. What capacities did I desire for myself? ... A better sense of humor? The ability to speak in public? Social graces? ... What things, what possessions, did I want? ... What kinds of ideas interested me? ... What persons in my life? What kinds of friends? Suddenly I realized how important friends could be as a part of this dreaming. Is not aloneness every man's problem? And what can any one of us achieve apart from other human beings?

It was suggested that in all of these areas, we make the wishing as specific as possible.

After the desires were down on paper, then they were to be submitted to a series of hurdles to test whether or not they were dreams true to one's own nature and therefore requests that one had a right to make in prayer. Would the dreams fulfill the particular talents, temperament, and emotional needs that God had planted in one's being?

These are not easy questions to answer. But they are so important that any degree of probing or length of time required to answer them is worth the effort.

In the beginning I had wondered why the author of the book had implied a connection between constructive daydreaming and prayer. Psychologists tell us that no creativity is possible unless the subconscious and the conscious are both brought into play and working together and that the subconscious responds only to suggestion through visualization. Thinking along the same line, the author suggested that praying can take the form of visualization—which is dreaming in specifics. Jesus often insisted that people not only ask but be definite about what they wanted. There was a blind man who kept calling after Jesus, "Have pity on me! Jesus, have pity on me!" The man's chief problem—blindness—must have been obvious to Christ. Yet He required that the man make his request specific by asking the leading question, "What do you want me to do for you?" [2]

As I pondered it, it seemed to me that guided day dreaming also lays a solid base for prayer, because it is certainly the Creator's will that the desires and talents that He Himself has planted in us be realized. God is supremely concerned about the fulfillment and productivity of the potentially fine person He envisions in each of us.

How foolish it would have been for Fritz Kreisler to dream of becoming a world-known labor leader. What wasted effort for Einstein to have dreamed of being a movie star!

On the other hand, would not Fritz Kreisler actually be committing a "sin of omission" if his whole life were not a prayer aimed at making a contribution to the world through his music? Knowing that, he has the strongest foundation possible for answered prayer. His music, written into his being, is "the will of God" and he can pray with absolute confidence for the overcoming of every obstacle in the way of its fulfillment.

Since those days at the little inn thinking about the Dreaming Prayer, I have discovered that there are those who are wary of the prayer that makes dreams come true on two counts: they have doubts about the rightness of praying for material needs; and they are cautious—correctly—about trying to use God and spiritual principles for selfish ends.

Both are valid objections that need to be considered. As for whether God means for us to include material needs in our petitions, one answer would be that Christ was interested in the bodies of men along with their souls. He was concerned about their health and their physical hunger.

Christianity acknowledges material things—bread and wine, water, good and bad soil, the lilies of the fields, the birds, men's bodies; it seeks to lift all these material objects to serve man's spirit and God's purposes. I believe that is why the Scriptures make no distinction between the secular and the sacred, the everyday and the religious. The ideal is that all of life, every vocation and profession, is to be used to glorify God.

As for the danger that our heart's desire may be our selfish human will rather than God's, there are ways by which we can test this. Only when a dream has passed these two tests (so that we are certain that our wish is also God's dream) can we pray the Dreaming Prayer with faith and thus with effectiveness.

The first hurdle is simply our recognition that God's laws are in operation in our universe. Does our dream involve taking anything or any person belonging to someone else? Would the fulfillment of it hurt any other human being? If so, then we can be sure that this particular dream is not God's will for us.

Are we willing to make all our relationships with other people right? If we hold resentments, grudges, bitterness—no matter how justified we think they are—these wrong emotions will cut us off from God, the source of creativity. After all, no dream can be achieved in a vacuum of human relationships. Even one such wrong relationship can cut the channel of power.

Do we want our dream with our whole heart? Dreams are not usually brought to fruition in divided personalities. Only the whole heart will be willing to do its part toward implementing the dream.

Are we willing to wait patiently for God's timing?

Are we dreaming big? The bigger the dream and the more persons it will benefit, the greater will be God's blessing on it. If our heart's desire can pass this first series of tests, then we are ready for an even greater hurdle. My experience has been that the last necessary step in the Dreaming Prayer sequence is that we hand our dream over to God to fulfill or not, as He wishes, and then go off and leave it with Him. This is where the prayer that makes dreams come true must also include the Prayer of Relinquishment. With this final test available to us, we need have no fear of trying to use God for selfish ends. We are asking only that His will be fulfilled in us.

One day soon after I returned from Europe in 1958, a close friend and I were discussing Raymond's story. Tessie is an attractive, lively brunette whose husband, Phil, had died suddenly at thirty-two, leaving her with three small children. She had loved Phil with all her being and, so far as I could tell, there had been a fine relationship.

Tessie's widowhood and mine had drawn us together. We had formed the habit of eating dinner together regularly. One of Tessie's deepest desires, which she had confided to me, was for remarriage.

"You know," she said one evening, "it's funny how our society is about courtship and marriage—that is, as far as women are concerned. It's all right for men to be frank about what they want and go after it. But we women have to be hush-hush and hole-in-corner. We have to sit and wait.

"So here I am, lonely, needing help with my children, and needing love—physical love, too, why not admit it? What am I supposed to do? Go around keeping up the false front that all is well? Everyone says that if we women appear too eager, *that* drives men away.... Where and how do we meet eligible men, anyway?"

As we talked it over, the story of Raymond and my mother and Radical Hill prompted Tessie and me to try the Dreaming Prayer for her problem. I pledged myself to work with her on it for as long as necessary. As I considered my lively friend and her three children, it seemed highly probable to me that happiness and fulfillment through a second marriage were God's will for her. Yet neither of us dared assume that. The last word would have to be God's.

Tessie's first steps were practical ones toward self-improvement. In her grief over Phil's death and her battle to be both mother and father to her children with no household help, she had neglected her appearance. She heard of a Charm School and managed the money to enroll.

The results—psychological as well as physical—were well worth the effort. After that came some new clothes. Tessie joined an informal dance group that met once a week and consented to her first dates since Phil's death. Yet she found many of these men unexciting, some even boring. It seemed to be a constant effort for her.

After talking that over, she and I decided on several other steps. It was time for Tessie to begin thinking specifically about what she wanted in a husband and in a marriage. This did not mean that she must decide on a man over five-eight tall, a blond with blue eyes, between thirty-five and forty-five who did not wear glasses. It was rather a question of the character of her man and the values she wanted in marriage.

The second step was that Tessie decided to stop thinking of dates simply in terms of having fun herself. She began concentrating more on the art of *giving*, for instance working hard on an occasional home-cooked meal for a date rather than always expecting him to take her to an expensive glamour spot.

These efforts led Tessie to a deeper realization. One evening she confronted me with a surprising confession: "Remarriage may be God's will for me, but I'm not sure it's Tessie's will for Tessie."

"What on earth do you mean?"

"I've wanted the icing on the cake—the romance, the ego-satisfaction of being sought after by men. But lately something inside me has been asking questions, and they're making me squirm. Such as, do I realize that love isn't getting but giving? And what do I have to give to some man with deep needs? What qualities can I contribute to a new marriage? And am I willing to pay the price of the adjustment that will be necessary? Or suppose a man with some handicap fell in love with me, or one without much of an income, or a widower with children of his own? ... See what I mean about the questions being disturbing?"

I saw, all right. I also recognized in this incisive realism the Spirit of God hard at work on Tessie and her dream. "I suppose all those questions point to the fact that it's dangerous to have any inner division about your heart's desire," I commented. "You have to want your dream with your whole heart."

My friend had a rueful look on her face. "Right! So this is as far as I've gotten. I've admitted to God that I *am* divided. For instance, at the moment I don't feel a bit enthusiastic about taking on a widower with children. So since I am divided—what's the next step?"

She and I pondered that one for a while. "You're being honest, Tessie," I said finally. "That's a big step in itself. Why don't we try asking God to mend those inner cleavages, make you completely willing for His will."

And both of us were silent, startled by the revelation that we are the ones—not God—who have to be persuaded to be stretched enough to receive from Him the realization of our dreams.

The next bit of progress did not come until three months later. It amounted to Tessie's realization that falling in love is more than a spontaneous burst of sentiment, through happenstance. She finally saw that it would be her capacity for love that would draw love to her.

We spent many evenings trying to think through how one can develop this capacity to love. I wanted the answer for myself as well as for my friend. We concluded that the ability to love is not limited to sexual or romantic love. If one cannot be loving in all areas of life, he or she is not capable of enduring love for the opposite sex either. So there is nothing for it but the hard assignment of giving love and being lovable in every area of life with people of both sexes, of all ages, shapes and sizes.

We tried to think through some of the qualities wrapped up in that word *loveableness*. This was a start on the list that we made together.

Outgoingness
Interest in other people
Vitality—physical, intellectual, and spiritual
Joy and a sense of humor
Sex appeal (the kind that's unself-conscious, not artificial)
Femininity

In the midst of this, Tessie and I were learning that the Dreaming Prayer, like all serious prayer, can be a difficult business, difficult in the sense that God can ask for many changes in the one praying, and changes are never easy.

One year and four months after my friend and I had embarked on the prayer-project, Tessie met a crisis. A married man with four children fell in love with her. There was a great physical pull between them, and some undesirable circumstances in the man's marriage provided the rationale: he suggested a quick Mexican divorce in order to marry Tessie.

This period was painful. Tessie felt cut off from God. "I

used to have a sense of adventure about this Dreaming Prayer, the feel of getting somewhere, no matter how slowly," she told me. "Now I've hit a dead spot." Then she was defensive. "But I do love this man, and our love is a beautiful thing. So— What's wrong?"

In the end, Tessie answered her own question. I had admiration for the courage of her conclusion that this friend was not the answer for her, because the situation could not pass one of the acid tests for any right dream: the fulfillment of our heart's desire cannot take anything or anybody belonging to someone else. In spite of the rapport and the physical attraction between them, this man was an essential part of someone else's life pattern—not Tessie's. So with anguish and tears, Tessie sent him back to his wife to make a new beginning in his own marriage.

For a while, my friend was disconsolate. Then she concluded that since she had been "a good girl" God would surely reward her by sending her dream man quickly. It was a nice thought, only we found out that God does not work that way. We cannot bargain with God and buy His blessings by being good. Another year and a half passed, and Tessie was still a widow.

This dramatized for us the fact that the Dreaming Prayer can require patience. God's perfect timing oftener than not seems slow—slow—slow to us.

In the meantime, the changes in Tessie were more apparent to me than to her. After her relinquishment of the man who had wanted to marry her, the loveableness that she had wanted so much suddenly wrapped her round like a cloak. Perhaps the difficult experience had mellowed her. Undoubtedly untouched emotion potentials were now released. Whatever the reason, suddenly she seemed all woman, with a tenderness and an aliveness that had not been hers before. Looking at her, I knew that the fulfillment of her dream could not be far away.

As it turned out, only one more hurdle lay between her

and her deepest wish. This was an important one, and it grew out of profound discouragement. More than three years had passed since that first evening when Tessie and I had discussed the Dreaming Prayer and had decided to try it for her problem. It had been three years of intense, sincere effort at self-evaluation, self-improvement, and cooperation with God. Yet the dream still remained unfulfilled. Was our joint effort at the prayer a failure, a mockery? For several weeks my friend thought so and went into a mental slump. She grew almost bitter as she talked about "prayer being just self-hypnosis anyway. Why do we bother? Why don't we just throw out the whole experiment as a bad job?"

Then one day we met over luncheon downtown, and I found Tessie's mood changed. In fact, she was impatient to get the ordering done so she could share what was on her mind.

"It's about six years now since I gave my life to God," she began. "Since then, He's had a stake in me. From His point of view, I'm His child—even though I'm inclined to forget it sometimes. I suppose there are certain lessons He must teach me."

The waitress came with our order, and Tessie was silent until we were alone again. "I've come to the reluctant conclusion that right now one of these lessons is that He wants me to stop running off in all directions, trying to force the fulfillment of my dream. I've tried Charm School, new clothes, the dance group, socializing, trying to be outgoing and thoughtful in dating. the art of listening—you know, a hundred things. Let's face it—these are all valuable, but they simply have not worked."

"So what's your idea of a solution?" I asked.

"Well—I think God is trying to tell me to relax and let Him take over now. If He wants me to remarry, somehow I think He's capable of arranging it."

"Tessie, you've just said 'if God wants me to remarry——'

Does that mean that you're ready to let Him decide whether or not remarriage is in the picture for you?"

Tessie grimaced. "What alternative do I have? My best efforts have failed. At this point I feel defeated. So—either God does this for me, or it doesn't come off."

There it was again—relinquishment! When Tessie made that decision, a lot of tension drained out of her. There were some surprising psychological and social results. By some radar which I do not pretend to understand, Tessie's male friends sensed the new relaxation and inner freedom in her. Their response was immediate. Soon she was having a difficult time finding enough evenings.

Apparently when she had finally handed her problem over to God's management, she had also relinquished that over-intensity that puts men on the defensive. The new contentment and poise that resulted seemed to disarm and attract them.

About three months after our luncheon talk, she met Van at a dinner party. He was a bachelor from Cleveland, in Washington on business. It turned out that six years before Van had been engaged to an Army nurse who had died of pneumonia while stationed in Germany. His reaction to Tessie was instantaneous, though he did not reveal it that night. But frequent long-distance calls from Cleveland were soon revealing a confident man who knew what he wanted and was going after it with every power he possessed.

Tessie had often commented to me that she was wary of all bachelors over thirty-five or so. "In my opinion," she had insisted, "they're usually warped in some way, else they'd be married. They're momma's boys or women haters or something. Anyway, I can't imagine any bachelor having the courage to take on a ready-made family of three squirming youngsters."

Van turned out to be an exception on both counts. The idea of assuming greatly increased responsibilities not only did not deter him but his masculinity responded to it. His proposal of marriage came just three weeks after they had met. Later Tessie confided to me, "Of course, my immediate reaction to his proposal was a sputtering 'Why, Van, you've lost your marbles! I scarcely know you at all.' "

I laughed. "And of course, that was true. You'd only had— what was it—three dates?"

"Four," corrected Tessie. "Van made it clear that he expected no answer right then. He wanted me to know how *he* felt, that he was positive in his own mind and determined. Then he added that if, at that moment, I was certain that he couldn't be a part of my future, he needed to know, so that he wouldn't go on hoping."

"That certainly is the direct road to courtship," I marveled.

"Yes, and what left me gasping," Tessie added, "was the way Van made himself so vulnerable, so naked to hurt. It was a kind of raw courage ready to risk the rejection of the life that he was offering me."

I saw that there were tears in Tessie's brown eyes. "After that I began to realize that here was a man with rare qualities. Then came the special moment when it seemed as if Christ was standing over our courtship saying, "This is My gift. Take it with joy and My blessing."

Van and Tessie were married that April.

And with the fulfillment of Tessie's dream, I saw all over again what Mother had taught me so many years before: when the dream in our heart is one that God has planted there, a strange happiness flows into us. At that moment all of the spiritual resources of the universe are released to help us. Our praying is then at one with the will of God and becomes a channel for the Creator's always joyous, triumphant purposes for us and our world.

12

Ego-Slaying

I SHALL LONG REMEMBER a certain June day in 1955. It was spent with a group of thirteen Christian friends at a rustic lodge in the rolling Maryland countryside. This day in the woods was to be a time apart. The plan was to share portions of two books—C. S. Lewis' *Beyond Personality* and A. W. Tozer's *The Divine Conquest*. Then we would separate for some individual meditation on what had been read; after that lunch, more sharing, and some prayer. It was hoped that the day would end with some definite step forward toward Christian maturity.

Tozer's thoughts and Lewis' are now merged in my mind. But as I remember, what we were studying could be summarized this way: A misconception that many church people have is the theory that with Christ's help we can become "nice people." This teaches that the good in man can be separated from the bad, and the good developed. It says that education is the answer to most problems. It admonishes us to self-effort, human endeavor. Our lives are to be "man's best with God's help."

The main trouble with the "nice people" theory is that when we try living by it, we find ourselves getting nowhere.

What is more, it is not Christianity. Nowhere do the Scriptures tell us that, with God's help, we can sort out the good and the evil in ourselves and cultivate the good. Rather, these writers insist that ever since the first man and woman were tempted to pull away from their Creator, hoping that they would be "as gods," all men have been tainted with the same desire to bow the knee to no one but themselves. Our nature might be compared to an apple shot through with brown specks of imperfection. There is no way to cut out every brown speck and save the apple; the doom of decay is on the fruit.

Just so, each of us is tinctured with self-will; with self-ambitions; with the desire to be pampered, cushioned, and admired; with overcriticalness of everyone else and over-sensitiveness about ourselves; with a drive to enlarge the self with an accumulation of things. Thus, try as we may to separate these self-centered qualities from the unselfish ones, the self keeps cropping up again and again, tripping us every time.

What is Christ's solution to our dilemma? It is recorded for us in the eighth chapter of Mark. "Whosoever will save his life shall lose it," He says, "but whosoever shall lose his life for my sake.... shall save it." [1] To put it another way, there is no solution apart from the painful, all-out one of handing over to Him all of our natural self to be destroyed (the good parts of the apple along with the brown specks) so that Christ can give us a new self, one born from above, one in which He will live at the center of our being.

If the idea of Christ living at the center of life frightens us, it may be because we fear that by handing over self-will we would then become spineless creatures, colorless carbon-copy personalities. We need not be afraid on either count. Actually, it's when selfishness and self-will progressively take over in our society that we become carbon copies of one another. When an adolescent is still unsure of his selfhood, he has a horror of being in any way different from his friends. When adults are not in the least concerned about pleasing God, they are desperately concerned about pleasing each other. When we have few inner resources, we hold up masks to hide our poverty. And all the masks seem to be turned out by the same factory—suburbia, the "organization man," "the man in the gray flannel suit," all aided by mass advertising, extended by the media of mass communication.

Whenever we exchange self-will for God's will, we find greater strength, a finer quality of iron in the new will given us. And, by a strange paradox, we then become more individualistic, with more unique personalities than we would have thought possible. That is because we have exchanged the mask for the real self.

On that day of retreat, I remember being impressed with how vividly C. S. Lewis expressed it. I copied several sentences in my notebook:

Christ says, "Give me *all*. I don't want so much of your money and so much of your work—I want *you*. I have not come to torment your natural self, but to kill it. No half-measures are any good. I don't want to cut off a branch here and a branch there, I want to have the whole tree down. I don't want to drill the tooth, or crown it, or stop it, but to have it out. Hand over the whole natural self, all the desires which you think innocent, as well as the ones you think wicked—the whole outfit. I will give you a new self instead. In fact I will give you myself, my own will shall become yours." [2]

To the Apostle Paul this matter of handing over the whole man to Christ to be annihilated was at the heart of Christianity. "For we know that our old self was crucified with Him (that is, with Christ) to do away with our sinful body, so that we might not be enslaved to sin any longer...." [3]

To Paul the essence of sin lay in a man's life being ruled by "My will be done" rather than by God's will be done. There is, he was saying, a fundamental choice at the heart of life.

It is simply "Who is going to be master?" And if we fail to make a conscious choice on this, then we make it by default. In that case, self will rule from the throne of our hearts.

As we sat in the living room of the rustic retreat lodge that day, some of us on cushions on the floor, Sheldon Turner, the lawyer and lay leader who was guiding the discussion, pointed out that the relatively new science of psychology has—independently of theology—arrived at the same conclusion: there is no maturity or fulfillment of man's personality apart from the slaying of egocentricity. A psychiatrist put it this way:

> Egocentricity in any form... always leads to difficult experiences which we call crises.... The more we are egocentric, and therefore rigid, the less we are able to bear life's burdens.... [Increasing egocentricity destroys itself! He who tries to save his life kills himself.] This is as it should be, since the breakdown of the Ego—the collapse of the system of mistaken ideas which like a shell encase the Self and limit the expression of its power—is one basic aim of human destiny....[4]

Just before lunch that day, paper and pencils were handed around, and each of us tried putting down the characteristics of the self-centered person as opposed to the God-centered person. Combining the lists, they looked something like this:

THE EGOCENTRIC PERSONALITY *"My will be done"*	THE GOD-CENTERED PERSONALITY *"Thy will be done"*
Is intent on self-glory.	Has true humility.
Is concerned about other people's opinions of self; craves admiration and popularity.	Is increasingly free from the necessity for the approval or praise of others.
Is rigid, self-opinionated.	Is flexible.
Cannot stand criticism.	Handles criticism objectively; usually benefits from it.
Desires power over others; uses others for his own ends.	Is devoted to the common good.

THE EGOCENTRIC PERSONALITY	THE GOD-CENTERED PERSONALITY
"My will be done"	*"Thy will be done"*
Wants ease; is self-indulgent.	Ease given up when necessary; knows that many comforts precious to the self may have to go.
Holds self-preservation of supreme importance.	Is aware that you lose your life to find it.
Tries to be self-sufficient; has a practical atheism by which he feels he does not need God's help.	Is acutely aware of his need of God in everyday life.
Feels that life owes him certain things.	Realizes that life owes him nothing; that goodness can not earn him anything.
Is oversensitive; feelings easily hurt; nourishes resentments.	Readily forgives others.
Springs back slowly, painfully from disappointments.	Has capacity to rise above disappointments and use them creatively.
Trusts in material possessions for security.	Know that security is in relationship to God, not in things.
Indulges in self-pity when things go wrong.	Has objective resiliency when things go wrong.
Needs praise and publicity for his good deeds.	Works well with others; can take second place.
Is tolerant of, even blind to, his own sins; appalled at the evil in others.	Understands the potential evil in himself and lays it before God; is not shocked at any evil possibility in self or others.
Is self-complacent; craves the peace of mind that relieves him of unwelcome responsibilities.	Knows that warfare between good and evil will not allow undisturbed peace.
Loves those who love him.	Can love the unlovely; has a feeling of oneness in God toward all humanity.

When the group gathered again after lunch, one girl asked immediately: "But *how* does one deal with the 'My will be done'? Who can ever get rid of self completely?"

"Perhaps not in this life," Sheldon said thoughtfully. "But no human progress could have been made in any field had we followed the line that if we can't do everything perfectly, we won't try. Remember—Christ promises us a miracle with this ego-slaying, a much bigger portion of self slain in this life than we think possible."

The girl repeated her question, "All right, how do you go about it?"

Sheldon then quoted Paul's words: "For you died, and your life is hidden with Christ in God." [5]

It was pointed out that the "have died" is the past perfect tense; it looks back to a definite point in the past. Therefore this matter of getting rid of the old tyrant self is a deliberate step, exactly as entering into the Christian life is a definite step.

We worked out a plan for ego-slaying which goes something like this:

1. We see the limitation of self-centered living and the danger of it in every area.

2. We pass sentence on the natural self by telling God that we are willing to have Him slay it. Our statement of willingness is a definite act at a given time.

3. We accept by faith the fact that God has heard us; that the next action will be His. We reckon by faith that He has indeed undertaken the execution.

4. There will be a crisis or series of crises. We live through them step by step. This is the overt evidence that the slaying of the self has been undertaken.

5. Every day of our lives we shall still have to choose between selfishness and unselfishness. But the big decision to let Christ rather than self rule makes all the smaller deci-

sions easier. This is the "taking up the cross day after day" of which Jesus spoke.[6]

Sheldon warned the group that we had better not tell God that we desired ego-slaying unless we meant it. For no one can predict what painful experiences God will allow in order to make the experience real. After all, each man's self-will takes a different form, and God is going to touch self-interest at its most vulnerable spot.

Then he went on to add wryly, "But I don't want to sound too grim. Maybe this will be some comfort to you. For you who have already embarked on the Christian life, this execution of self is something that has to happen sooner or later, here or in the next life. So you may as well get on with it—get it over with, so that you can break through to real happiness now."

He grinned at us, and his blue eyes held a special light. We had known this remarkable layman for a long time. Somewhere back in his past he had left self behind to a degree that scarcely seemed possible. Yet he had not only survived the experience, but became one of the most delightful personalities I know, successful in his profession, powerful in his way with other men.

What Sheldon called "the execution of self" is the great "crisis," or the series of smaller crises, of which the psychiatrist spoke in the quotation above. This is Paul's "old self" in the process of crucifixion—and it is only human to flee that. Christianity, most of us think, is fine up to a point, so long as we can make it serve us. So long as it gives us peace of mind, settles some of the dust of our inner conflicts, makes us more likable people—well, fine! But of course this is peripheral stuff. This is interpreting Christianity as a rosewater philosophy to make a comfortable atmosphere for nice people. But nice people have no cutting edge. Nor have they any answers for the problems that beset our world.

We begin to see that no man is worthy to rule until he has been ruled; no man can lead well until he has given himself to leadership greater than his own. Even Jesus Christ was no exception. Repeatedly He said that He was not carrying out His own will, but the will of the One who sent Him.

I found Sheldon Turner's thought disturbing: "The Christ of the cross isn't going to become real to you until you come to terms with this hard core of reality at the heart of Christianity. How could He be real to you when you—not He—are still at the center of your life?"

As the woods around the lodge grew dark and the retreat drew to a close, we had much to think about. Those of us who decided to take the plunge, did not do so lightly. In fact, we felt rather as if we were agreeing to a sort of spiritual Russian roulette.

Before parting and driving back to Washington, we agreed that we would check back with one another to find out what had happened to us following the retreat. In actual fact, how would God make real to us this slaying of self? Looking back now, I know that not one of us could have guessed.

It would take a book in itself to tell the details of what happened to the seven of us who said *yes* to the risky adventure of ego-slaying. For what I can tell here, I have changed names and a few details in order not to embarrass the friends concerned.

One businessman, Ed, was touched at two points—his masculinity and his professional reputation. He was the sort of married man who enjoyed flirting with women up to a point, especially with women much younger than he. He had told himself that the flirting game was harmless fun, so long as he always stopped short of actual affairs. I do not think it had occurred to him that in feeding his masculine ego with the adoration and flattery of young secretaries, he ran the risk of their falling in love with him and getting hurt.

It seems that for weeks he had been driving Isobel, the youngest girl in the office, home from work each afternoon. The attention of an older man, especially the boss, had been flattering. In her room at night, Isobel built dream-castles, romanticized every gesture, every remembered sentence. She even wrote the boss a series of love letters. She had no intention of mailing them, kept them locked in a leather jewelry case in her dressing-table drawer.

One night she forgot to lock the case.

In the process of cleaning her daughter's room the following day, Isobel's mother found the letters. From them she concluded that her daughter was having an affair with her boss. Incensed at the idea of an older man seducing an innocent girl, she decided on a course of action.

Soon Ed received an anonymous letter. It accused him of adultery and threatened to reveal the matter to his wife and to his board of directors. At first he regarded the letter as a joke. He was not guilty of adultery! No doubt the letter had been written by some crackpot. Contemptuously, he tore it into small bits and tossed the pieces in the wastebasket.

But by the time the second, the third, and the fourth letters arrived, each more violent than the last, and now threatening blackmail, Ed was in a fine state of nerves. The reiterated threat of the anonymous writer to go to his wife made him decide to tell her about it himself. In addition, he went to the District of Columbia Chief of Police with the letters in hand and told him the story.

Using the United States mails for attempted blackmail is a penal offense, so the officers went into action. Through clever detective work, the mother was apprehended. When the Chief of Police telephoned Ed to tell him that the anonymous writer was Isobel's mother, he was horrified. How could just driving a girl home from work a few times result in such serious misunderstanding?

Then he had a clear-eyed look at himself and his old habit

of using women for what he had regarded as harmless ego-satisfactions. With a new humility, he paid a call on Isobel and her terrified family. It must have been quite a scene in their family living room that evening. Ed said afterward that during those hours he became a man.

He assumed full responsibility for what had happened. He assured the girl's parents that there was no affair. Gently he tried to spell out to Isobel how much he loved his wife and valued his marriage, and he asked her forgiveness for what she had interpreted as unspoken promises.

Isobel's mother would actually have received a prison sentence had not Ed personally gone to court and pleaded for leniency. He knew the judge, having played golf with him at the Burning Tree Club. Realizing by now the connection between the sequence of events and the ego-slaying he had pledged, Ed felt that—pride or not—there was nothing for him to do but tell the whole story to the judge in his chambers. Surely, he told the judge, this woman had learned her lesson and would never repeat such an offence. It would be devastating to the family to have the mother taken away. And Isobel and her two younger brothers might never live down the stigma of their mother being sentenced to prison.

So, after a stern lecture to the mother, the judge suspended sentence and paroled her. But the detectives who had worked so hard to apprehend her at Ed's request felt that justice had not been done and made no attempt to hide their anger at Ed and his "softness." This was hard on his pride, too.

Thus the crisis ended. It had come only two weeks after Ed's decision at the retreat. Though the seven of us had known one another for a long time, we marveled that Ed wanted to share so intimate an experience with us. He insisted on doing so. "Telling it to this one group of close friends is part of the therapy, I guess. Besides it will make it harder for me ever to repeat such immature nonsense. Sheldon warned us all that this process would be painful. It sure was! Yet I'm grateful, ever so grateful, that it happened to me."

Out of Ed's experience, and those of others, we began to see some of the characteristic ways God handles the slaying of the old self. In one sense, the crisis is not sent by God—that is, imposed from above. In each instance, the emergency is the direct result of weakness, the rigidity, the lack of wisdom of one's own self-centered actions. However, the timing of the various crises in the weeks following the retreat seemed remarkable.

Another feature common to all the emergencies was that they never got so completely out of hand that permanent damage resulted to the individual involved or to other people. The dagger thrusts were against the false values, against the evil masquerading as good. The real self emerged unhurt, indeed stronger than ever, with a fresh ability to stand up to life's problems. As in Ed's experience, God seemed to keep His finger on the situation, directing it, stopping it short of disaster.

This seemed to us awe-inspiring proof of God's love for the individual—that Divine love that combines in such an inimitable way tenderness and the iron of discipline. Ed told us that he thought he understood now what the writer of Hebrews had meant when he wrote: "The Lord disciplines the man he loves.... God is treating you as sons.... Discipline always seems for the time to be a thing of pain, not of joy; but those who are trained by it reap the fruit of it afterwards...." [7]

Included in the group of seven was one minister. Roger had an impelling personality and had been born with a gift for preaching. Some thirteen years out of seminary, he was then the popular pastor of a thriving Lutheran church in northern Virginia.

Roger's crisis was merely uncomfortable compared to the pain Ed suffered, probably because Roger had already dealt more forcibly with the old self-centered tendencies than the rest of us.

"In the last few years," Roger explained to us, "I've had several overtures from other churches about becoming their pastor. Some have been important churches in our Lutheran conference. It's quite flattering to be waited upon by a pulpit committee, to be asked to preach a trial sermon to a congregation in some distant city, to be dined and feted and wooed, to be offered all sorts of inducements to accept their call.

"I'd been telling myself that I had no way of knowing what God wanted me to do with each of these offers unless I investigated them. Sometimes that resulted in carrying the negotiations quite far. So the pulpit committees would be most hopeful that I would come. In the interim, my own church would plead with me not to go, sometimes offer inducements for me to stay. Then in the end I would know that I had to turn down the offer of the pulpit committee."

"But wasn't that a sort of ecclesiastical flirting?" someone asked.

Roger smiled. "I know that now. It was similar to the flirting Ed has told us about, and for the same reason. My ego got well fed every time by the process."

"What was the crisis?" I asked.

"Shortly after the retreat I received an overture from a church in Denver, Colorado. My wife and I went out there at the church's expense. Delightful trip!

"There were flowers in the hotel suite, corsages for Betty. There were newspaper stories with pictures of Betty and me. Headlines like VISITING PASTOR LIKES HOSPITALITY OF DENVER or VIRGINIA MINISTER TO PREACH AT 11 A.M. SERVICE TOMORROW; POSSIBLE SUCCESSOR TO DR. ————.

"We found the church divided down the middle theologically. Their previous minister had been an arch-conservative who had split hairs about the second coming of Christ. It was unfortunate for me that my visit got newspaper publicity. Two days after we got home, I received a letter saying that the pulpit committee had recommended that the congregation call me, but that the congregational meeting had voted 608 to 462 not to. They didn't think me doctrinally sound—or something.

"I know this may seem trivial to the rest of you, but my pride smarted for days. Betty laughed and said it was good for me. She's right, of course! But that newspaper publicity! Especially the headline that read: DENVER CHURCH WON'T CALL PASTOR; VIEWS ON CHRIST GIVEN AS REASON. My views on Christ weren't the reason at all. That hurt, because Christ is everything to me. Don't think the whole story didn't filter back to Virginia, too! Well, as a result I've had to face up to the fact that trifling with the feelings of groups of people —like churches—just won't do. And I've been probing for my motives in what you've called my 'ecclesiastical flirting.'

"Mixed up in it is always the temptation to run away from problems in my own church. Then there's the flattery of being wanted by two congregations. But the worst part of it has been lack of strict honesty with myself and with everyone else. From now on," Roger concluded, "I've got to be honest, completely honest in the most transparent sort of way."

I lived through Beverley's crisis with her, since she and I were the closest of friends. We had the intimacy that comes through sharing the deeps of life together. At first, we had been drawn together because we were both widows with sons to rear. Beverley had two boys, Kenneth, a teen-ager, and his younger brother, Sam. Her husband had been lost in World War II in the New Guinea jungle. At first he had been declared missing in action. But as the months melted into years, Bev's initial hope died and was replaced by a conviction that Jim would never come back. Nor did he; his body was never found. All of this she had shared with me—and much more.

During one of the recesses at the retreat, Bev and I had been sitting out under the trees. "I certainly needed this retreat," she confided. "I've been so mixed up recently. There's a barrier between me and the boys, especially Kenneth. Can't seem to get through to him at all. No zest in my work. I don't even get my fun out of recreation these days. The other night a friend took me to the Blue Room of the Shoreham. Suddenly, right in the midst of dinner, it was as if some part of me had detached itself and was standing off to one side watching objectively."

"And what did you see?" I asked.

Bev leaned her brown curly hair back against the tree trunk. "Oh, a lot of people, including me, determinedly working at trying to have fun. There was pretense at the heart of our play. You know—a sort of attitude of 'this evening is costing me plenty. I've paid for it, so I'm going to have fun, if it kills me.' "

We both laughed. "I know what you mean."

"Well, anyway," Bev continued, "already today I've found out what's wrong with me."

My friend toyed with a piece of grass reflectively. "Right after Jim went away, I did ask God to take over my life, rule it. But self has crept back and has been doing a lot of ruling in God's place."

"Looking on from the outside, it doesn't strike me that way," I objected.

"It's true, though. I've been compromising in the matter of drinking, for instance, and that can't be best for my boys. I find myself taking a cocktail sometimes when I don't want one at all, just so folks won't think I'm different. That's caring far too much about other people's opinions of me and not enough about my own.

"Then there's the matter of selfish use of time. I haven't been putting myself out for the boys. Some of their interests, like baseball, I find beastly boring. But I'm not making enough effort to identify with them. There's more, too."

We were called back to the lodge then, but with this much new insight into herself, Bev was one of the seven who decided to take the plunge in ego-slaying.

Her crisis began on a certain Monday morning which was to hold heartache and drama for her. At seven-thirty the telephone rang. It was Detective C——— of the Sixth Precinct, Juvenile Squad. His voice was gentle. He well knew that what he was about to tell this young widow would be a blow. Her Kenneth and three other boys had gotten into trouble on Saturday night. They had taken some property from their school—two axes and a fire extinguisher—and had broken the headlights of two school buses. Bev told me later that she began trembling so violently that she could scarcely hold the telephone.

"You and your son will have to appear at the Sixth Precinct Station at three-thirty this afternoon," Detective C——— concluded.

Bev hung up and immediately dialed me. I was shocked for her but asked no questions over the phone. "I'll be over as soon as I can get dressed," I told her.

Her voice was quivering. "How on earth could Kenneth do something like that? I just don't understand?" She started crying, and we both hung up.

When I got to Bev's home, I found Kenneth with her in the den. She had kept him home from school, so that we could talk with him before the three-thirty hearing.

The boy was fourteen, tall, in the gawky stage. His face was alternately flushed and pale that morning, his features pinched beneath a reddish shock of hair. His mother kept insisting, "Kenneth, you've got to tell us everything. It would be awful if anything else were sprung on us this afternoon. It's time for honesty now—real honesty. Otherwise, how can we help you?"

But Kenneth had little to say, plead and probe as we would. He claimed that we knew everything there was to know. The barrier between him and his mother was there, all right.

Then the school principal telephoned. He wanted to see Kenneth later that morning. After the boy had gone, Bev and I prayed together. It was one of those real prayers—when two people mean business and get down to cases. Both of us wept.

That afternoon we spent three hours at the Precinct Station. Two men from the Juvenile Board were an hour and forty-five minutes late arriving. We waited with the other parents in the front room, watching the hands of the clock move with maddening slowness. I remember one father in particular—a man with black hair peppered with gray and large luminous brown eyes. He was wearing clothes that didn't match and tennis shoes in the middle of winter. And the sad shocked face of another father, his eyes with the look of a hurt animal's.

One mother with a lined, seamed face had brought along the little family dog. She held the little terrier close to her with a leash made from her son's tie. The parents of one boy were abroad and in their place had come a relative who was a psychiatrist, young and prematurely gray. I could almost see his trained mind wrestling with the question of what had happened to these boys from good families.

Finally the two officials arrived, and we were asked to go into a back room. Though it was informal, there was, nevertheless, a courtroom atmosphere. The Juvenile Board sat behind the one long table. There were several benches for the boys and their parents. I looked at Bev and knew that her head was throbbing, and that tears were close to the surface.

While we waited for the hearing to begin, one of the boys, the son of the man with the shocked, hurt eyes, put his head down on the table and began sobbing. He cried softly, not wanting to attract attention, trying to smother the sound with his arms. Later we found out that since early childhood the boy had wanted to go to West Point. If this incident went down on a police record, he would never achieve his heart's desire.

Through it all Kenneth seemed to have a permanent blush. He kept chewing on his fingernails long after there was no bit of surplus nail to chew. It came out in the questioning that he was the one who had bought beer for the other boys. How much had the beer been responsible for their conduct? Who could tell? I knew that Bev would be connecting her recent leniency on drinking with her son's buying the beer.

Kenneth stood straight and said, "Sir." I looked at him and suddenly felt sure that this boy would turn out all right. But that didn't lessen the agony I felt for Bev and Kenneth.

The men on the Juvenile Squad could not have been more compassionate and understanding in their handling of the situation. No word appeared in the Washington newspapers. Wisely, they strung the matter out enough so that Kenneth was badly frightened. A week after the first hearing, he and Bev had to go down to the Juvenile Court again. Of course, they were required to pay for the property damage. But in the end, convinced that these boys had learned their lesson, the Board dismissed their cases with no record against them.

Once again God had permitted circumstances to go only so far as severe discipline would dictate but not to permanent hurt.

A week later Bev was saying to me, "I didn't know a mother's pride of ownership in her children could make her so vulnerable. *My* sons . . . the fear that *my* reputation would be hurt . . . the possible reflection on *my* dead husband's good name . . . all self-pride!

"I know that my insistence on owning my children was the crux of my problem with Kenneth. Kenneth is an individual in his own right. He belongs to God, not to me; he's just been loaned to me for a few years.

"Since then I've been talking to my son, person-to-person. I've admitted some of my mistakes and fears and weaknesses, where I need his help. Catherine, this one week I've watched a miracle unfolding."

Bev's face glowed with her discovery. "That wall between us has come crashing down like the walls of Jericho." Once again quick tears swam in her eyes—this time tears of happiness, relief, gratitude.

One cannot live through experiences like the seven of us had and retain any doubts about the thrust of a living Lord into contemporary life. We learned much in a short time. The literalness of His standing outside the door of our hearts and never intruding until we invite Him in ... The immediacy of His invasion of our lives when we do open the door. His overweening concern that we call a halt to our trifling with life and move on toward maturity and effectiveness. His incisive knowledge of the most vulnerable weaknesses in each of us. Who but Christ could know so unerringly that point of mutiny, so covertly hidden even from ourselves?

All this left us wondering, awestruck. Worship Him? Of course! How can we help it? For He is the only One worthy of worship, supremely worthy! And yet the first step in the direction of that great love must always be ours.

13

The Gospel of Healing

Our Sunday-school teacher was telling us the story of
the man born blind who had received sight from Jesus. We
were impressionable twelve-year-olds. I can remember hugging delightedly to myself the thought of the big commotion
the healing must have caused. Surely everyone in the man's
home village would have talked of little else. I imagined the
conversation something like this:

"Isn't he the beggar, the one who's been blind all his life?"

"It looks like him!"

"It isn't possible. Who could cure a man who was *born*
blind?"

"Let's ask his parents. They'll know...."

And so they sought out the man's father and mother, who
were noncommittal: "We don't know what happened. Why
don't you ask our son about it?"

While people wrangled and talked excitedly, there stood
the man saying over and over, "All I know is that I used to be
blind; now I can see. Isn't it wonderful?"

"But what did he do to you—how did he make you see?"
his questioners had persisted.

Then the man had grown impatient. "I've told you before.

He put a paste on my eyes; I washed it off, just as He told me to in the Pool of Siloam. Now I can see. Don't you understand? I can *see!*"

But the elders of the church had not thought it wonderful at all, because the healing had upset their intellectual fruit-cart, and the fruit was rolling helter-skelter in all directions.

A certain exuberant quality in the story appealed to the rebel in me. I wondered if Jesus had enjoyed the ruckus too....

Then, a few Sundays later, I heard a sermon that seemed to contradict the wonderful story that we had heard in Sunday school. I cannot remember the precise words of the man in the pulpit, but the gist of it went something like this:

"We should not expect miracles in our day like those recorded in the Bible. After all, the New Testament miracles were for a particular time. They were a special dispensation from God needed to authenticate the fact Jesus had really been sent from God. Also they were needed to get the Christian movement started. Gradually the miraculous element in Christianity died out, because it was not needed any more, indeed might have been dangerous. Today God answers our prayers in other ways, through drugs and the skill of modern physicians and men of science...."

I felt let down and indignant. If the preacher was right, then why had they bothered to tell us the story of the blind man in Sunday school? At the time I had not enough knowledge of the New Testament to know what the holes in this man's position were. Later I discovered that he was reflecting the popular eighteenth- and nineteenth-century Protestant position regarding miracles. To these men it seemed a safe middle position, because it effectively preserved the inspiration of the Scriptures, yet did not put the theologians in conflict with the new discoveries of science.

For the next fifteen years I was not at all concerned with whether healing came about through miracles or science. I took health for granted. College, romance, marriage, the birth of a son filled my days to the crowding point. The question of whether those New Testament stories of supernatural cures have relevance for our time touched my life not at all—until . . .

Until that afternoon in May 1943, when the illness I have already mentioned stalked into my life. Over in Baltimore, where I had gone for a physical check-up, Dr. Thomas Sprunt told me as gently as he could that I had an early case of tuberculosis in both lungs. I would have to go to bed full-time. It might take a long while to get well.

It did take a long while—three weary, endless years. Most of this time I spent in the big front bedroom of the manse with its five windows and five Peter Marshall seascapes on the walls. I traveled every tiny design in the pale yellow wallpaper with my eyes hundreds of times. I even remember two stains on the ceiling over my bed where Peter had swatted mosquitos the summer before.

How tired the muscles of one's back can become from too much lying in bed! What is there to fill the hours, the days, the weeks that stretch on and on? I could still work out the week's menus and make marketing lists. But as time went on, the kitchen seemed farther and farther away and food became of little interest. I would lie there, longing to know what was going on downstairs, hearing the hum of voices in the living room. If only I could listen in on the conversations and take an active part in something!

At the beginning of my illness, Peter John was three years old. I could tell him an occasional story and help him with a wooden puzzle, if he would perch on a stool by the bed. I had the late afternoon to look forward to, when Peter would come back from the church office. Through him, I could get glimpses of the world beyond the bedroom walls.

But there was never much for me to tell him. All too often he came home to my discouragement, even my tears of weariness and rebellion. He was patient with me, loving, wise. But not even Peter could answer my pleading questions: "Why—oh, why do I have to lie here month after month? Why can't the doctors do something?"

As it became increasingly apparent that they could not, my need sent me back to the New Testament in eager search for an answer to the question that had so troubled my child's mind: did Jesus mean for healing by faith to be limited to His days on earth?

I made an honest search. Neither self-deception nor wishful thinking about what the gospel narratives meant would help me. The shadows on the X rays of the lungs plus the weakness that chained me in bed were real enough. I was in search of truth as clearly as I could perceive it.

The results of several months of reading and pondering might be summarized like this: Jesus said that He had come to earth to reveal His Father's nature and will to man. Then what was God's attitude towards sickness and disease as reflected in Jesus? I found that He placed any deviation from health in the same category as sin: He saw both as the work of an evil force, both as intruders in his Father's world. Jesus consistently "rebuked" disease precisely as He did demons.[1] At the beginning of His ministry, He declared an all-out offensive against sin, disease, and death.[2] Practically speaking, that meant that Jesus' attitude toward sickness was exactly that of any doctor today: He fought it all the way.

Nowhere in the gospel could I discover any hint of retreat or compromise with this position against disease. Jesus never refused to heal anyone who came to Him for help. He reproved every question of His unwillingness or His inability to heal.[3] Never once did He say, as we so often do, "If it is God's will to heal...." For Him there were no *if*s about His Father's will for wholeness of body as well as of spirit and mind. In fact, roughly one third of Christ's public ministry was taken up with the healing of men's bodies.

He seems never to have suggested that any individual was unworthy of healing. Worthiness or unworthiness were not the condition of receiving God's gifts. The criterion was rather the most practical one imaginable—the individual's need. He "cured those who needed to be healed." [4]

I could find no record of Jesus implying that an individual's spiritual state or the Kingdom of God would be furthered by ill health. Not once did He say that sickness is a blessing. I was impressed with the fact that there is no beatitude for the sick or for those who suffer physically, while there is a beatitude for those who suffer persecution. [5]

Clearly it was Jesus' desire that we be rid of disease. What was his plan for achieving this? He said that faith in His Father's willingness and ability to give His children all good gifts is the key. In His eyes there was no evil that faith could not vanquish, no need that faith could not supply.

I had not gone far in my study before I discovered that there were some religious leaders in Jesus' day who tried to interpret His miracles exactly as had that preacher in my childhood: that God used the miracles to prove to us that Jesus was divine. This was what Jesus called wanting "a sign" and He had harsh words for it: "Only an evil generation would demand a sign...." [6]

Jesus' chief motive in healing seems rather to have been nothing more or less than pure compassion. The word *compassion* is used over and over to describe His attitude toward the sick. That was why He often went out of His way to heal when the sufferer had neither asked for nor thought of His doing so. [7] He delighted in straightening a bent back. [8] He rejoiced in that moment when a man gleefully flings away his crutches. He was glad that He could break up a funeral and give a beloved son back to his mother. [9] It was a gratifying thing to Him to see the light of reason and sanity return to the eyes of a violent demoniac. [10] Jesus healed because the love of God flowing irresistibly through Him in a torrent of good will, simply swept evil away as the debris that it is.

Before Christ's crucifixion He commissioned His apostles to carry on His healing work and sent them out on several test missions.[11] When they returned, after having healed successfully, He rejoiced with them, "I watched Satan falling from heaven like a flash of lightning."[12] As restrained and stripped as the narrative usually is, a lilting, triumphant quality breaks through here. The physician-apostle Luke says that Jesus "thrilled with joy at that hour," breathed a prayer of thanksgiving and then turned to his disciples, exulting, "All has been handed over to me by my Father..."[13]

But then the next question to which I sought an answer was this one: Did Jesus mean for His disciples to continue with their healing ministry after His ascension? I found no doubt that He assumed that they would. How else could we interpret the solemn words spoken on the night before his betrayal, "Truly, truly I tell you, he who believes in me will do the very deeds I do, and still greater deeds than these...."

Moreover, after the resurrection, Jesus' commission to His followers for all ages contains the admonition: "Go ye into all the world, and preach the gospel to every creature.... and these signs shall follow them that believe;...they shall lay hands on the sick, and they shall recover."[14]

Matthew's version of the same great commission stresses the "teaching all nations...to observe all things whatsoever I have commanded you...." The "all things" and the "whatsoever" are inclusive enough. Certainly Jesus meant that the whole gospel should be taught and practiced, not an effete, watered-down version of it.

The Acts of the Apostles leaves no doubt that Peter and Paul and the other apostles interpreted the whole gospel to include healing. For these men proceeded to heal on many occasions.

Going back to my original question, "Did Jesus mean for healing by faith to be limited to His days on earth?" I found that the New Testament cries a consistent, unequivocal, resounding "*No!*"

For me those were days of engrossing discovery. The four walls of my bedroom no longer confined mind or spirit. I was off adventuring in another realm, and I felt like a discoverer who had stumbled into a hidden valley rich with deposits of gold. Something of the pristine intoxication of those first followers of "the Way" winged out of the ancient records into my heart.

Obviously the next step was to appropriate what I had learned. My faith was simple, perhaps even naïve. I reasoned that had I been living in Jesus' day, I would have been among those who sought Him out for healing. I knew that the Scriptures insist that nothing has changed about His compassion or His power, that He is "always the same, yesterday, today, and forever." [15] And we have His unequivocal promise, "Lo, I am with you alway, even unto the end of the world." [16]

Then since He was with me—though I could not see Him or even feel His Presence—I pictured how the scene might be. I saw myself bowed before Him, looking up into His eyes, "Lord, I need Your help. You made my body. You can heal it. Will You do for me what You have for so many others?" He would have smiled at me, I thought, and stretched out His hand to lay it on my head. Then I proceeded in the simplest way to ask for His healing.

After that I waited impatiently for the next routine chest X rays.

Usually I received the doctor's telephone report several days after the X rays. The moment finally came; I found picking up the telephone by my bed for this particular call something of a traumatic experience. During the pause while the nurse transferred the call to the doctor's inner office, my heart began to race, my throat went dry. Every sense had its antennae out to catch the mood and timbre of the doctor's first words.

My imagination toyed with what I would say to him when he told me of his amazement in finding my chest healed. Would I tell him the truth? But what if—no, I wouldn't even admit the thought. I had read somewhere that real faith entertains no doubts. By a process of will power that I found somewhat wearying, I clung resolutely, desperately to the thought of complete health.

Finally at the other end of the phone there was a click and the doctor's voice came on. He sounded casual, "We find no increased density in either lung. The shadows and infiltration are just about the same. No real change ... the sedimentation rate has gone down one point. Just carry on! I'll see you in a few days."

Slowly I rested the telephone back on its cradle. The doctor's words had already pricked and burst the self-inflated balloon that I had thought was faith. For that day and the next I was too numb, too stunned even to try to reason out what had happened. Then came rebellious tears, followed by a period of feeling sorry for myself and by hours of black depression. Finally my mind began to function again.

I knew that I had come to the boundaries of my human reason. I stood on the edge and stared off into an abyss of despair. Since medical skill was not solving my problem and my spiritual efforts—so far as I could evaluate them—had gotten me nowhere, what now?

Was it possible that Jesus Christ and Christianity were myths *in toto*, a carefully wrought system of nonsense? Or if God did exist, was He so bound by the natural law that He Himself had created that He was helpless too?

In that mood of near-despair, I went for a visit to my parents' home on the Eastern Shore of Virginia. My doctors still did not want me out of bed for more than thirty minutes at a time.

The trip was made possible by my taking a boat to Norfolk. I remember that Peter actually picked me up in his arms and carried me up the gangplank to the bunk in my stateroom.

A few nights after my arrival—on September 14, 1943, to be exact—something happened to me that defies analysis. I have relived it in my mind hundreds of times since that night. All I can do is to describe it exactly as it happened....

I awakened about 3:30 A.M. There was blackness all around me, not a sound. I had no idea what had awakened me. Nor did I understand why I had emerged suddenly from deep sleep into alertness with no interim drowsiness.

Then it happened, I was aware of a Presence, a Power, a Personality in my room. My physical eyes saw nothing, yet a new way of seeing was instantly available. My body tingled as with a shock of electricity.

The new set of senses which I had suddenly been given enabled me to perceive the vivid Personality who stood at the right side of my bed. There was in Him a curious combination of kingliness and tenderness.

Through His tenderness shone the fact that He looked upon me as a child, quite a foolish child at times. And He had a sense of humor—and the light touch. With my new eyes I saw that He smiled at me. His attitude was, "Why do you take yourself and your problems so seriously? Relax! There's nothing here I can't take care of."

I realized too that He knew every detail of my life and household. And with my new ears I heard Him speak in contemporary language. There was never a "thee" or a "thou."

"Go and tell your mother," He said. And then He smiled again. "That's simple enough isn't it?"

My humanness immediately asserted itself. "Go and tell my mother—what?" I thought. I wanted to argue, "It's the middle of the night, what will mother think?"

But again, I was conscious of that note of mastery in the One who had just spoken. And I understood something else:

He was standing there waiting, leaving me entirely free to obey or to disobey. For an instant I wavered between my disinclination to obey and that compelling quality in Him, sensing that something terribly important—as important as my whole future—hung on my decision. Then resolution welled up in me. "I'll do it, if it kills me," I told Him as I threw off the bed covers.

And once again, He smiled at my intensity . . . and stood aside for me to pass.

Mother wakened immediately and sat up in bed. Father was still asleep. "What's happened?" There was alarm in her voice.

"Don't be frightened. Something wonderful has happened. I just want you to know that I'm going to be all right now. I'll tell you about it in the morning."

This was scarcely fair, since Mother must have been consumed with curiosity. Yet because she sensed the combination of excitement and restraint in me, she did not question me further.

A few minutes later when I returned to the bedroom, it was empty. I lay there wide awake until dawn marveling at what had happened. Now I knew what the New Testament writers meant when they spoke of Jesus "speaking with authority." I had felt His kingliness. I could understand how it was that the skeptic Thomas could in the same Presence pass in an instant from unbelief to worship before this Christ, saying "My Lord and my God."

In the morning I wondered if I was healed. Would the next X ray finally show healthy lung tissue? But something far more important even than healthy lungs and body tissue was now clear to me. I knew that Christianity is no myth. I could understand why no intimidation, not even the threat of death, could shake Peter and James and John and the other apostles from their insistence that Jesus Christ was alive!

How was His resurrection possible? I had no idea. But suddenly all theological controversy as to *how* it had happened seemed unimportant in the face of the fact that it was so.

As for my health, I dared not assume that Christ had healed me. He had made no such statement!

As it turned out, this experience was the turning point in my illness. For the first time the next X ray showed progress, as did every X ray thereafter. Even so, months were to pass before I was pronounced well.

Why did it take so long? The tardiness was not God's will. Of that I am sure. Rather it was due to two deficiencies of mine. The first was an inner difficulty. As time went on, I began to realize that the psychologically penetrating question Jesus had once put to a man at the Pool of Bethesda—a man who had been ill for thirty-eight years—also applied to me: "Do you want your health restored?" [17]

This seems a ridiculous question. Who wouldn't want to get well? Yet many doctors today believe that one of the root causes of much illness is a deep-seated retreat from life. Psychosomatic medicine has much to say about the will to live and its converse, the subconscious death-wish. Apparently any interior division about this, any chronic state of indecision about facing some necessary adjustments to life, can directly contribute to illness.

So I had to ask myself, "Am I willing to go back into life ready to assume full responsibilities? Am I willing to make adult adjustments to whatever life hands me? Can I accept such robust health at Christ's hands that no one need ever feel sorry for me again, that I shall never again be able to use poor health as an excuse for avoiding some responsibility? This had to be a clear-cut decision of my will. I was aware of Christ standing aside for me to make it, even as He had stood aside that night of September fourteenth while I decided whether or not I would obey Him.

But the second reason for the delay in my convalescence was not so easily resolved. It was my inability to grasp an inviolable spiritual principle—one that is seen everywhere in the New Testament—that faith must always be in the present tense. The most succinct statement of the principle is in Mark: "So I tell you, whatever you pray for and ask, believe you have got it, and you shall have it." [18]

I puzzled for months over this one verse. The verb tenses seem contradictory. How can one believe that he already possesses health, for instance, at the same moment that he is being promised health in the future? Yet I wondered if that was not exactly what Christ had been asking me to believe that night of September fourteenth: that X rays and medical reports notwithstanding, I was healed right then.

Every time that Jesus forgave sins or healed, he demonstrated this principle. One could pick examples almost at random. Though Zacchaeus had spent a lifetime in sin, Jesus told him, "This day is salvation come to this house." [19] The woman in the synagogue who had been bowed over [with arthritis probably] for eighteen years was told, "Woman, you are released from your weakness" [20]—right now, at this moment.

About this time, I came across Hannah Whitall Smith's statement that God's inevitable order is Fact, then Faith, and last, Feeling. In relation to health, this order would mean that health would precede one's faith for it; that feeling well, the disappearance of symptoms, and the clinical proof of health would come last of all. This too substantiates the formula that Jesus gave us.

I came to realize that our mortality, which forces us to divide time into past, present, and future is probably the simplest key to the seeming contradiction in the verb tenses in the verse in question. In the world of spirit, there is only the eternal Now. But Jesus was trying to explain the principle to men still in the flesh. Even with this much understanding, the most my faith could grasp was that my healing was *in the process* of coming. I felt that this was scarcely good enough. No wonder my recovery was so slow.

There are those who are able to grip this principle of

present-moment faith more firmly than I did, enough to act on it. In such cases, the healing process is accelerated accordingly. This was dramatized for me by what had happened to another tubercular patient. Her story was to be a decisive factor in my own recovery.

One afternoon in the late spring of 1945, during a period when my progress toward health seemed especially slow, a former college friend came to call. I had not seen her in years. Apart from her news of our classmates, one thing seemed uppermost in her mind—the story of Rosa Bell Montgomery. "She's just had a remarkable recovery from TB," the friend told me. "Her case was much worse than yours! In fact she was in a sanatorium in New Mexico and not expected to live out the month. Hers was a case of spiritual healing, pure and simple. She's fine now. In fact, she's getting married next month."

As I sat in bed propped up against pillows listening to this, I kept questioning, probing for more details.

My friend saw my eagerness. "I'll tell you what. I'll write Rosa and tell her about you. I think she'd be happy to write you herself and give you the story firsthand. Would you like that?"

Would I like it!

The promised letter, however, was slow in coming. When it finally arrived, I could understand why. It was a lengthy letter for a girl to write in longhand on her honeymoon. It was postmarked New York.

How sorry I am to have waited so long to write to you. My only excuse or reason for this delay is that the letter telling me about you reached me in Los Angeles just a few days after I was married, and I have been on a lovely but hectic honeymoon ever since.... Now that we are in New York, far from the sweet attentions of friends and family, I can chat with you undisturbed....

It has been more than three years now since I turned my case over to the Lord and He really did a good piece of work on me. No one talked me into it—in fact no one talked to me about it at all—and I didn't read anything that influenced me. This is how it happened, and I shall be as brief as possible....

Rosa had been a bed patient in a sanatorium in Albuquerque for almost ten months, a cavity in the left lung, fluid on the right, losing weight steadily. There came the night when Rosa took a long look at herself spiritually. She felt that her heart had been wayward and proud. In her mind she went over all the things that she had been hugging to herself. Suppose God should want her to give up these things? For example, her deep desire to find a husband. Perhaps marriage wasn't in God's plan for her because of her health problem. But how could she bear the thought of never marrying?

Then suddenly, none of these things seemed to matter any more. She decided that she wanted Christ more than she wanted anything else. Lying on her hospital bed, watching the shadows from the desert moonlight on the ceiling, her will bowed itself before Christ and called Him Master. Immediately there was a feeling of peace.

The next day she had the same keen desire I had to search the Scriptures on the subject of healing. Rosa had grown up in a physician's home. She had been taught all her life that God uses doctors and medicine to heal today. But she also knew that medicine still had no real cure for tuberculosis. The doctors could cooperate with nature to achieve an arrested case —and that was all. So she determined to drop all previous ideas and to find out for herself what the Scriptures had to say on the subject.

Her conclusions were just what mine had been from the same sort of search. So she turned her case over to God.

Jesus had talked about the agreement of like-minded people as being one prerequisite for answered prayer. "If two of you agree on earth about anything you pray for, it will be done for you by my Father in Heaven. For where two or three have gathered in My Name, I am there amongst them." [21]

So one March afternoon, a few friends met Rosa in the sanctuary of a local church. Rosa was too ill to get dressed, so she went in her bathrobe. There, before the altar, the group gathered around her and prayed. It was simple and direct. Yet when they prayed nothing dramatic happened. Rosa felt no different, except for an inner assurance that the answer was on the way.

That being so, she no longer asked for healing but began thanking God for it. Here Rosa was demonstrating that principle that had so puzzled me, "Believe you have got it and you shall have it." She decided that she would begin acting her faith by getting up and walking about, so far as her strength would permit.

The fact that faith has to be in the present then led her to a daring decision: she would permit no more pneumothorax treatments.

Rosa's doctor at the sanitorium was appalled. Dr. Werner cajoled and threatened. Once the lungs were collapsed, it was suicide to stop the pneumothorax before healing was complete! But his warnings were to no avail; Rosa quietly stood her ground. She knew how foolhardy her decision seemed to the medical men. Nor was she implying that others should act in so drastic a manner. But this, she felt, was what Jesus was telling *her* to do. She must obey. It was as simple as that. God would take care of the results.

Rosa found all the pressure harder to withstand than she would admit. Many symptoms of her disease were still bothering her—fever, a cough, the fluid in her left lung. Yet she knew that she had to keep her attention fixed on Christ, not on her symptoms; that she had to listen for His directions, not those of others, however well-meaning and loving they were.

Her doctor made one last desperate try. He asked that Rosa's father, Dr. Nelson Bell, in Montreat, North Carolina,[22] be appraised of the situation. "But I don't think it would do for me to talk to him just now," Dr. Werner told Rosa. "I'm too upset about this." So a friend at the sanitorium put the telephone call through.

Dr. Bell did some sharp questioning. When he had satisfied himself that Rosa was firm in her decision, and that she would agree to stay in the sanitorium where the doctors could keep an eye on her, he gave her his blessing.

After that, Dr. Werner battled Rosa no more, only watched her more closely than ever. By April she had begun to gain weight. Her pulse had gone down to normal. The afternoon fever was decreasing.

By June, Rosa was out of bed most of the time. By July she had formed the habit of walking sixteen blocks down the hill for an afternoon milkshake, then sixteen blocks back up the hill. In October she pleaded for and got a position in the institution's laboratory.

The following February—not quite a year since the little group of friends had gathered in her room for prayer—the leading radiologist of New Mexico compared a new set of X-ray plates with the old ones. He was dumfounded at the change.

In April the same technician found the cavity of her right lung "completely obliterated." At that time he also wrote Dr. Bell that Rosa's "explanation of her healing is the only adequate one."

Then Don Montgomery walked into her life, and God gave her the one joy she had thought He might ask her to relinquish —love and marriage.

I am still in touch with Rosa. She has never had any recurrence of her old trouble. Nor has health required her to live in the Southwest. She is no fanatic on the subject of healing, but her experience has made her relationship with Christ an intensely personal one.

In all her letters to me she stressed Christ's individualized treatment of each case. "You must listen for His orders, not copy mine," she warned.

The first hint of my directions came in an odd way. I dreamed that the lung specialist said to me, "There are people who don't get well until they get up and go about their business. Of course, as a doctor I couldn't take the responsibility for telling you that, but——" and I woke up.

I mentioned the dream to my mother. "That's queer," she answered as a startled look crossed her face. "The same thought has been coming to me over and over."

Still I was cautious about acting on this. After all, perhaps the dream had been nothing more than wishful thinking in my sleep. But in time, my orders did come in an inner conviction that did not fade with the passing of days: *As you give strength to others, strength will be given to you. Stay under the doctor's care, but start getting out of bed.* And that is just what I did.

I began with a small chore, tidying up the linen closet once a week; I could sit down to do that. Then I assumed the responsibility and fun of dressing Peter John each morning. After that came a short afternoon walk with Jeffrey, our cocker. First, a half a block. Then to the corner. After a few weeks, we were circling the block. I was inching my way, but little by little vitality was flowing back to me.

Then came the day when the doctor's nurse telephoned to report that the sedimentation rate had returned to the normal range. This meant that there was no longer evidence of infection in the blood stream. So far, so good. But the X-ray pictures still showed trouble.

By now X rays were being taken three months apart. Two months after the good laboratory report, I went down to add the next routine chest film to the doctor's fat file. It was on a Tuesday morning that I was to telephone to hear the result.

The first time I called, the doctor was in the midst of a consultation. Would I please try again in about an hour?

During the hour, some of my old fears of those telephone reports came creeping back. *What if*—I thought— *No, "what ifs" are always silly, because they borrow trouble.* Nevertheless, when I dialed the number again it was with an unsteady hand.

The doctor's voice was as calm as always. "The appearance is that of perfectly healed lesions—"

"Perfectly healed!" I almost shouted at him. "You mean I'm well?"

There was a smile in his voice. "That's what I mean. But wouldn't you like to hear the remainder of the report?"

I listened impatiently to the droning technical language. How could he be so maddeningly placid about it? He was reading it as if this were a weather report! The first minute I could hang up, I dropped the telephone and rushed downstairs shouting the great news.

In a few hours when I could be calmer about it, gratitude of a deeper kind welled up. I was grateful not only because I was well again, but because of my personal encounter with Christ, which had settled certain questions forever. Inestimable blessings had come out of a difficult experience. I had discovered myself and what I wanted out of life. The woman who rose from bed and went out to meet life was a different woman.

After such an experience, I of all people should have been convinced for all time of God's power to heal. But there was still an area that continued to trouble me. I now had no doubt that an individual can open himself to the healing love of God. But can that love be sent winging to someone else? Can prayers affect another person's illness?

In the intervening years I have had this question answered for me again and again. The answer is definitely *Yes!*

I have chosen to use Karen Emmott's story out of many, because the medical facts are indisputable. Not only is the man who initiated the prayers for her a surgeon, but her father too, is a doctor. Karen is the eldest daughter of Dr. Ralph Emmott, a specialist in urology in Oklahoma City.

Her physical problem began soon after her fifteenth birthday in the spring of 1960. It was nothing serious—just an abscess which required a minor operation, incision, and drainage. Twenty-four hours in the hospital (the one where her father practices) seemed to clear everything up.

Karen plunged into a busy summer. Before me as I write this is a small picture of her as she was then. Yes, she was a charmer: short curly hair, sparkling eyes, a piquant quality about her. At the close of the school year she had been voted drum-majorette. Her five younger brothers and sisters were proud of her. She seemed to be following in the footsteps of their mother, who had been a campus beauty queen in Canada.

On July first, Karen noticed that another abscess was forming. Again her doctor recommended the minor operation and drainage. The operation was set for 1 P.M. on July fifth. It was such a routine matter that Karen's father went on to his regular afternoon clinic in the urology department.

As Karen was placed on the operating-room cart, she gave her mother a puckish kiss. It was to be her last volitional act for many months.

The first indication that Karen's father had that tragedy had struck came when the Operating Room Supervisor—a friend of the Emmott family—summoned him from the clinic. Hastening to the operating floor, he learned that toward the close of the ten-minute operation there had been sudden cardiac arrest. The chest had been incised. The heart had been massaged. Now it was beating again.

But during the emergency, no one in the operating room had paused to look at the clock. How long had it been from the cessation of heartbeat until circulation had been restored? Four minutes? Five? It was a question that was to haunt everyone concerned with Karen's case. For with cardiac arrest, time is of the essence. The sensitive brain tissues are damaged almost immediately when the constant supply of oxygen is cut off.

Karen's mother shut herself in her husband's office and tried to pray. In the recovery room, two doors away, everything that science knew was being done for Karen—a hypothemia blanket to keep body temperature at thirty-one degrees and prevent further swelling of the brain; a tracheotomy to help the paralyzed lungs to breathe.

Kneeling by a leather chair, Mrs. Emmott groped for a way to pray. "Oh God, let me have Karen back again. These fifteen years are so brief and unfinished. . . ." Then her thoughts would wander off. *Such a fine thread between this world and the life beyond. How can we be so indifferent to God when things are going well?* "God, will You take care of our girl? Oh, God. . . ." *This can't be real . . . Karen will wake up soon and this scare will be in the past.*

But by nine o'clock that night, it was apparent that Karen was not going to wake up.

Except for the beating of her heart, Karen was dead. On the morning of July sixth, those watching beside her bed saw one eyelid flicker. Weeks went by and there was no other sign of life. Then the convulsions began. Sudden seizures with bloody froth on her lips and soaring temperature alternated with deep coma.

By mid-August the convulsions were under control. But the consensus of all the specialists on the case was that the outlook was hopeless, the brain damage beyond repair.

Every body function had to be artificially maintained. The girl's mother could scarcely bear the sight . . . a tube in Karen's chest; cutdowns in her leg veins for some limited nutrition; the tracheotomy tube; a catheter, even needle electrodes stuck in her scalp and legs to monitor her heartbeat.

At last the doctors spoke the brutal truth. "Your daughter will always remain in a vegetative state," they told the Emmotts. "Alive, but unknowing. It is possible that we will be able to keep her alive for years. But we advise you to put her out of your minds and your lives. Forget she ever lived."

Forget? A mother and father forget part of their own hearts? Their lovely intelligent Karen alive, and yet not alive; dead and yet not dead. For Isabel and Ralph Emmott, horror closed in. There is no blackness like the eternal night of no hope. Isabel had long since stopped praying. Surely there could be no God of mercy, else He would not allow this to happen. Death could have no sting compared to this.

On August 16 to free a hospital bed for a patient whom the doctors could help, the girl was moved to a Children's Convalescent Home. A month passed. There was no change in her vegetative existence except a steady loss of weight.

On Thursday, September 28, Isabel Emmott was invited by a friend to hear a talk at a local church. She went only because the speaker was to be Dr. William Reed, Consulting Surgeon at Samaritan Hospital, Bay City, Michigan. Mrs. Emmott was mildly curious as to why a physician would be speaking in a church.

Dr. Reed was a tall, earnest young man in his late thirties. He told about the sequence of events by which he had learned that medicine plus prayer can bring about cures otherwise impossible.

"Science, mathematics, and physics, as a result of Einsteinian thought, have left the realm of the material and have in certain ways become mystical sciences. There is a sense in which medicine too must go beyond the material. The whole man must be treated. I am now convinced that neither medicine nor surgery can achieve maximum effectiveness—especially for the case which is beyond the scope of the physician to cure —so long as the body is treated to the exclusion of the spirit."

It was not the usual religious talk. Isabel Emmott was fascinated. In all her years of churchgoing she never heard anyone mention healing through prayer. Nor had she heard of a doctor who prayed in the presence of the operating room personnel before he began each operation. Mrs. Emmott smiled to herself as she thought of how he had put it. "I used to bow my head and pray silently. But then I thought the nurses might just think I had a headache. Now if I hesitate about the prayer, they remind me." And this was a doctor, not a minister!

At the conclusion of the talk, her friend told her, "I've done something without asking you. Hope you won't mind. I've already told Dr. Reed about Karen. If you'd like it, he has agreed to ride out with us to the Convalescent Home this afternoon." Her eyes searched Isabel's face.

Light sprang into the black eyes. "Like it? Of course!"

That afternoon at the door of the Convalescent Home Karen Emmott's father was waiting. Dr. Reed judged him to be about his own age. As the piercing brown eyes of the girl's father looked him over, the thought crossed his mind that probably Dr. Emmott had already looked him up in the American Medical Association's directory.

In dispassionate medical terms, Karen's father told Dr. Reed the history of her case. As the words of hopelessness poured out on him, Bill Reed was thinking, "Lord, you've handed me a tough one this time." He had never tried praying for such a difficult case. Yet he could not dislodge from his mind the words, "With God all things are possible . . . all things. . . ." Obviously his first task was to give hope back to Karen's parents. This would not be easy when one of them was a knowledgeable doctor.

Dr. Emmott's face was a study in skepticism. "I'd advise you not to form any opinion until after you've seen Karen," he said. "Come on in, my wife is waiting for us in the room."

The first glance was shocking. A once-beautiful girl, now emaciated, spastic, her black eyes—so like her mother's—wildly staring, without recognition. Constantly there were aimless thrashing movements. The sides to her bed were high to keep her from falling out. Dr. Emmott was watching his face.

Cautiously Dr. Reed told how it had been shown by some

men working in the field of hypnotism that the subconscious mind of a patient under anesthesia is aware of what goes on in the operating room. "And I believe that it may also be true in coma," he added.

Dr. Emmott seemed mildly interested in the thesis. As for Isabel Emmott, a faint light of hope flickered in her tired eyes.

"Now what I suggest," Dr. Reed said, "is that we begin to treat Karen as if she were spiritually awake and spiritually perceptive. Do you think you could do it?" Both parents nodded. They had nothing to lose. "Then shall we begin right now?"

So Bill Reed placed his hands on Karen's head and prayed, not about her, but with her, taking her situation to God, thanking Him for His loving care. Nothing happened. The violent jerking and twisting did not even momentarily subside.

"I haven't the least idea how God will answer this prayer," he admitted. "But we've got to keep reminding ourselves that in His eyes, there are no hopeless cases. Now let me explain what I think your role will be in getting Karen well again——"

Getting Karen well again? Mrs. Emmott could scarcely believe what she was hearing. In all the long months since the tragedy, no one—no one at all—had even mentioned the possibility of Karen getting well. And here was this stranger...

Dr. Reed outlined several steps: (1) Prayer continuous and confident; (2) Daily conversations with Karen, always assuring her of complete recovery; no negative words or even thoughts in her presence; (3) as soon as possible discontinuance of all artificial aids—sedation, catheter, breathing-tube, intravenous feeding, etc.

The following morning Mrs. Emmott drove to the Nursing Home and sat down beside her daughter. Karen was showing the same thrashing movements as before. Gently she placed her hand on Karen's forehead. "Karen," she said softly, "you are going to get well. Your friends have been asking about you. They're missing you at school and at majorette practice."

Did she imagine it? Were the movements a little less violent? Day after day Mrs. Emmott talked to Karen—about family activities, about Karen's friends, about what was happening at school. Always she would come back to the same persistent theme: "You are going to get well, Karen. God loves you, Karen. We love you. Won't it be wonderful to be well again?"

After the first day there was a definite change; Karen's spastic contortions were less violent. Two days later her mother and the nurses were able to put her in a wheelchair and take her into the sunshine for the first time in three months. But still she showed no sign of awareness.

The next step—taken in faith—was the removal of the catheter. With that, the severe urinary infection began to subside.

Then came the matter of food. Isabel Emmott decided to try letting Karen eat in the normal way. Three friends took turns helping her. At first, chewing was impossible for Karen; even swallowing was hard. But gradually she learned to eat baby foods and mashed potatoes.

Slowly the miracle unfolded. One evening in mid-November Karen's father put a ball-point pen in her hand. She punched the release button and began to scribble on the blanket cover.

Almost frantic with joy, her parents began handing her other familiar objects—a stick of gum, a Chapstick, sunglasses. She put the sunglasses on upside down, then righted them.

That night they went home jubilant. Now they set themselves a new goal, to have Karen home for part of Christmas Day. And it happened as they pictured it: on Christmas afternoon the whole family was together. Around the table at Christmas dinner every one of her brothers and sisters thanked God that Karen could be with them for a few hours.

Back at the Convalescent Home, Karen began rebelling. She hated the tube feedings that still had to be used to supplement the baby foods. Unless her hands were tied, she would pull the tube out. Then she began refusing the baby foods too.

Her mother had an inspiration. She would prepare a tuna-fish sandwich. In the old days that had been one of Karen's favorites. She asked a group of friends to meet and pray for the little venture.

Karen gobbled the sandwich down with better coordination in chewing and swallowing than anyone had thought possible. In the next few days ice cream, French fries, and hamburgers met equal enthusiasm. Soon there were no more tube feedings, and Karen's weight at last started up.

Isabel and Ralph Emmott were learning. They would take a step at a time, each launched by hope, taken in faith. After this, they recognized rebellion in Karen as her readiness for another step.

December was drawing to a close. Still Karen had not spoken. Getting rid of the tracheotomy tube was next. During a ten-day period, successively smaller tubes were placed in the wound. On the tenth day, the tube was withdrawn entirely. The girl breathed normally but still seemed incapable of speech.

But with the tube out, now Karen could be brought home to st⁓, . January fourth was a gala day for the Emmott family. Isabel could scarcely hold back tears of gladness over Karen's homecoming.

And then a few days later the girl began to whisper. Her first sentences in a low voice and with precise enunciation were a series of revelations. Her mother wrote them down, "I want to live my life in the old natural normal way." ... "If heaven and hell are worlds, then I want to go to the heaven-world." ... "I want to meet and greet the man Jesus." ... "Please assure me that my life has been a successful thing. I need the reassurance if it has been."

Each evening as she tucked Karen in, Isabel would repeat the Lord's Prayer and the 23rd Psalm. On Easter Sunday, 1961,

Karen repeated the Lord's Prayer by herself—with a few flourishes of her own: "Who art in heaven—way up in that world we call heaven. . . ."

Progress is slow, but progress there is. Karen now feeds herself, reads, walks unassisted. Last June she developed a new rebellion. Unless she is watched, she will slip out of the house and try to drive the family car.

Whenever Isabel Emmott needs more prayer-stamina and physical stamina for the long road ahead she gets down on her knees and thanks God for the long way Karen has already come from her vegetative state. Hopeless! No! The Emmotts know now that Bill Reed was right: in God's view there is no such term as *hopeless*.

Surely the preacher in my childhood was mistaken in thinking that the miraculous element in Christianity has died out because it is not needed any more. Not needed? When always there are so many—like Karen—for whom the doctors have no answer?

No, it is not the absence of need that has caused the sharp decline of the miraculous element in Christianity. Something has chilled and contracted our faith in God's love and in His freedom to stoop to our need and to heal our bodies. Healings through prayer are still the exception rather than the rule. Yet it takes just as much power to forgive sin or to release men and women from enslaving habits as it does to heal. And the truth is that these other miracles are just as rare in our day as are healings.

Still spiritual progress is being made, for in the last two decades there has been a groundswell of interest in spiritual healing among all religious denominations. The National Council of Churches recently surveyed a number of Protestant ministers to find out what they thought about healing through prayer. Thirty-four per cent of the clergymen answering the questionnaire said that they had attempted spiritual healing, in many cases with success astonishing even to them.

The new collaboration between ministers and physicians is also a sign that there is no longer an imagined conflict between religion and medicine. On the religious front, all those I know who are interested in healing believe that divine healing should always be undertaken in cooperation with doctors, never in competition with them.

On the side of medicine, every adequately trained modern doctor recognizes the connection between his patient's mind and spirit and the tissues of his body. Many hospitals (like St. Luke's in New York City) have full-time chaplains on their staffs.

Meanwhile, psychologists like Adler, Jung, and Fritz Künkel have steadily closed the lag in our understanding of how mind and spirit affect body. They are also bringing us closer and closer to Jesus' teaching that man's being is a whole, that he can in no way be separated into compartments.

Practically speaking, we shall have taken our greatest step forward in the realm of spiritual healing when the average Christian becomes as sure of God's will for health as he is of his doctor's. Only those who have settled this in their own minds, can press forward in the adventure of spiritual research. And press forward we must, for Christ has commanded us to do so.

Of course, we shall not always succeed; neither do the doctors. Jesus Himself had some failures in His home town of Nazareth "because of their unbelief." [23]

But above all, let us not be stopped by a particularly subtle roadblock. "Isn't it a dangerous thing to ask for healing through prayer?" this argument goes. "Suppose you pray for health and fail.... Mightn't you then lose your faith in God altogether?"

One minister who has had a healing service every week for

twelve years answers this by saying, "In twelve years I have never had anyone come to me and say, 'I followed your suggestions. I went all out. It hasn't worked. I will have nothing more to do with religion and the church.' But I have had marvelous experiences with people who have received answers that are even better than what they asked for."

In my own case, it was precisely while my prayer was still unanswered that I received the most vivid assurances of God's reality.

What this comes down to is the simple but powerful truth that God can be trusted in this regard as in all others. Hope is always of God; hopelessness is always of evil. Faith is always right; fear and despair are always wrong.

We can rest on the love of God, knowing that His love for us boundlessly surpasses our own. Nothing can ever separate us from that love except our own blind unwillingness to receive.

14

Journey into Joy

SOME TIME DURING the second year after my entering-in experience, I found myself with a lively curiosity about what seemed an odd subject—the Holy Spirit. Like most people, I had thought of the Holy Spirit as a theological abstraction, a sort of ecclesiastical garnish for christenings, weddings, benedictions, and the like. As for the term *the Holy Ghost*—that I regarded as archaic, if not downright eerie.

However odd the subject seemed, the fact remained that this was no passing curiosity. As is often the case when something is brought sharply to one's attention, everywhere I turned during those months, I seemed to hear or read something about the Holy Spirit.

During our vacation at Cape Cod, the church that Peter and I attended with Peter John included a talk for children as part of its regular Sunday service. The first Sunday we were there, the guest preacher gave as his sermonette an object-lesson talk on the Holy Spirit as related to the Trinity.

Three glass containers had been placed on a table before the young preacher. One was filled with water, the second with ice, the third with what appeared to be steam, probably dry ice.

"Children," he began, "perhaps you've heard of 'The Trinity.' *Trinity* means 'three.' When we speak of the Trinity, we mean the three Persons that go to make up God: God, the Father; Jesus Christ, the Son; and the Holy Spirit.

"Now look at these three jars. This one has water. This one has ice, and that one, steam. They all look different, don't they?

"Yet you know that ice is only frozen water. And that when your mother boils water in a pan on the stove, steam rises from it.

"That means that water, ice, and steam are really the same thing.

"Now, the same thing is true of the Trinity . . . Jesus Christ, the water of Life, is different from the Father—yet the same too. The Holy Spirit, like the powerful steam that can drive an engine, is different from Christ and the Father, yet the same."

I listened, as interested as any of the children. What the young minister said that morning gave me a new concept and provided a background for approaching the subject that continued to occupy my mind.

Then about two months later something happened which took this interest out of the realm of theory and placed it on a personal basis. It was in the early fall of that year that my friends Tay and Fern told me of the experience of guidance that they had had in Florida the previous winter (pp. 131 ff.).

I had known Tay for a long time. Often she had inner nudges and proddings of the kind that had sent her out to help her friend Grace at a time of desperate emergency. Curiously I asked her, "How do you explain these intuitions—this —well, Voice on the inside?"

"Some people call them intuitions," Tay answered promptly. "But I would prefer to call the help I got at Delray Beach that morning the direction of the Holy Spirit."

So there it was again!

Tay was looking at me curiously. "What does the Holy Spirit mean to you?" she asked.

I remembered the sermonette at the Cape Cod church. "Oh —one of the three Persons of the Godhead—the third Person of the Trinity."

"But I sense something in the offhand way you say that——" she looked at me sharply. "Let me guess that in your mind the Spirit has an insignificant and unnecessary place. Isn't that right?"

I nodded. "That's right."

"But I know from personal experiences that the Holy Spirit is just as great, just as needed as the other two Persons of the Trinity. Anyway you still haven't answered my original question, what is He to *you?*"

Tay's intensity seemed to demand a candid reply. "I've got to be truthful, Tay," I replied. "He's nothing to me. I've had no contact with Him and could get along quite well without Him."

Although at the time I believed my own statement, I was soon to find out that it was not so. As a matter of fact, I could not get along at all well without the Holy Spirit. Some searching in the Bible told me why.

Using a concordance and a notebook, I began methodically looking up all the references I could find on the third Person of the Trinity. Gradually I worked the findings into a logical outline in the notebook.

I learned that the Holy Spirit is not "an influence" but a Person; not "a thing," an "it," but "He." In a sense, He is both the most basic and the most modest member of the Trinity, for His work is to reflect Christ and to glorify Him.

The obvious meaning of the word *glorify* is "to give homage to, as in worship." But there is a deeper meaning. Dr. Leslie Weatherhead, in a 1952 Lenten sermon in the City Temple,

London, brought out this richer meaning: "I would define glory as that expression of the nature of a person or thing which, of itself, evokes our praise."

Then the "glory" of a sunrise must be in the beauty of its delicate pinks and oranges reflected in the sky just before the sun itself appears over the hills. In this sense the glory is in the qualities or characteristics of the sunrise which we can perceive.

The "glory" of Jesus Christ lies in the characteristics of His nature that makes us want to adore Him. These traits are not kingly trappings or the halo placed around His head by medieval painters. Far from it! Men saw His glory in His humanity—His instant compassion, tenderness, understanding, fearlessness, incisiveness, His refusal to compromise with evil, His selflessness which culminated in His ultimate self-giving on the cross.

The Apostle John puts it in unforgettable words: "And the Word was made flesh, and dwelt among us, (and we beheld his glory, the glory as of the only begotten of the Father) full of grace and truth." [1]

But then I found the New Testament declaring that these qualities of Jesus' nature are not apparent to us any more than a sunrise is apparent to a blind man. That is why we need the Holy Spirit to make Christ's glory perceptible to us. It is as if the Spirit gives us a new way of seeing, with which we can perceive spiritual truth where all has been darkness before.

I found that Jesus had his own preferred names for the Spirit. Christ spoke in Aramaic, the tongue of His own people. This was the dialect of the bazaars and the seaside, replete with colorful idioms, metaphors, and probably picturesque humor. There is good reason to believe that the tone of Jesus' speech was quite unlike the English of the King James' Version of the early seventeenth century. The King James' translators often rendered the Holy Spirit the "Holy Ghost." But Jesus liked to call Him "the Helper," "the Spirit of Truth," "the Teacher," "the Comforter," "the Counselor."

The gospel of John was especially helpful in giving me more understanding about the Holy Spirit. In His last talk with the eleven (Judas had already left the group), Christ made it clear that they were to experience Him through the Spirit. On that last night, He had important things to say to His apostles, most of them concerning the Comforter.

The disciples knew that their Master was in imminent danger. They were frightened, sorrowful men.

"Do not be frightened about my leaving you," Jesus told them, in effect. "It is actually to your advantage that I go away."

Then He outlined His plan:

When He could no longer be with them physically, Another would take His place. This One—the Helper—would be the continuation and extension of His [Christ's] life on earth.[2] All the wonders that the disciples had witnessed of teaching, preaching, forgiving, cleansing, healing would go right on. But even greater accomplishments would be possible through the Helper, ones that had not been possible during Jesus' earthly ministry.[3]

This had to be so, because there was more truth, much more, to be discovered. And it would be the Spirit of Truth that would lead men into these undreamed-of areas of exploration.[4]

This is the only plan by which men in all centuries could have fellowship with the risen Christ. Without the Spirit transmitting His continuing presence to us, we would have no more than the memory and recorded words and deeds of any good man, such as St. Francis of Assisi or Lincoln or Gandhi.

Jesus made a surprising statement that last night to His apostles: the plan was that this Spirit would dwell in men's bodies. We were being offered the privilege of presenting our bodies to the Helper, so that He could not only be with us, but *in* us. This would be God the Father coming closer to men than He had ever been before. This is expressed in a variety of ways in Scripture. It is "God tabernacling with men." Paul was later to cry: "I live; yet not I, but Christ liveth in me." [5] And, "Do you not know that your body is the temple of the holy Spirit within you—the Spirit you have received from God?" [6]

Christ promised His disciples that if they would thus offer their bodies as an abiding place for the Helper, the Father's power and wisdom, as well as His [Christ's] would be theirs. [7]

He also warned that people in the world would think all of this odd, and could not possibly see or recognize the Spirit until they too had experienced Him. [8]

Then He instructed the eleven what to do in order to receive the Spirit. [9] And He admonished each of them not even to try to be His witness until *after* the Spirit had come to Him. [10]

Probably the apostles understood little of this at the time. Even so, it must have been obvious to them that Jesus was putting maximum value on the Helper. And this brought me back full circle to my own statement to my friend Tay that I could "get along quite well" without the Holy Spirit. On the contrary, I found that according to the New Testament if we are without the Spirit, then we are without:

Joy
The awareness of God's love for us
The conviction of who Christ is
The ability to communicate the gospel in a life-changing way
The conviction of sin
Guidance
Healing
An intercessor with the Father
The gifts of the Spirit
The fruits of the Spirit
The pledge (or inner proof) of eternal life

For anyone who has the least desire to be a Christian, this seems like an extensive list of blessings to forego. Even from my incomplete examination, it was obvious that Jesus saw the presence of the Helper as the one gift encompassing all other gifts.

Having learned this much, my next question was "How does one go about receiving the Holy Spirit?" From the stories in the Acts, telling how different men received Him, it is obvious that there are many ways and no set techniques. Thus the outline I culled from Scripture at that time cannot be taken as final or rigid:

1. We have to be convinced that the Scriptures teach the indwelling of Christ in our bodies through the Holy Spirit, and we have to want His Presence for ourselves.
2. We have to go to Christ and ask for the gift.
3. We then reckon that the Spirit has taken possession of our bodies and is dwelling in us.
4. We receive proof of this, what some have called "the manifestation" of the Spirit.
5. We keep His Presence through obedience to the inner Voice.

Next I proceeded to ask for the Holy Spirit for myself. Nothing dramatic happened to me—no rushing wind or ecstasy or "speaking in tongues" as happened to the disciples at Pentecost. To this day I have experienced only a modicum of all that there is to know about the Helper. This is still a growing point for me, where further adventure awaits. But the little I have already learned about the Comforter I am eager to share, because it is exactly at this point that Christianity has become for me most practical and most provocative.

My first discovery was that there is nothing ethereal, no trace of the sanctimonious humbug that most people expect to find in the Holy Spirit. Nor is there any saccharine sentimentality. Quite the contrary; there is a down-to-earth quality of personality about the Holy Spirit so marked that I still would not believe it had I not experienced it.

The Spirit delights in mediating Christ to us in the everydayness of life. For instance: About two years after Peter Marshall had his first heart attack, one morning I was plagued by the insistent thought that I should learn to drive the family car. I mentioned the idea to my husband. He was not wildly enthusiastic; he knew that two drivers for one car could result in complications.

Over a matter of months the idea kept coming back, so persistently that I concluded that this was the Helper insisting. Finally Peter agreed to my taking driving lessons.

At the time of Peter's sudden death, I had been driving just long enough to have confidence to carry on. But if I had had to learn during the period of emotional turmoil immediately following his death, I might never have attempted it. Later on I realized that being able to drive also had significance in helping me towards the independence necessary to begin my new life.

The effect this sort of loving concern has on one is indescribable. To me this seems proof, as only the Comforter can give it to us, that God exists, and that He cares about us. It is one way that we can know, finally and forever, that we are loved and that this love can be expressed in simple, everyday ways straight from the unselfish heart of God.

Thus I discovered that no detail of life is too small for the Helper's concern. For years I had been hearing Christians discuss the question "Have we any right to bother God with the small details of daily life?"

Those who thought not would argue, "After all, it would be a low grade of Christian who would treat God as if He were a celestial bellhop created to serve our petty needs. Besides, since God has given us common sense, He expects us to use it for these small matters."

Certainly we should be wary of any interpretation of religion so self-centered that it continually seeks, "What can my faith do for me today?" We should have a healthy fear of making our God too small. They are right who see Him as the God of history with far-flung designs for man's destiny. Yet the fact remains that Jesus added for us another dimension to the nature of His Father. "By all means you *should* bother the Father with details," Jesus seems to say in so many places in the gospels. He was constantly "bothering the Father" with the practicalities of life—with people's health problems, with securing the money for Peter's temple tax, with supper for a crowd of hungry listeners, with the wine running out at a wedding reception.

And after Jesus' resurrection, what then? Would men then have to revert to the God of the Old Testament—high and lifted-up, majestic, remote? No, the heavenly plan was that the Spirit would go on showing us this intimate side of the omnipotent God exactly as Jesus had. For in all ways the Spirit reflects Jesus.

Jesus cared about the everyday needs of men; so does the Spirit. Jesus stirred men's hearts, turned casual inquirers into passionate believers. Just so, the Spirit will recharge our emotions today. Sometimes I think this is the most vital work of the Spirit in the twentieth century. It has been said of our civilization that it deadens emotion. For millions of people in our thing-surfeited Western world, life has become tasteless. Nothing is as much fun as we thought it would be. Creative thought and work wither, since there are not emotional springs to nourish it. Strength and romance go out of love.

Society assumes a tepid state in which it admires detached neutrality, shows mild contempt for strong feelings. We are suspicious of anyone who becomes agitated about a principle or an issue.

This kind of apathy places our nation itself in jeopardy. Upon his retirement as Chief of Naval Operations in July 1961, Admiral Arleigh A. Burke sounded a note of warning:

"I wonder if the American people have such strong convictions as they used to? We don't seem to see the necessity of living by our convictions and dying for them, if need be. I am concerned about comfortable living in relation to the people's determination to stand firm for what America believes."

If part of our problem today be lack of great passions, intense beliefs, then how is the Holy Spirit an answer? Because of His power to revive man's emotional life. For in the first century or the twentieth, people have never been able to confront Jesus Christ face to face and remain coolly impassive. Something about Him kindles either a total devotion or provokes men to violent opposition. And Jesus Himself seems always to have preferred antagonism to apathy. For apathy is the symptom of a sick and dying spirit.

Strong emotions surge through the gospels. Virile men did not leave their businesses and their homes to follow Christ without intense convictions. Men did not risk persecution and death out of lukewarmness. Those who were healed, who had sight restored, their children given back to them, could not be phlegmatic about it. The exuberance of the men who experienced the Spirit at Pentecost was such that they were accused of being drunk with new wine. Emotion beyond embarrassment, beyond caring what other people thought, towards the release of bound personalities—all this is there for anyone to read.

I have watched the same process today in those whom the Holy Spirit touches. Feelings are sensitized. Life takes on relish. Joys are heightened. Here is the way one woman described her encounter with the Spirit:

...I saw no new thing, but I saw all the usual things in a miraculous new light. I saw for the first time how wildly beautiful and joyous, beyond any words of mine to describe, is the whole of life. Every human being ... every sparrow that flew, every branch tossing in the wind, was caught up in and was a part of the whole mad ecstasy of loveliness, of joy, of importance, of intoxication of life....[11]

In the experience of everyone to whom I have talked about the Spirit, the word *joy* stands out. In the rebirth of our emotional selves this seems to be the essential missing ingredient which the Holy Spirit supplies.

I have written earlier in this book of the joy of childhood. For me it was in the fragrance of mint and honeysuckle, the feel of bare feet on moss, ice-cold apples, the magnificent fury of a thunderstorm, the far horizons of blue Appalachians. And all my life I have felt that this early joy was trying to teach me something, that it was not just a sentiment restricted to childhood. It seemed to reveal something fundamental and basic about the nature of the universe itself.

Surely I was right; surely this is the way things are in God's world! But only now do I see how God intends for us to know this. It is the Holy Spirit who is to open our eyes to the joy which undergirds the universe.

It was the Holy Spirit who opened Marianne Brown's eyes. Mrs. Brown is the wife of the Presbyterian minister in the small town of Parkesburg, Pennsylvania, mother of five children and mistress of an old-fashioned rambling eleven-room manse. The details of her story come directly from her.

Six years ago, if you had asked Marianne Brown what was the most basic truth about life, the last thing she would have answered would have been "joy!" She might have said "duty" or even, if she had been feeling brutally honest, "exhaustion."

Like many another minister's wife, Mrs. Brown was trapped in a maelstrom of activity—church meetings, the presidency of the women's organization, constant entertaining, a neighborhood kindergarten, supervising the area recreation program. She had a merciless conscience that drove her and a concern about other people's opinions that made her unable to say *no* to any request. Like most ministers' wives, she was not able to afford any household help.

Her one escape from exhaustion was to be ill at frequent intervals and go to bed for rest. This was not too difficult to manage, because the constantly overtired woman was an easy target for assorted viruses and disorders. Furthermore she had been born with a congenital heart defect, diagnosed by the doctors as mitral stenosis.

Marianne would lie in bed and brood. Why was her vitality so low? Why did black moods descend so often, periods of retreating within herself? Sometimes she would go for days, speaking grudgingly even to her family. She introduced every other thought with the words, "The trouble is——" It was indicative of her joyless outlook on life.

"Looking back now," she told me, "it seems to me that all my life had been a search for the joy that had been denied me. I remember once seeing a ragged child standing at the great wrought-iron gates of an estate, his hands clasping the bars. His eyes were glued wistfully on the winding walks among the great trees, the sweep of lawn in which he might have run and tumbled, the flower-beds, even a brook where a small boy might have gone wading and fishing . . .

"Well, I was like that little boy, hungrily staring at vistas of joy that seemed forever closed to me. That is, until six years ago."

Then six years ago a new life began for Marianne—quietly enough. A neighbor dropped in one morning. Over a cup of coffee at the breakfast table, the harassed minister's wife poured out her troubles. The friend admitted that she had no answers for Marianne but suggested that they pray together.

They did. There was nothing unusual or dramatic about the prayer. Yet it seemed to relieve the pressures, so they prayed together again. Then, one by one, other friends joined them. Eventually there was a small group of husbands and wives who met in each other's homes each Saturday evening.

A family crisis overtook the Browns soon afterward. Their high-school-age daughter suffered a nervous breakdown. The group that met in prayer gave them important support through the crisis. And once again prayer brought startling results.

Their daughter's early recovery filled the Browns with gratitude to God and to the friends who had shouldered their problems with them. On a certain Saturday night, as the meeting was being closed with a circle of prayer, Marianne found herself slipping to her knees as deep feelings of thanksgiving to God for His nearness and goodness bubbled up and spilled over into words, words that came and kept coming in a torrent.

Then suddenly—to Marianne Brown in Parkesburg, Pennsylvania in 1955—the Holy Spirit came. She had done no studying or thinking about the Comforter, indeed, was scarcely aware of Him at all. Let Marianne tell it:

God's Spirit took over and seemed to immerse my whole being— body, mind, and spirit. The Spirit came like tidal waves of "joy unspeakable and full of glory" and inundated me. Torrents of God's love swept over me for what seemed only a few minutes but lasted a long time. More than once I wondered if my human body could bear the ecstasy, and I both begged God to stop and feared that He would!

That night my emotions found perfect expression. I know now that my emotions had been starved. I had been only half-living, because I had been only half-feeling.

In those minutes God revealed more to me than I had ever learned in books ... I knew that for the remainder of my life Jesus Himself would be my first love. In Him every desire I had ever had was fulfilled. And I knew that such communion with God is His will for every human being!

Marianne's friends, even her husband, were stunned at what they were witnessing. The Reverend Mr. Brown had preached about Pentecost, talked about the Holy Spirit, sometimes in knowing theological tones. But witnessing Him in action—that was something else again! He and most of those present had always been wary of emotionalism in religion. We Presbyterians usually are! With the erudite John Calvin of Geneva and starchy John Knox of Edinburgh as the fathers of our church, this is only natural. And the educated clergy upon which the Presbyterian church has always insisted, usually puts inordinate emphasis on the mind, little emphasis on the emotions.

So it was a confused and wondering group that at a late hour reluctantly told one another good night and went back to their respective homes. Though they were not yet ready to admit it to each other, already something had happened to each of them through Marianne's experience: they too wanted the Holy Spirit and joy!

In the weeks that followed their wish was granted. It was like a fire that had descended on Marianne and then leaped from person to person, including her minister husband! As the fire spread, the group was welded together in a way none of them had ever known before.

There was no difficulty now in sharing with one another thoughts, joys, fears, hopes, disappointments, problems, triumphs. They lived in each other's lives, not just spiritually, but in practical fashion too. They were discovering *Koinonia*, the fellowship of the Holy Spirit that the first-century infant church had experienced following Pentecost. Eventually the one group grew into a series of them throughout the local church community.

As for Marianne herself, "Six years have passed since then," she told me. "I have not spent one day of them in bed. I find myself able, without fatigue, to care for my big house and the needs of my family, still without outside help. And there is more entertaining than ever. Our home is open house to friends from all over the world.

"The guidance of the Helper about my daily tasks is quite specific. He has enabled me to say a sure 'No' to what He does not want me to do. For what He directs me to undertake, there is an unfailing supply of vitality. Sometimes I have taught as many as five Bible classes a week."

Marianne Brown no longer searches for joy. She bubbles over with it. Her voice lilts with it. Life itself is joy.

It is the same exuberant joy that we experience as children. Christ said: "Except ye become as little children, ye shall not enter into the kingdom of heaven." [12] It is the Spirit saying *yea* to man's *can I?*

At the beginning of the book, I referred to the point, so often made now, that the only hope for our world is a change in human nature itself. Is it possible that the rising tide of interest in the Spirit all across the United States today is evidence that the Helper is undertaking this task?

One day last year two friends and I spent part of an afternoon in the apartment of Dr. Henry Pitney Van Dusen, President of Union Theological Seminary, discussing this very possibility. Dr. Van Dusen's book on the Holy Spirit, *Spirit, Son, and Father*, reflects his own increasing emphasis on the Spirit as the most effective agent in human life.

The conversation turned to what each of us there that afternoon had at one time discovered: that the Spirit repeatedly brings us back to Jesus' emphasis—that real faith is no otherwordly affair. I know that again and again in recent years He has plucked me out of the clouds of theoretical Christianity back to earth where I belonged.

For when we allow the Spirit to guide us He will concern Himself with how we use our time and spend our money; with honesty and moral integrity and Christlike quality of character; with what is happening to our children; with the health of our relationship with other people and with our God. And, if our need is severe enough, the Holy Spirit will turn our lives upside down.

For man's chief problem is still man. The search that begins at the point of our need—the longing for Something More—in the end brings us back full circle to the inner man. With the threat of thermonuclear war hanging over us, civilization's problem is still unredeemed individuals. No summit meeting is held, no international conference convened but that our quandary is dramatized for us.

How, then, can human nature change? Men have demonstrated that they cannot change themselves. Nor can men change other men. We have seen that education does not necessarily achieve it, nor legislation, nor raising incomes, nor plying them with all the gadgets that money can buy. That brings us to the crown of the Holy Spirit's work among men. Only Christ can change human nature, and it is the Holy Spirit that makes Christ available to needy mankind.

That is what happened to Saul of Tarsus, to Augustine, to Ignatius Loyola, to St. Francis of Assisi, and to thousands through the centuries. It is still happening to men and women in our day.

How drastically and profoundly the Holy Spirit can turn a man's character upside down was demonstrated in the case of Starr Daily.

It was the year 1924. In a courtroom in the Midwest, the judge's voice was grave as he looked down at the prisoner standing before him. "I am about to sentence you to a major prison for the third time. I know you are sick. And I know that more punishment is not the remedy. But your record leaves me powerless."

And so "hopeless criminal" was society's judgment of Starr Daily. The verdict seemed justified. At sixteen Starr's only ambition had been to build a reputation as a dangerous man. He dreamed of the time when the police would refer to him with a shudder.

He achieved his aim by becoming the leader of a gang of safecrackers. There was no safe he could not open, no time lock he could not take apart. But finally liquor made him careless, and he was caught.

There followed fourteen years of penal farms, chain gangs, and two extended penitentiary sentences. Through all that time Starr's father never lost hope that his son might be redeemed from his life of crime. His best efforts failed. He lived to see his Starr re-enter prison for the third time. Starr never saw his father after that. The broken-hearted man died with a prayer for his son on his lips.

In prison Starr made two futile attempts to escape. Then he evolved a plan to instigate a prison riot. The deputy warden was to be seized and used as a shield and hostage. A stool-pigeon betrayed the plan, and Starr was sentenced to the dungeon.

Most strong men could not survive "the hole" for more than fifteen days. American prisons thirty-five years ago could be grim and brutal places. It was winter, and the walls of the dank cell seeped moisture. At six every morning, the prisoner would be given a piece of bread and a cup of water. Then he would be left hanging in handcuffs for twelve hours. At six in the evening, he would be let down for the night and given another piece of bread and another cup of water.

Starr survived fifteen days of this. By the last day in the cuffs, he could no longer stand on feet black with congealed blood. That morning "the Bull"—the keeper of the hole—had to lift the almost-unconscious man into the cuffs.

For weeks after that, the prisoner was allowed to lie on the icy stone floor—emaciated, unspeakably filthy, near death. He lost track of time. Mired in the lowest hell imaginable, only hate was keeping him alive—hate for the Bull, hate for the deputy warden who had vowed that he would force Starr to crawl to him like a dog, begging mercy.

Then there came a moment when the man on the floor was too weak to hate. Through that momentary opening crept a strange new thought: *All of my life I have been a dynamo of energy. What might have happened if I had used that energy for something good?*

Then the thought faded. *It's too late now; I'm dying.* There followed a half-waking, half-sleeping state of unconsciousness: moments of delirium, times of awareness.

This was followed by disconnected dreams, like mists floating across the brain. Time was no more. The prisoner was aware no longer of the frozen stone floor, of his filth, or of anyone who came or went.

Finally, the dreams began to take on meaning, to become rational in form and sequence. Suddenly Starr seemed to be in a garden. He knew that he had been in this same garden before—many times in childhood. It was in a shoe-shaped valley surrounded by gentle hills. At one end of the garden a great white-gray rock jutted out. Then Jesus Christ, the Man whom he had been trying to avoid all his life, was coming toward him. Now He stood face to face with Starr, looking deep into his eyes as if penetrating to the bottom of his soul. Love of a quality that he had never before felt was drawing the hate out of his heart, like extracting poison from an infected wound.

With a strange clarity, one part of Starr's mind thought *I am submerged in Reality, I'll never be the same again, now and through all eternity.*

There followed another dream in which all the people Starr had ever injured passed before his eyes. One by one, he poured out his love to them.

Then all who had injured him appeared, and on them too he bestowed the love needed to restore and to heal. The love flowed from beyond him, poured through him in a torrent of caring and ecstatic gratitude.

When the prisoner returned to consciousness, the cell did not look the same. Its grim grayness was gone. For him it was illuminated with a warm light. His feelings too were different. The prison environment no longer had the power to give him pain, only joy.

The next thing Starr knew, the door opened and the Bull

said in a tone of voice Starr had never before heard him use,
"Are you hungry? I could steal a sandwich from the kitchen
and bring it to you."

The prisoner stared in amazement. But he was even more
startled at his own reply, "No, don't do that. Don't risk your
neck by breaking a rule for me."

It was the Bull's turn to be astonished. He went off wonderingly, came back with the doctor, and Starr was carried to
the prison hospital. Through a swift and surprising series of
events, prison doors swung open for Starr Daily in March
1930, five years ahead of the time set for his release.

Was his experience on the cell floor a hallucination? No,
not unless we would call what happened to Saul of Tarsus a
hallucination. The proof was the change in the man. He who
had been declared incorrigible by penologists, was from that
moment cured of all criminal tendencies.

Peter Marshall loved the man that Starr Daily became and
delighted in telling his story from the pulpit of the New York
Avenue Presbyterian Church in Washington. In 1954, when I
was in Hollywood for script conferences on *A Man Called
Peter*, I drove out to the Daily's home in Van Nuys, California, for an overnight visit with Starr and his wife Marie.

A tall spare man, graying now, Starr's face bears the lines of
the long hard years. But flashes of dry humor, spoken in a
Midwestern drawl, light up the face.

From this man who had only a sixth-grade education have
come eight books. He has lectured all over the nation. His
knowledge of the criminal mind has contributed to valuable
rethinking of prison techniques. He has personally been the
Holy Spirit's vehicle for the reclamation of scores of criminals.

In speaking to me recently about the experience that
changed his life, Starr Daily said, "The Holy Spirit came to
me through the glorified Christ. He did not give me the gifts
of the Spirit, rather the fruits of the spirit to be worked out
in a day to day discipline. Perhaps that was necessary in my

case, so that the fruits could be integrated with the drastic character changes necessary. Anyway, you remember that St. Paul said that this was "the most excellent way."

Can we change human nature? No, but the Holy Spirit can. His all-encompassing love is Jesus' love for us, the extension of Jesus' life and power in our day. The Helper takes our needs as His own. Our dangers He enters into with us. Our perplexities He illumines. Our joyousness, He sanctifies.

The Spirit was with John Sherrill that day when he entered into Life by saying *Yes* to Christ. He was with Stuart Luhan that night when the Winecoff Hotel caught on fire.

The Counselor helped my friend Beverley through the crisis with her boy, Kenneth. He enabled Raymond Thomas to dream of a better life than Radical Hill could bring him. He is with Betty Elliot and her small daughter, Valerie, in the South American jungle. And even now He is with Karen Emmott out in Oklahoma City—Karen of the piquant face, who still hopes to live her life in "the old natural normal way."

Do without Him? How could any of us who have embarked on the pilgrimage that is Christianity do without Him? For we who long for something more, for strength and hope and wisdom beyond our selves, discover to our joy that as the Comforter reveals Christ to us, in Him we have our heart's desire.

15

Afterglow

IT WAS THE AFTERNOON of May first. I sat at the typewriter in my basement office. Through the picture window, I could see the first faint traces of green on the sweep of trees down the hill. Spring had come late to New York state this year.

Suddenly the telephone rang shrilly. Mother's voice leaped at me over the wires from Evergreen Farm in Virginia. Her voice sounded strange, I thought.

"Catherine, I have bad news," she said. Then there was a long pause. "Dad's gone——"

"Dad is gone—?"

She rushed breathlessly on. "Dr. Oliver just came to tell me——"

"How? When?"

"About fifteen minutes ago. Dad left the house, saying he was going up to the store for the mail, that he'd be back right away. He never came back."

"You mean——?"

"He was sitting on a wooden chair in the store, talking and joking with Mr. Janney and some other men. All at once he gave two faint sighs—and that was it."

I sat staring at my typewriter, trying to take this in.

"Dr. Oliver tells me that when he got there, Dad was still sitting in the chair, his legs crossed, his hands on his lap. His head was bowed a little. There was a peaceful, happy expression on his face——"

"Oh, Mother—darling——" Desperately I tried to collect my thoughts. "It will be forty minutes or so before I can tell Len. He's on his way home from the New York office now. He will know about plane schedules to Washington. I'll get there just as soon as I can."

"Catherine, will you telephone Peter John at Yale——?"

"You know I will. Immediately."

As it turned out, Peter was in glee club rehearsal, where the group was working on numbers for the concert tour of South America scheduled for the summer. He did not get the news about his grandfather until early that evening.

How suddenly death interrupts life!

Yet two nights later, as the family gathered in the living room at Evergreen, it was not so much grief that we felt, but gratitude. In seventy-six years, Dad had lived a rich, full life. Forty-six active years in the ministry, nearly five wonderful years on the farm.

He had lived to give his blessing to Leonard LeSourd and me by performing our wedding ceremony on November 14, 1959, in the little Presbyterian Church in Leesburg, Virginia. Though he had shared the service with Len's father and with Dr. Norman Vincent Peale, it was he who had insisted on pronouncing the solemn words that launched us on our new life: "By the authority vested in me as a minister of the Church of Christ. . . ."

A lifetime dream had been fulfilled the preceding summer in a trip to Europe to see the Passion Play. And at Eastertime, as if to round out his last year, every member of Dad's large family had been gathered around him, including the three new grandchildren—Jeffrey, Chester, and Linda LeSourd.

Then there had been the Golden Wedding Anniversary celebration. Just a year ago, the old farmhouse had glowed and shone and overflowed with friends, some of whom had driven long distances to share Mother's and Father's joy. Exactly a year later on this third of May, Mother had memories that blessed and burned. On this, the evening of their fifty-first anniversary, Mother could not bear the thought of leaving at the impersonal funeral parlor the earthly form that Dad had cast off. That was why the casket was close by now in the farmhouse where our family had gathered.

"But how wonderful it was," Mother said, "that John had all this last year."

We spoke of our gratitude too for the gracious small providences of the last hours. How hard it would have been for Mother if she had been alone with Dad at the end. And what if heart failure had occurred at the wheel of his car on the way to the store? He had been spared invalidism too. How he would have hated giving up his projects! To the end, he was busy with them. We began enumerating them . . .

Only three days before he had finished building a wagon bed so sturdy that we wondered if the farm tractor could haul it.

Then, with as much delight as a small boy with a first wagon, he had painted it bright, shiny red. On the day of his death, he had been wondering about how many baby chickens to buy this year; how many new strawberry plants to set; how soon he and Earl Cook, our helper on the farm, could start work on the second terrace by the chicken house. Then of course, the base for the sundial had to be built——

My brother-in-law, Harlow Hoskins, said at that point, "But I thought Dad was planning on using the stump of the bee tree as a base for the sundial——"

"You mean," and there was a certain supercilious note in Peter John's voice, "the stump of that tree that Mother made forever famous with her deathless prose."

"Make fun of it, if you will, young man," his grandmother retorted. "Believe it or not, lots of visitors have wanted to see the stump of that locust tree."

"I can give you some new material, Catherine," my brother Bob added teasingly. "This happened when I was a little boy. Did you know about the Christmas that Pop was standing at the top of a ladder, trying to plug strings of outdoor Christmas lights into the socket on the porch ceiling? His hand slipped and he stuck his thumb in the socket. He let out a roar, almost leaped off the ladder, and out came a word that was hardly—um—ministerial. Then he looked down at me sitting on the porch floor, staring up at him with my mouth hanging open.

" 'Just forget I said that, son,' he said in a gruff voice."

Bob chuckled. "What Pop didn't know was that suddenly I felt a new and close bond with him. We men had shared something rather special."

A childish shriek in the hall pierced our conversation. Mary, my sister-in-law, and Em both rushed for their respective children, who had been playing tag on the stairs. Voices in the hall quieted down immediately, and we resumed our conversation. But a few minutes later, seven-year-old Mary Margaret crept into the room.

"Bobby is sitting on the top step and won't play any more and won't come down," she reported in her soft voice.

"Never mind, Mary," Mother said. "I'll take care of this."

Then we heard her voice. "Bobby, you misunderstood. Your mother wasn't shushing you because she thought you were being disrespectful of your grandfather. Why, Grandfather wouldn't want you children to be sad and long-faced. He's happy, and he wants you to be happy too. Besides, he loved having you children around him. You know that——"

"Oh, thank you, Grandmother," we heard Bobby say. She started to speak but then her voice trailed off, smothered in a little boy's hug.

Peter John shook his head wonderingly. "And on the night before the funeral. What a woman!"

"I suppose my children come by their exuberance naturally," Bob grinned. "Remember the lard-can story, Em?"

"Remember it! How could I forget it?"

Then they both started talking at once.

I looked up at Peter Marshall's portrait. It was easy to imagine what he would be saying at that moment, "Same old family.... Haven't changed a bit!"

Peter John observed, "We need Grandfather's booming voice to referee."

"All right," Em conceded. "I'll pass. You tell it, Bob."

"Well, Father was always immaculately dressed before he went into the pulpit of a Sunday morning. If possible he liked to wear a flower in his buttonhole. On this particular Sunday morning, he was wearing a freshly pressed white suit and white shoes—the only pair of white ones he owned. Just before leaving for the church, he headed for the back garden where he knew some Ragged Robins were in bloom.

"What he didn't know was that Em and I had boobytrapped the garden. We had begged empty lard cans from Mother—big ones—fifteen-pound tins. Then we'd sunk the cans in the earth, filled them with water, and neatly laid twigs and tufts of grass across the top to camouflage them."

"It was a dirty trick," Em muttered.

"Anyway, Father walked right into one of the traps set in the middle of the garden path. Em and I heard him bellow like a wounded bull and we ducked for hiding places. But he was in a fine fury and promptly rooted us out. One of his pant legs was wet halfway up and, of course, his shoe was sopping. I'm afraid Em and I didn't further his spiritual state that Sunday."

My sister Em picked up the conversation. "I was lying awake last night, remembering a lot of things too. Len, you've never heard this one...."

Then she related an incident from Father's West Virginia pastorate. One day he had been seeking out a newcomer in town who worked in the Round House at the Baltimore and Ohio railroad yards. When Father finally located the man, he found him repairing an engine.

"Sorry, I can't shake hands with you, Preacher," the man said, holding up hands black with coal dust and engine grease.

Impulsively, my father stooped over and rubbed his hands in the soot that lay an inch thick on the floor. "Now there's no difference between us," he said. "You see, sir, I *want* to shake your hand."

"That man," Em added, "was father's friend for life."

"I can believe that story," Len said. "I've never known a man who loved people so much—all kinds of people. In Europe last summer, while Catherine and her mother would be looking at monuments or museums or paintings, Dad would be carrying on lively conversations with a bellhop, a guard, a policeman, or assorted shopkeepers."

Len was right about Father's love for people. How wholeheartedly people responded was dramatized for us by this incident, among many. Frank Scott and others from Dad's Eastern Shore Church drove all night to get to the funeral. Mr. Scott is a farmer and a man of few words. "I loved Mr. Wood," he said simply as he gripped my hand. "I had to come."

The funeral service was anything but somber. David Crawford, the minister, had told me earlier, "Your father and I had a fine relationship. In fact, so good that he could tease me almost constantly. I couldn't possibly be long-faced in any service for him. If you don't mind, I'd like to make this a model of what I long for every funeral service to be."

So there was congregational singing. We sang Martin Luther's triumphant hymn

A mighty fortress is our God,
A bulwark never failing. . . .

I looked round and saw Earl Cook standing in the back of the church, cap in hand, his dusky face glowing, singing more lustily than any of us. Mr. Crawford stood in front of the almost-full church. His head was lifted high, a look of exaltation on his face. He had picked passages of Scripture with the same ringing note in them. One sentence from the 121st Psalm leaped out at me:

The Lord shall preserve thy going out and thy
coming in from this time forth, and even for
evermore.

Not a member of our family could escape the feeling that for Dad the Lord had fulfilled that promise exactly. Sitting there in the little church, my thoughts went back to the final afternoon of his life . . .

"I'm going out for the mail," he had said. "I'll be right back."

The love of God had tenderly overshadowed him as he went. The end must not come at the little single-land bridge abutment. No—not there. Nor at the sharp bend in the road by the Quaker Meeting House. No, he must have friends near, like Mr. Janney who owns the store—Mr. Janney, so much a part of the tiny community, the great-great-great-grandson of Hannah Janney. Why, as father was driving to the store, he passed the spot where Hannah is buried. . . . I like to remember Hannah. About the time another Quaker family was building Evergreen, she had been busy having twelve children. But she still had time to be the leader of the Meeting and the arbiter for the community to the end of her ninety-three years. . . . Yes, somehow it was fitting that it was Mr. Janney who had been with Dad at the end. . . .

So if the Lord had preserved Dad's going out in that minute

way, we were sure that He had preserved his coming in to his new life as well. That was why we could not be gloomy during the fifty-mile ride to the cemetery.

The procession traveled over the new George Washington Memorial parkway where the first glimpse of Washington is the spires of Georgetown. . . . Across the Memorial Bridge where the gold Italian statues glitter in the spring sunlight . . . Circle the Lincoln Memorial and let the eyes rest on its white symmetry. Surely the most beautiful building in Washington. . . . The cherry trees around the Tidal Basin are fading now.

Down Constitution Avenue—so familiar, so familiar. How many times I have traveled it. And on into the Maryland countryside to Fort Lincoln Cemetery . . . Peter Marshall had preached so many sunrise Easter services there. Now father will lie close to him. . . .

On the day after the funeral, Mother and I were going through Father's desk. From one drawer, I pulled out a letter that I recognized. It was a love letter I had spontaneously dashed off to Dad several months before.

"I'm surprised that he kept it," I commented.

"He read it over and over," Mother said. "You'll never know how much it meant to him."

I had forgotten what I said. Curiously I opened it:

I knew you were not feeling well when I told you goodbye at the airport. I've been thinking about you ever since then. This is being written on an impulse. Sometimes it's good to follow these spot impulses, speak what's in the heart. . . .

You and Mother gave me the most gorgeous childhood any little girl ever had, because you gave me so much of yourself. Remember all the things you built for me? That set of doll furniture . . . The little cupboard with the glass doors . . . And the dresser with its swinging mirror and the tiny glass knobs. I can see it yet.

Then there was the house in the cherry tree you made for me. And the croquet court with lights strung overhead. These were the myriad ways you entered so deeply into the lives of us children.

But of course, the greatest thing that you and Mother did for us was to bequeath us the sure knowledge of the love and goodness of God abroad in the world.

Am I getting too sentimental? What I really want to say is, you're very dear to me....

Slowly I returned the letter to its envelope and put it back in the drawer. I was glad that I had followed my heart and written it.

Then I picked up Dad's final bank statement. I could scarcely believe what I was seeing. His balance was sixty-five cents.

It is true that you can't take it with you. But who ever heard of anyone coming out *that* even at the end of life?

How typical of Dad! He never did have any money. The salaries of preachers in small towns are notoriously small. Yet always he had been supplied with every need—even to a college education for each of his children and Evergreen Farm for his retirement. His sixty-five-cent statement somehow seemed right.

Father's life had taught me the one thing that really matters—human relationships. The bonds that unite families and friends are not forged for a little while, they are for eternity. They stretch across every boundary of space and time. They twine and intertwine from one generation to another, weave and interweave, priceless beyond measure. They are something to be cherished, to be fought for, to be kept intact at all cost. People—with their fears and their foibles and their dreams. People—with their struggles toward faith, with the pain and the exaltation of their pilgrimage. People—with personalities that live on and on, growing, learning, loving, lending helping hands to others. *People*—that is what life is all about.

Mother broke in on my soaring thoughts. Her mind was darting ahead in several directions: "Probably the baby calf will be born in a few days. . . . Oh, and Catherine, we must let Mrs. Ten Wolde in the Netherlands and Ray in Vienna know, as soon as possible, about Dad's death. . . . Oh, and I've been thinking. There are some fine young people down at the orphanage in the Valley of Virginia. You know, it might mean a lot to one of those high school boys to live and work on the farm this summer——"

In her eyes I saw the promise of the future.

Notes

CHAPTER 1 *Something More*

1. *Life* (November 28, 1960), p. 101.
2. The material that follows is from a speech made by Major William Meyer, Army Medical Corps, in San Francisco in 1958. This material has now been declassified by the Department of Defense.
3. Russell W. Davenport, *The Dignity of Man* (New York: Harper & Brothers, 1955), p. 25.

CHAPTER 2 *The Unselfishness of God*

1. Deuteronomy 33:27
2. Taken from Romans 8:35-39
3. Romans 8:28
4. This and what follows is detailed beginning on page 219 of Hannah W. Smith's *My Spiritual Autobiography, Or How I Discovered the Unselfishness of God* (New York: Fleming H. Revell Company, 1903).
5. Psalm 145:9
6. John 6:38 (Moffatt)
7. John 14:9 (Moffatt)
8. Luke 15:11-32
9. Matthew 7:9-11 (Moffatt)
10. Cairns, D. S., *The Faith That Rebels* (New York: R. R. Smith, Inc., 1930), pp. 211-213.
11. II Timothy 1:12 (Moffatt)

CHAPTER 3 *How to Enter In*

1. Luke 6:46
2. Matthew 12:43–45 (Moffatt)

CHAPTER 4 *The Secret of the Will*

1. Revelation 3:20
2. This and the quotes that follow are from Oursler's *Why I Know There Is a God* (New York: Doubleday & Company, 1950), pp. 17–20.
3. Philippians 2:13

CHAPTER 5 *Dare to Trust God*

1. Luke 7:50
2. Matthew 9:29
3. Mark 9:23
4. Matthew 21:22 (Moffatt)
5. Psalm 34:8
6. John 16:24 (Moffatt)
7. Matthew 7:11 (Moffatt)
8. Matthew 6:33
9. Psalm 81:10
10. Luke 12:33 (Moffatt)
11. James 2:17 (Moffatt)
12. I John 5:10 (Moffatt)

CHAPTER 6 *The Prayer of Relinquishment*

1. I Corinthians 1:25 (Moffatt)
2. Matthew 27:11–24; John 19:9–12
3. J. B. Phillips, *The Gospels Translated into Modern English* (New York: The Macmillan Company, 1942), p. 104.

CHAPTER 7 *Forgive Us Our Sins...*

1. John 1:9
2. John 6:37
3. Isaiah 1:18
4. Psalm 86:5
5. John 15:3
6. I John 5:19, 3:19 (Moffatt)
7. C. G. Jung, *Modern Man in Search of a Soul* (New York: Harcourt, Brace & Co., 1933), pp. 39, 40.
8. From Peter Marshall's sermon "Letters in the Sand," *A Man Called Peter* (New York: McGraw-Hill Book Company, Inc., 1951), p. 321.

CHAPTER 8 ...*As We Forgive Those Who Sin Against Us*

1. Matthew 6:14, 15
2. Matthew 5:23,24
3. Ephesians 4:32
4. Matthew 6:15

CHAPTER 9 *How to Find God's Guidance*

1. Proverbs 3:6
2. John 10:3,6
3. James 1:5
4. John 16:13
5. Hannah Whitall Smith, *My Spiritual Autobiography*, pp. 70-72.
6. Romans 8:14 (Moffatt)

CHAPTER 10 *The Power of Helplessness*

1. Psalm 4:1 (Moffatt)
2. Romans 8:28
3. Fritz Künkel and Roy E. Dickerson, *How Character Develops* (New York: Charles Scribner's Sons, 1947), pp. 131-32.
4. John 15:5 (Moffatt)
5. *The Interpreter's Bible*, Vol. 8., p. 715.
6. John 6:44 (Moffatt)
7. John 6:15-16
8. Ephesians 2:8,9
9. John 5:30
10. A. B. Simpson, *The Gospel of Healing* (Harrisburg, Pa.: Christian Publishers, 1915), p. 169.
11. Genesis 45:5,8
12. Genesis 50:20
13. Matthew 26:52 (Moffatt)
14. John 19:11 (Moffatt)
15. John 10:17,18

CHAPTER 11 *The Prayer That Makes Dreams Come True*

1. Glenn Clark's *I Will Lift Up Mine Eyes* (New York: Harper & Bros., 1937).
2. Mark 10:47,51 (Moffatt)

CHAPTER 12 *Ego-Slaying*

1. Mark 8:35
2. C. S. Lewis, *Beyond Personality* (New York: The Macmillan Company, 1947), p. 40.

3. Romans 6:1–11
4. Künkel and Dickerson, *How Character Develops*, pp. 105, 114.
5. Colossians 3:3 (Moffatt)
6. Luke 9:23
7. Hebrews 12:6,7,11 (Moffatt)

CHAPTER 13 *The Gospel of Healing*

1. Luke 4:39
2. Luke 4:18
3. Luke 5:12; Mark 9:23,24
4. Luke 9:11 (Moffatt)
5. Matthew 5:10
6. Matthew 16:1–4
7. Luke 6:8–10
8. Luke 13:10–13
9. Luke 7:11–16
10. Luke 8:27–35
11. Luke 10:1–16
12. Luke 10:18
13. Luke 10:21,22
14. Mark 16:15,18
15. Hebrews 13:8 (Moffatt)
16. Matthew 28:20
17. John 5:6 (Moffatt)
18. Mark 11:4 (Moffatt)
19. Luke 19:9
20. Luke 13:12 (Moffatt)
21. Matthew 18:19 (Moffatt)
22. Another daughter of Dr. Bell, Ruth, is Mrs. Billy Graham.
23. Matthew 13:58

CHAPTER 14 *Journey into Joy*

1. John 1:14
2. John 7:39,16:14
3. John 14:12
4. John 16:12,13
5. Galatians 2:20
6. I Corinthians 6:19
7. John 16:13–15
8. John 14:17; I Corinthian 2:14
9. John 1:33; Luke 11:13; John 14:16
10. Luke 24:49; Acts 1:4,5,8
11. Margaret Prescott Montague, "Twenty Minutes of Reality," *Atlantic Monthly* (November 1916).
12. Matthew 18:3

Index